Al-Qaeda's Post-9/11 Devolution

Al-Qaeda's Post-9/11 Devolution

The Failed Jihadist Struggle Against the Near and Far Enemy

Anthony Celso

Bloomsbury Academic
An imprint of Bloomsbury Publishing Plc

B L O O M S B U R Y
NEW YORK • LONDON • NEW DELHI • SYDNEY

Bloomsbury Academic
An imprint of Bloomsbury Publishing Inc

1385 Broadway	50 Bedford Square
New York	London
NY 10018	WC1B 3DP
USA	UK

www.bloomsbury.com

BLOOMSBURY and the Diana logo are trademarks of Bloomsbury Publishing Plc

First published 2014
Paperback edition first published 2015

© Anthony Celso, 2014

All rights reserved. No part of this publication may be reproduced or transmitted in any form or by any means, electronic or mechanical, including photocopying, recording, or any information storage or retrieval system, without prior permission in writing from the publishers.

No responsibility for loss caused to any individual or organization acting on or refraining from action as a result of the material in this publication can be accepted by Bloomsbury or the author.

Library of Congress Cataloging-in-Publication Data
Celso, Anthony.
Al Qaeda's post 9/11 devolution: the failed jihadist struggle against the near
and far enemy/Anthony Celso.
pages cm.
Includes bibliographical references and index.
ISBN 978-1-4411-5589-4 (hardback)
1. Qaida (Organization) 2. Terrorism. 3. September 11 Terrorist Attacks, 2001. I. Title.
HV6433.M6283.Q34 2014
363.325–dc23
2013034733

ISBN: HB: 978-1-4411-5589-4
PB: 9781-5013-1244-1
ePUB: 978-1-4411-5289-3
ePDF: 978-1-4411-8042-1

Typeset by Newgen Knowledge Works (P) Ltd., Chennai, India
Printed and bound in the United States of America

This book is dedicated to my wife Alicia for all of her love and support over the years.

Contents

Acknowledgments		viii
Introduction: Al-Qaeda's Post-9/11 Devolution and Its Diffuse Network of "Associates," "Affiliates," Insurgents, and "Homegrown" Terrorists		1
1	Al-Qaeda's Jihadist Worldview	15
2	Al-Qaeda's Formation and Its *Far Enemy* Strategy	31
3	Al-Qaeda's Post-9/11 Strategy and Organizational Devolution	55
4	Al-Qaeda's Role in the Madrid and London Bombings	81
5	Zarqawi: Al-Qaeda's Tragic Antihero and the Destructive Role of the Iraqi Jihad	105
6	Al-Qaeda's Affiliates and Insurgent Groups in Somalia, Yemen, and the Maghreb	129
7	West Africa: The Latest Jihadist War	143
8	Al-Qaeda Plots and Attacks against the United States after 9/11	159
9	Is Al-Qaeda on the Brink of Defeat? Bin Laden's Death and the Impact of the Arab Spring	181
Notes		201
Bibliography		227
Index		235

Acknowledgments

There are a number of people and organizations that I would like to acknowledge that have assisted in the writing of this book. First and foremost, I would like to thank my two colleagues at the Department of Security Studies at Angelo State University Dr Bruce Bechtol Jr and Dr Robert Ehlers for their consistent support, advice, and encouragement in the writing of this book. Additional thanks must be given to the work of the Foreign Policy Research Institute of Philadelphia (FPRI), the Combating Terrorism Center (CTC) at West Point, the *Long War Journal* and Madrid's *Real Instituto Elcano* (RIE) whose reports, analyses, and studies have immeasurably assisted the development of the arguments established in this book. Special recognition must be given to the work of Spanish terror expert Fernando Reinares, whose analysis of the Madrid terror attacks and al-Qaeda's penetration of the 3/11 network has played a critical role in my analytical framework regarding al-Qaeda's post-9/11 strategy, and mention must be made to the pioneering analysis of FPRI's late scholar Michael Radu whose assessment of Radical Islam in my view has no peer. His untimely death greatly hurts the study of terror groups and deprives us all of his brilliant insight. I am also deeply indebted to one of the blind reviewers working for Bloomsbury Press whose potent suggestions and criticism of my book proposal helped immeasurably in the writing of this project. His/her wise counsel propelled my exploration of al-Qaeda's historical and tactical evolution. I also feel moved to acknowledge the role of the editors of *Mediterranean Quarterly* including Nikolaos Stavrou whose support for my past research has culminated in this book. Finally, I must recognize the "help" of my adorable 12-year-old Maine Coon cat Jezebel who sat on my lap during the writing of this project and while physically she hindered my work, her sweet and loving disposition in some mysterious way assisted the book's completion.

Anthony Celso, July 16, 2013

Introduction: Al-Qaeda's Post-9/11 Devolution and Its Diffuse Network of "Associates," "Affiliates," Insurgents, and "Homegrown" Terrorists

I begin this message with condolences for myself and you on the death of our dear brother Shaykh Sa'id, God rest his soul. May the Almighty honor him with what he desires.... I also offer condolences on the deaths of our dear brothers Abu-'Umar al-Baghdadi and Abu Hamza al-Muhajir and those who waged Jihad with them until they died.

Osama bin Laden[1]

This book is about the post-9/11 *devolution* of al-Qaeda and the emergence of its affiliates, insurgent and associated organizations. Al-Qaeda's jihadist war against the United States has been transformed into a complex fractured struggle waged by determined and fanatical Islamists. Some of the battles have been triggered by international interventions in Afghanistan and Iraq. Most, however, are the consequence of local grievances cojoining with the dramatic growth of jihadist intellectual currents that have engulfed the Muslim world. These struggles as the Syrian civil war vividly demonstrates have a pronounced sectarian and localized nature that has blunted al-Qaeda's emphasis in attacking the American *far enemy.*

Devolution involves the *erosion of an organization's central authority and the empowerment of its local branches to develop and implement policy.* Prior to 9/11 al-Qaeda was very much a hierarchy where specific decisions and policies were made by a few key leaders. Peter Bergen's early work on al-Qaeda describes it as corporate enterprise with bin Laden as its Board Chairman.[2] Secure in its Afghan sanctuary between 1996 and 2001 bin Laden and his Shura Council was able to direct al-Qaeda's military, financial, and media operations. The historic Saudi leader determined targets, selected attack teams, and allocated funds for each project. The American military retaliation after 9/11 shattered al-Qaeda command and control capability and effectively fragmented the organization into a loose network of aligned groups and affiliates.

Al-Qaeda's post-9/11 predicament is similar to the plight of criminal organizations facing severe law enforcement pressure.[3] The experiences of Mexican cartels during the past decade are illustrative of al-Qaeda's post-9/11 organizational diffusion. Faced with prosecution of key leaders the Juarez, Gulf, and Sinaloa began to fragment into loose networks of criminal gangs acting autonomously and often at cross-purposes. Chris Dishman describes networks as involving "disperse nodes of cells or individual interknitted by common beliefs, ideologies, doctrines and goals."[4] Given law enforcement and financial pressures this diffuse network of individual cells began to pursue agendas that diverged from the wishes of a weakened central headquarters. The fragmentation can be severe enough that individual nodes break from the parent organization and become their competitors and antagonists.

The rise of the paramilitary *Los Zetas* is emblematic of the organizational fissures affecting the Mexican drug trade. Composed of ex-Special Forces personnel, *Los Zetas* were originally hired killers for the Gulf Cartel that eventually formed their own ultraviolent criminal organization eventually challenging the hegemony of its Gulf parent organization.[5] Weakened by government criminal prosecution that decapitated their central leaderships, cartels have devolved into dozens of ultraviolent armed gangs impervious to hierarchical coordination. Dishman describes this process as "every cell for itself" and argues that al-Qaeda has undergone a comparable process.[6]

With its hierarchical chain of command disrupted after 9/11, al-Qaeda experienced severe centrifugal pressures. Organizationally bin Laden's group flattened out with regional and local emirs taking on more responsibility to develop policy. The progression of al-Qaeda affiliates in Iraq, the Maghreb, Somalia, and Yemen is a consequence of regional emirs joining with local jihadists who swore *fidelity* to bin Laden's leadership. The severity of al-Qaeda's losses in the US military counterstrike forced the organization, furthermore, to reach out to other jihadist organizations to develop a common response to the US war on terror. Its previous relations with groups like the Moroccan Islamic Combat Group (MICG) and the Southeast Asian Jemaah Islamiyah (JI) facilitated this process where al-Qaeda hope to inspire these groups to attack Western interests.

Some analysts have viewed this organizational fragmentation as a source of al-Qaeda strength and a few even saw it as a confirmation that the West is losing the *war on terror*.[7] This narrative reached its apogee during the 2005–7 period in Iraq as it appeared that the country was headed toward civil war and inevitable American military defeat. This pessimistic view was reinforced when al-Qaeda attacked the Madrid and London transport systems producing mass upheaval and in the Spanish case al-Qaeda's attacks altered electoral and policy outcomes. Spain's military withdraw from Iraq seemed to foreshadow America's imminent defeat at the hands of a determined hydra-headed al-Qaeda menace. As the late Michael Radu cynically noted in one of his commentaries for the Foreign Policy Research Institute of Philadelphia (FPRI), the Spanish Socialist government's decision to withdraw forces from Iraq after the Madrid attacks proved "terror works!"[8]

Al-Qaeda's appendages in Yemen, Somalia, Iraq, Afghanistan, and the Maghreb hoped to draw the United States into many fronts *vexing* and *exhausting* the American superpower. Faced with mounting troop losses and economic burdens created by the *war on terror*, the American monolith would disengage from the Middle East allowing al-Qaeda the ability to exploit a power vacuum. Al-Qaeda theorists Abu Musab Suri and Abu Bakr Naji wrote voluminous treatises on the inevitable defeat of the United States beleaguered in its ability to subdue *valiant* bands of Muslim fighters.

They believed that the West would inevitably succumb to this *vexation* and *exhaustion* strategy. Some Western academics agreed with his prediction. In fact, it was "expert" opinion in 2006 that al-Qaeda had succeeded in Iraq and the country was inexorably headed for civil war.[9] These analysts reckoned that the best "realist" strategy" was to withdraw and cut American losses. It is now clear that had this advice been taken that an al-Qaeda "victory" would be a foregone conclusion.

While the al-Qaeda is winning the *war on terror* perspective still has adherents, the potency of their arguments has diminished. Al-Qaeda reverses in Iraq, the hollowing of its leadership by Predator drone attacks in Waziristan, the travails of many of its affiliates and the death of Osama bin Laden (OBL) are one of many factors that suggest the jihadist movement has stalled. Significant declines in al-Qaeda's support across the Muslim world reinforced by the emergence of the prodemocracy Arab Spring movement has weakened the jihadist cause.

This is especially true with the rise of Islamist governments in Tunisia, Morocco, Jordan, and Egypt that after democratic elections pose major strategic challenges for al-Qaeda. Despite the recent military overthrow of Muhammad Morsi's Islamist government in Egypt, al-Qaeda's *near enemy* narrative of apostate governments implacably hostile to Islam looks increasingly hollow.

Al-Qaeda's principal agenda of forcing a US disengagement from the Middle East has floundered as have its efforts at violent insurrection against Muslim *apostate* regimes.

Where regimes have been overturned it has been the consequence of nonviolent civil disobedience campaigns in Tunisia and Egypt and a NATO supported insurrection against Qaddafi's Libyan regime. In each case al-Qaeda was uninvolved and unprepared for the rapidity of events. The Syrian revolt, similarly, is a consequence of internal dynamics and long simmering sectarian conflicts. At most al-Qaeda can hope to exploit the resulting turmoil in Syria and gain a temporary sanctuary governed by the fanatical al-Nusra Front. Such sanctuaries are precarious. French and African forces, for example, easily displaced al-Qaeda in the Islamic Maghreb (AQIM) and its allies from their northern Malian "safe haven."

Al-Qaeda affiliates in Iraq, Yemen, and Somalia have witnessed reverses with many of their leaders killed or imprisoned. The list of al-Qaeda fallen (Abu Musab Zarqawi, Anwar al-Awlaki, Abu Yahya al-Libi, Mohammed Atef, Abu Hamza, and Amir Azizi) continues to mount. Increasingly local actors are taking responsibility in the fight against al-Qaeda affiliates with Pan-African forces in Somalia supporting Sufi militias to fight al-Shabaab. The Economic Community of West African States (ECOWAS) with European and North American financial and technical assistance is training a Pan-African force to stabilize North Mali after France's January 2013 military intervention. The Gallic effort drove Islamist forces from their Kindal, Gao, and Timbuktu bastions into the northern mountains near the Algerian border where many of their key leaders have been killed. The French contingent will be replaced by regional forces. The jihadist war has fractured and devolved into a struggle against local enemies reversing bin Laden's strategy to attack the United States *far enemy*.

Most significantly al-Qaeda has failed to strike decisively against the American homeland. Inspired by al-Qaeda in the Arabian Peninsula (AQAP) ideologue Anwar al-Awlaki lectures and e-mail conversations, Palestinian-American US Army Major Nidal Hassan killed 13 of his fellow serviceman at his Fort Hood Texas base. It remains al-Qaeda's most successful post-9/11 attack to date on US territory. The Obama Administration continues to mistakenly describe Hassan's shooting as "workplace violence."[10]

The greatest evidence of al-Qaeda decay and failure, ironically, comes from al-Qaeda's Abbottabad correspondence. Seized by US forces in their storming of OBL's Pakistani compound, the 17 declassified letters authored by bin Laden and his key associates paint a picture of a weakened, dysfunctional organization incapable of controlling its "affiliates" and "insurgent" groups.[11] The letters describe "aligned" groups as driven by fanatical, counterproductive violence against largely local enemies. Bin Laden chastises al-Shabaab and AQAP for their pursuit of local struggles. They, in his view, did not know the correct path to jihad.

The historic leader's letters laments al-Qaeda's association with Zarqawi's Iraqi jihad and his repulsion at al-Qaeda in Iraq's (AQI) nihilistic violence against the Shi'ite Muslim community. His correspondence reinforces Ayman al-Zawahiri 2005 letter that expressed dissatisfaction with AQI's sectarian campaign. The Iraqi jihad, bin Laden recognized, damaged al-Qaeda's brand name in the Muslim world. Al-Qaeda's media expert American Adam Gadahn urged his organization to break all ties to its "affiliates" in his Abbottabad correspondence. Significantly, bin Laden never formally recognized any other group as an al-Qaeda appendage. Prior to his death, bin Laden appeared troubled and insecure. When recognition of affiliates was forthcoming, Ayman al-Zawahiri granted it.

Bin Laden was so worried that "affiliates" were damaging his organization that he proposed an al-Qaeda office to centralize media operations for its diverse branches. Had it been implemented, this measure would surely have failed. Al-Qaeda *affiliates* and *insurgent groups* are preoccupied with an ideological and military war against their "apostate" *near enemies*. At best al-Qaeda can give advice, training, and augment aligned groups armed capability against local enemies. It cannot, however, completely transform their jihadist struggle toward attacks against the United States or its European allies. Significantly, al-Qaeda has not launched a major successful attack in the West since its London subway and bus bombings some eight years ago.

Osama's exasperation with his affiliates' struggles with local adversaries is somewhat puzzling. Al-Qaeda's post-9/11 alliance with regional jihadist networks conflated the *near* with the *far enemy*. By providing expertise and training to such groups al-Qaeda was assisting their struggles against their *apostate* enemies. Al-Qaeda in essence was joining their war against predominately Muslim regimes forcing these governments to assist the United

States in the *war on terror*. Given the immediacy of the struggle against local adversaries these groups largely targeted native security services and their civilian supporters. This is even true of AQAP which is alone in having a sustained policy of targeting the United States.

Ayman al-Zawahiri's leadership of al-Qaeda's network furthermore aggravates the terror organizations problems. West Point's Combating Terrorism Center analysis of the Abbottabad letters argues that Zawahiri and bin Laden where at odds on the incorporation of regional jihadist groups into al-Qaeda's organizational umbrella. The Egyptian is widely disliked by the bin Laden Saudi-Yemeni branch of al-Qaeda and his lack of charisma impairs the effectiveness of an organization dependent upon a mythic heroic figure. Given his decades long struggle against the Egyptian regime, Zawahiri's commitment to bin Laden's *far enemy* approach is suspect.

The jihadist struggle against "apostate" governments is anything but promising. Al-Qaeda "affiliates" and "insurgent groups" have not succeeded in their struggles against their opponents. The AQAP, AQIM, and al-Shabaab have been unable to seize political power. Their quest for an extremist Islamic state purified of Western influence has been frustrated by stubborn local, regional, and international resistance. Al-Qaeda's "affiliates" and "insurgents" have been able to create partial safe havens for terror operations that are tenuous and reversible.

Al-Qaeda's numerous branches operate on the margins of failed states and their ideological extremism breeds more enemies than friends. AQIM's ten-month sanctuary in Mali was punctuated by such ideological extremism that it invited French military intervention that easily drove Islamist forces from major urban centers. French troops were cheered by Timbuktu and Gao's inhabitants weary of repressive Islamist rule that included stoning and amputations. Several AQIM leaders have died in the ensuing fighting in northern mountains close to the Algerian border and the group's prospects for rejuvenation are grim. They may be able to mount a protracted guerrilla campaign against Pan-African forces and persist on criminal finance. So far their counterattacks have resulted mainly in the death of their own militants

Some observers interpret al-Qaeda inroads in West Africa and the rise of Ansar Dine (AD) and Boko Haram (BH) as a harbinger of a new jihadist war against the West.[12] Here too local concerns are paramount and the ultraviolent sectarian agenda of these movements has aroused much local opposition. Once a group adopts a jihadist worldview of Islamic purity it often is impervious to reason. Invariably it resorts to reflexive unproductive violence that becomes a source of intraorganizational division and popular revulsion.

Senior al-Qaeda commanders have been unable to control the excesses of their local militants. The Associated Press discovered a letter in a building abandoned by retreating Islamist forces in Timbuktu. Written by AQIM's historic leader Abdelmalek Droukdel the letter urged his followers to curb their destruction of Sufi shrines, moderate their imposition of Sharia, and cooperate with local groups.[13] His advice went unheeded. Droukdel accurately predicted that the excesses of his lieutenants would invite international military intervention.

The overall fragmentation of the al-Qaeda movement is underscored by recent events in Syria and the dispute between Islamic State of Iraq (ISI) and the Syrian al-Nusra Front. On April 2013, the ISI leader announced al-Nusra's integration into his movement. Baghdadi's hasty announcement was repudiated by both al-Nusra and al-Qaeda's current leader Ayman al-Zawahiri. In a subsequent letter ISI leader Baghdadi's reproaches Ayman al-Zawahiri's response.

The jihadist struggles in Yemen, Somalia, and the Maghreb predate the advent of al-Qaeda. They reflect internal economic, tribal, and political quarrels abetted by the global surge in jihadist fundamentalism. These factors drive such groups in which al-Qaeda alignment can provide ideological impetus to gain recruits, bequeath a modicum of prestige, and enhanced armed capability to fight local enemies. Within this context, the death of bin Laden's and al-Qaeda's inability to launch major strikes against the West is likely to diminish the terror group's appeal to local groups.

Al-Qaeda joined with these groups hoping to revive its operational capability that was degraded after the 9/11 attacks. The loss of its Taliban safe haven and the death of many of its militants in the US Afghan military campaign badly blunted its offensive capacity. Western countermeasures in North America and Europe, furthermore, had uprooted many al-Qaeda cells and broken up the networks financial resources.

Within this context, al-Qaeda's outreach to regional jihadist groups was logical and reasoned. Past collaboration and mutual contacts could be the basis of a new jihadist struggle that cojoined the war against the *near* and *far enemy*. Such a struggle could be simultaneous and overlapping with al-Qaeda gaining increased offensive capability to strike the Western *far enemy*, while regional jihadist organizations acquired al-Qaeda's ideological legitimacy and expertise to batter local opponents.

Initially this alliance paid mutual dividends. Al-Qaeda was able to align with the Indonesian JI network to commit the 2002 Bali bombings killing hundreds of Western tourists. A few years later al-Qaeda partnered with the MICG to launch the Madrid 2004 attacks and its ideological and logistical connections with Pakistani jihadist groups facilitated the training of British born militants who committed the July 2005 London subway and bus attacks. AQI, AQIM, al-Shabaab, and AQAP gained al-Qaeda expertise that assisted the lethality of their operations. By 2005–6 AQI almost succeeded in driving US forces from Iraq.

Given the early benefits of the association, why were al-Qaeda and its regional allies unable to achieve their objectives and sustain their partnership? A casual review of the academic literature of this period 2005–7 suggested an imminent al-Qaeda victory over the West. Why were these expectations dashed? This book seeks to answer these questions. It will do sequentially.

The book's organization and argument

Chapter 1 begins with an examination of the jihadist worldview. It is this ideological perspective that provides the impetus for the ongoing struggles between the West and jihadist groups and Islamist insurgencies against "apostate" regimes in the Muslim world. Of the two conflicts, it is the war against the *near enemy* that impassions most jihadists and has been a paramount concern in the radical Islamist movement since its inception.

The war against Muslim *apostate* states has largely defined the jihadist struggle and it continues to be the dominant tendency of the movement. Al-Qaeda's effort to bridge the gap between advocates of the *near* versus the *far enemy war* by conflating these struggles has floundered. Bin Laden's Abbottabad correspondence repeatedly complains these networks failure to target the United States.

Al-Qaeda's war against the Western *far enemy* is largely an aberrant innovation within the jihadi world and is a marked departure from a struggle that began in the 1920s with the formation of the Egyptian Muslim Brotherhood. Strains and factions within the Islamist movement have consistently worked against a unified struggle with splinter movements emerging from many jihadist organizations. The rise of *democratic* Islamist movements who have made the transition to parliamentary rule will aggravate these frictional tendencies. al-Qaeda and its branches face the unenviable prospect of taking their war to

Muslim Brotherhood inspired governments in Tunisia, Jordan, and Morocco. This is a war that they will surely lose.

Once Jihadism and its various branches have been sketched, we will look at al-Qaeda's evolution from the Afghan jihad to its development as an organized network that declared war against America. Bin Laden's ascension within al-Qaeda was facilitated by his displacement of Abdullah Azzam as key leader of the organization in a 1988 power struggle. The Saudi and his Egyptian follower Ayman al-Zawahiri quarreled with Azzam on key ideological and strategic issues. Azzam's mysterious 1989 assassination outside a Pakistani mosque paves the way for bin Laden and Zawahiri more expansive vision of jihad that includes attacks against the *near* and *far enemy*.

Chapter 2 analyzes al-Qaeda organizational and ideological trajectory that propels the devastating 9/11 attacks. Al-Qaeda's partnership with its East Asian allies in the Philippines and Indonesia sets the context for the 9/11 attacks and al-Qaeda's post-9/11 strategy that started with JI's 2002 Bali bombings that targeted Western tourists. Al-Qaeda's ascension and its assaults against the United States were greatly facilitated by successive administrations who failed to take decisive action against the terror network.

Chapter 3 discusses the US military strike against al-Qaeda and the Taliban after 9/11 that resulted in the death of tens of thousands of Islamic militants badly weakening al-Qaeda. Bin Laden's miscalculation of the American response inspired a significant debate in the jihadi community. Surprised by the 9/11 attacks (whose secrecy was fiercely guarded) and the ferocity and innovativeness of the US counterstrike, al-Qaeda's leaders were uncertain of the way forward. Internal criticism of al-Qaeda's organization and leadership was significant. Committed to a war against the *near enemy*, many militants were openly critical of the attacks. Others saw al-Qaeda's leadership and structure deficient in its war against the *far enemy*. Some advocated far reaching reorganization.

One such critic was Syrian Abu Musab Suri who denounced al-Qaeda's hierarchical organization and direction. He reckoned al-Qaeda's central location in Afghanistan and left it vulnerable to American retaliation that laid ways to its offensive capability. Badly crippled al-Qaeda desperately needed an alternative strategy to attack its opponents.

Suri's 1,600 page *The Call for a Global Islamic Resistance* builds upon Che Guevara's *el foco* theory and his approach is preconditioned upon small bands of Muslims spontaneously rising up to defend the Muslim community or *ummah* against American retaliation.[14] Bands of tens and twenties across the

Muslim world, Suri reasoned would attack occupying Western troops in Iraq and Afghanistan. These assaults he believed combined with terrorist attacks by Diaspora immigrant communities in Europe and North America could defeat the Crusader-Zionist alliance sapping its will to wage war. Some Western academic observers claim Suri is the architect of al-Qaeda's post-9/11 strategy. Under Suri's conceptualization, al-Qaeda would provide an ideological stimulus that would trigger an uncoordinated decentralized jihadist war to defeat the United States.

With a safe haven across the Pakistani border after the US invasion of Afghanistan, al-Qaeda's leadership opted for a variation in Suri's strategy. Instead of a spontaneous disorganized jihad of small guerrilla bands, al-Qaeda sought alliances with preexisting terror networks operating in the Maghreb, Pakistan, Indonesia, and the Middle East. It hoped the notoriety of 9/11 attacks and the American involvement in the Afghan war would consolidate mujahidin forces transcending past ideological divisions.

Published on al-Qaeda websites in 2004 Abu Bakr Naji's *Management of Savagery: The Most Critical Stage through Which the Ummah Will Pass* sketches the terror group's post-9/11 doctrine of partnering with jihadist groups to *vex* and *exhaust* the West.[15] It speaks favorably of al-Qaeda's alliance with Indonesian militants to attack Western interests in Bali and suggests that the 2002 operation is a model guiding future action. Al-Qaeda provided Bali's Indonesian terrorists with money and expertise. The Bali operation would set the ideological and operational context for the Madrid and London bombings.

Naji outlines an al-Qaeda led strategy to draw Western forces and their apostate allies into protracted multiple battlefields in the Muslim World. Jihadist groups with networks in the West would also strike at soft targets in European countries to break the West's determination to pursue the *war on terror*. With its troops under attack abroad, its finances strained by military operations, and its citizens assaulted at home, Naji believed a *weak* and *effeminate* West would disengage its forces from the Middle East and Islamic lands.

The Management of Savagery also envisions a war against apostate regimes who badly weakened by Western abandonment would fall to Islamic forces. Much of Naji's book speaks to the consolidation of Islamic land by Muslim forces and the imposition of Taliban like rule.

This, not al-Suri's version of *el foco*, becomes al-Qaeda failed response to the US *war on terror*. By partnering with groups like the Pakistani Tehrik-e-Taliban (TTP), the Indonesian JI, MICG and by assisting insurgencies in Iraq, Afghanistan, and Somalia against foreign occupation forces and apostate regimes, al-Qaeda sought to defeat both the *far* and *near* enemy. Al-Qaeda's regional diversification strategy becomes the basis for the development of affiliated branches in Iraq, Yemen, Somalia, and the Maghreb.

Subsequent chapters of the book deal with al-Qaeda's *vexation* and *exhaustion* strategy and how the policy evolved in different regional contexts. Chapter 4 chronicles al-Qaeda sponsorship of the Madrid and London attacks that were a joint project between it and local-regional jihadi networks. Commissioned during the height of the Iraqi insurgency against US forces, these attacks represent the zenith of al-Qaeda's post-9/11 success. The Madrid and London attacks were not simply the work of homegrown terrorists but the product of a vast network of international, regional, and local jihadist organizations. Al-Qaeda's extensive involvement in both operations contradicts Marc Sageman's characterization that Madrid and London attacks were committed by homegrown terrorists.[16]

Since the July 2005 London attacks, al-Qaeda has encountered significant reversals. The failure of the Iraqi jihad discussed in Chapter 5 that so heavily weighs in bin Laden's commentaries has been particularly damaging. Formed in 2003 by Jordanian Abu Musab Zarqawi, AQI seemed positioned to implement Naji's *vexation* and *exhaustion* strategy. Zarqawi's high stakes strategy of attacking Shia religious centers and civilian populations almost provoked a full-scale sectarian war and an American military disengagement. By 2005 al-Qaeda was so firmly implanted in parts of the Sunni Triangle that it was on the verge of becoming a terror sanctuary.

The Jordanian's death in an American airstrike in the summer of 2006 left the organization without a charismatic and ruthless leader. AQI's subsequent reorganization under a variety of leaders was unable to regain its former dynamism. Zarqawi's AQI network, moreover, mistakenly challenged the tribal authority of Sunni sheiks in Anbar Province who confronted with al-Qaeda's killing of their members, aligned with US forces. America's formation of Sunni militias in late 2006 combined with Special Forces targeting of AQI leaders reversed al-Qaeda's dominant position in the Sunni Triangle. AQI's successor organization ISI hopes to capitalize on the sectarian bloodletting that has characterized recent events in Syria, Iraq, and Lebanon. ISI's attempted partnership with the Syrian al-Nusra Front declaring a regional Islamic state advances a policy that bin Laden and his associates rejected in their Abbottabad correspondence. The counterproductive violence and sectarian agenda of AQI's war against its adversaries resurfaces in the behavior of other al-Qaeda branches.

Chapter 6 analyzes al-Qaeda "affiliates" and "insurgent groups" in Somalia, Yemen, and the Maghreb whose ideological fanaticism has bred intense resistance and greatly limited their capacity to achieve strategic objectives. These groups have needlessly brutalized civilian populations. Al-Shabaab's 2012 retreat from the port of Kismayo to advancing African Union (AU) forces is one of many recent defeats. Al-Qaeda's diverse branches may survive on the margins of weak states but they have limited capacity or inclination (the Yemeni branch aside) to strike the Western homeland. Their reliance on criminal activity betrays and discredits their jihadist credentials.

Chapter 7 looks at jihad's advance in West Africa with the rise of BH in Nigeria and AQIM ally AD in North Mali. Characteristic of earlier jihadist movements like the Algerian Armed Islamic Group (GIA), both groups have entered an incipient ultraviolent phase that is likely to be their undoing. Signs are particularly telling in North Mali where AQIM and its allies have recently lost much of their territorial *safe haven* to French-Malian forces. Though it remains a force to destabilize Nigerian society BH and its splinter group Ansaru are unlikely to seize power in the country's northern region.

Bin Laden's pessimistic assessment of his *aligned*, *insurgent*, and *associated* groups sets the stage for Chapter 8 of the book. Al-Qaeda's inability to sustain its *vexation* and *exhaustion* strategy represents its greatest singular failure. The chapter addresses this issue by examining the organization's efforts to attack America. Only AQAP has demonstrated a desire to assault the US homeland after 9/11 and its efforts have been sporadic and largely ineffective. Within this context, AQAP's encouragement of US Army Major Nidal Hassan's 2009 killing of thirteen fellow servicemen at his Fort Hood military base represents its greatest post-9/11 *success*. This is true even if the Boston Marathon bombings of April 2013 which killed three persons but wounded hundreds are eventually linked to al-Qaeda or affiliate branches.

These few successes, however, must be weighed against numerous failures to strike America like Nigerian born Islamist Farouk Abdulmutallab inability to ignite his underwear clad explosives on a Christmas Day 2009 flight from Amsterdam to Detroit. Most of al-Qaeda's inspired terror plots against America since 9/11 have featured amateurs that have fallen prey to FBI or police sting operations.[17] It underscores the dangers of relying on local jihadists who lack sufficient training and stealth to launch attacks.

Chapter 9 is a retrospective of al-Qaeda's failed war against the West. With many of its senior leaders killed in drone strikes and its Taliban TTP ally weakened by Pakistani military incursions, al-Qaeda in Waziristan is under severe pressure. Equally critical has been Predator drone and Special Forces operations against the Haqqani-al-Qaeda network in Afghanistan and Pakistan where scores of midlevel commanders have been killed. Bin Laden's death, moreover, has triggered internal conflicts in the organization and it is unlikely that Ayman al-Zawahiri will be able to regenerate al-Qaeda's offensive capability. The Egyptian is greatly disliked by al-Qaeda's Saudi-Yemeni wing. Al-Qaeda's fracturing is likely to intensify.

The Arab Spring protest movement and the ascension of democratic Islamist political parties and governments offer several major ideological challenges for al-Qaeda. Among these are the Muslim Brotherhood governments in Egypt, Jordan, Morocco, and Tunisia accepting of democratic rules that the jihadi organization rejects. Confronting such regimes requires al-Qaeda to mount a terror campaign against Islamist governments that ideologically and organizationally will be difficult to sustain. Very few Muslims are likely to join al-Qaeda's jihad against Islamist governments.

While al-Qaeda may hope to capitalize on the instability generated by the overthrow of the Tunisian, Libyan, and Egyptian regimes, it has failed to develop a mass political movement or popular following capable of securing territorial control. Much of the region's political violence has an increasingly sectarian dimension. Jihadist mobilization in Iraq, Syria, and Lebanon against Shia and Alawite "apostates" is diverting Jihadism away from the organization's *far enemy* strategy.

Al-Qaeda is not yet defeated, but it is a badly crippled and failed organization. The terror network is unlikely to overcome its ideological, political, and strategic problems. Its future is likely to be confined to remote areas of failed states where it will continue to be harassed by local and international enemies. This is the book's main argument.

1

Al-Qaeda's Jihadist Worldview

Thus the plague that exists in the nations of Muslims has two causes: The first is the presence of American hegemony and the second is the presence of rulers that have abandoned Islamic law and who identify with this hegemony, serving its interests in exchange for securing their own interests. The only way for us to establish the religion and alleviate the plague which has befallen Muslims is to remove this hegemony which has beset upon the nations of worshipers and which transforms them, such that no regime that rules on the basis of Islamic law remains. The way to remove this hegemony is to continue our direct attrition against the American enemy until it is broken and is too weak to interfere in the matters of the Islamic world. After this phase comes the phase in which the second cause-rulers who have abandoned Islamic law are toppled, and this will be followed by the phase in which God's religion is established and Islamic law rules.

Osama bin Laden[1]

This book examines al-Qaeda's jihadist worldview as expressed in its ideology and practice. It is a study of the group and its progressive *devolution* since 9/11. Movements are about ideas that compel their adherents into action. For the jihadist movement this involves war and martyrdom. Jihad compels violent action against apostates and foreign aggressors in the defense and expansion of Islam.

The jihadist worldview entails a set of beliefs that impel some purposeful violent action. The connection between Islam and Jihadism can be quite complex and thorny.[2] The centrality of jihad in Islam has inspired much controversy among scholars.[3] Controversies are endemic to scholarly investigation of

Radical Islam and Jihadism for it is a minefield beset by definitional quandaries and methodological problems. Scholars continue to debate over the meaning of Islamism, Radical Islam, and Salafism.[4]

This book deals with al-Qaeda's reinterpretation of a variant of Radical Islamist thought known as Jihadism. It is not an effort to examine Islamism, Salafism, or Islam. Its central aim is to analyze al-Qaeda and how it has reconfigured the ideology and practice of jihad. Since al-Qaeda subscribes to jihadist ideology it is imperative to look at the tradition's core precepts and its historic-philosophical origins. It is a fairly complex and varied ideology.

Al-Qaeda's ideological and religious origins

Though Jihadism has roots in Islamism, Salafism, and Islam it is a conceptually distinct doctrine recognized by diverse theorists.[5] Jihad's meaning is a source of contention—classical Quranic interpretations view it as war in defense of Islam not as in later Sufi interpretations as personal struggle. Some view Jihadism as a perversion of Islam and Islamism because of its follower's takfiri tendency to view Muslims not committed to their cause as "apostates."[6] Though most Muslims accept jihad as an important religious duty, they view it as a defensive doctrine and not as an affirmative obligation to violently spread Islam. Historically jihad has been a collective responsibility undertaken by state entities in the defense and expansion of Islam.

Jihadism is pronounced in its violent agitation against impious Muslims and foreigners. It is an ideology that espouses multiple confrontations. While Jihadism seeks the recreation of the "enlightened rule" of Mohammad and his four "righteous" successors, it is not purely a Salafist doctrine, and is influenced by Marxist and fascistic ideas that transport it far from the classical tenets of Islam.[7]

Many Salafists who share the jihadist desire to recreate an authentic pure Islam want to achieve it by nonviolent evolution. Many prescribe preaching as a principal mode to achieve their desired ends. Whether the Salafists can achieve their Sharia state without the use of coercion is questionable. But at least conceptually one can make a distinction.

The exhortation to violence in the jihadist worldview sets it apart from Islam, Salafism, and Islamism. It is an ideology inspired by Islam but carried forth by political events, personal ambitions, and a doctrinal obeisance to European fascistic-communist ideas that extol violence, the glory of war, and the cleansing of impurity to achieve social justice. Like its fascist and communist brethren, it feeds off real and imaginary social injustices and the transcendental need for the recreation of a mythical past.[8] Frequently such beliefs lead to nihilistic behavior.

Jihadism's propensity for violence knows no bounds and seeks to eviscerate that which lies in its immediate path. A fact underscored by the bloody history of Jihadism waged primarily against Muslims some of whom today are Islamists. The jihadist use of unrestrained violence predates the Crusades and is instead imbedded in the theological and political struggles of the Muslim community called the *ummah*.[9]

Jihadism desires the recreation of a mythic idealized past based on the seventh-century evolution of Islam through violent means. Its emotive and spiritual power is based upon the exaltation of a glorious past, its castigation of an ignominious present and its promise of a transcendent future that restores God's sovereignty (*Hakimiya*) on Earth.

The ideology desires to purify the *ummah* of foreign influence for jihadists believe Westernization is responsible for Islam's regression. Accordingly, the Ottoman Empire's decline, its subsequent collapse and European colonization are vivid testimony to the *ummah*'s misguided acculturation of foreign influence. The West's unnatural ascendance is interpreted by jihadists as an aberration that can be transcended by internal purification, violent agitation, and revolution.

Jihadism has been defined as a modern phenomenon anchored in fundamentalist reactions to Western dominance.[10] While a correct interpretation is jihadist agitation has historical antecedents. Jihadism is also furthered by the Quran's later passages that hail violent confrontation against apostates and exalt Islamic conquest.

The theological impulse for war contained in the Medina *suras* contributed to violent confrontations in Islam's formative development.[11] Early Islam was beset by violent power struggles that contradict the jihadist conception of a mythic idealized past.[12] Internecine conflict over who should rule the *ummah* endures to this day and is a persistent theme of Islamic history.

The war within the Muslim world

The battle over Islam's development begins with seventh-century struggle between Ali and Othman over succession to the caliphate. The death of Mohammad's fourth successor left a leadership void with two claimants contending for power. Based on his status as the Prophet's son-in-law Ali claimed rightful passage to rule, a right that Othman a Syrian governor contested.

The resulting civil war ended when Ali retired his candidacy and was murdered by outraged supporters disgusted by his capitulation. Ali's conflict with Othman has enduring sectarian and ideological repercussions. Both the Shia-Sunni split and revolutionary jihadist traditions are anchored in this period.[13] The extreme violence witnessed in contemporary Syria is indelibly shaped by both sectarian and jihadist passions.

Othman's "victory" over Ali would never be accepted by Ali's supporters who mounted fierce campaigns against Othman's impious rule. Succession to the caliphate was plagued by multiple interpretations. Shiites centered on the genealogical connections to Mohammad's family while Sunni radicals fixated on the piety of the ruler and his fidelity to traditional Islamic principles. As Efraim Karsh reminds us, caliphate succession issues involve politics and personal ambition that comarry with sectarian and ideological passions.[14] Invariably these conflicts have frustrated the attainment of a unified ummah capable of achieving global dominance.

Efforts to control the *ummah*'s development have inspired fanatics who seek to recreate Mohammad's rule and luxuriate in Allah's divine radiance.[15] They have used unrestrained violence justified by religious mandates. It has given rise to a culture of martyrdom and retribution that has inspired multitudes.

These historical rivalries contribute to conflict in the Muslim world that has profound significance for Western security. The intersection of intra-Muslim conflict and foreign conspiracy is a central narrative of Medieval and Modern Islamic radicals. Much of their discourse alludes to conspiratorial anti-Islamic plots and insidious plans.

Jihadism has a significant historical pedigree rooted in the rejection of apostate "Muslim" rulers. According to this narrative, Greek and Persian influences under the Umayyad and Abbasid caliphates had corrupted Muslim rulers and created internal atrophy. This sets the stage for the collapse of the Ottomans and European conquests of the Middle East and North Africa.

Jihadists believe this occurred early in Islam's development. The eighth-century Kharajite rebellions against impious Sunni leaders exacerbated the sectarian divide and gave legitimacy to Shi'ite populist revolts against corrupt Sunni rulers whose foreign influence, inadequate genealogical lineage, and worldly ambitions disqualified their rule.[16]

The Kharajites would be followed by their eleventh- and twelfth-century ideological heirs the Assassins whose fierce terror campaigns struck fear in Sunni apostate rulers and European crusaders.[17] Such fanaticism remains a central characteristic of Shi'ite radicalism represented by elite formations like Hezbollah and the Revolutionary Guards.

Outrage over impious rulers reoccurs throughout Islamic history and explains the inability of Muslim leaders to achieve hegemonic dominance.[18] The desire to recreate a mythic past is reflected in the role of the Mahdi in Islamic philosophy.[19] He represents a quasi-divine figure capable of morally cleansing society, rectifying past injustice, and restoring past glory.

The Islamist response to foreign domination

Resistance to foreign corruption and Islamic revisionism is contained in the work of medieval Turkish-Syrian scholar Ibn Taymiyya who urged rebellion against Mongol rulers whose conversion to Islam was seen as unauthentic.[20] Modern Islamist theorists like Abul Ala Maududi and Sayyid Qutb make reference to Taymiyya in their philosophical works. Both see themselves in his tradition of radical violent agitation.[21]

Hostility to the non-Arab Muslims corrupted by Western or Asiatic influence may reflect Arab Islamic chauvinism that, despite Islam's international aspiration, seeks to recreate the early successes of Islamic Arab rulers. Ephraim Karsh argues this sentiment propelled the development of Pan-Arab nationalism that despite its secular orientation took great pride in past Arab caliphates.[22] The Pan-Arabists looked to Islam as an important factor in building a coalition against Israel.

The impulse toward rebellion against impiety and its concomitant desire to recreate a mythic utopian past has inspired many modern Islamist thinkers amenable to but not reflexive in their violent activism. Jihadist movements are inspired by foreign aggression and corrupting internal influence. While the Crusades and Colonialism had catalyzed jihadist movements, external aggression is an important but not necessary condition. Many Western analysts mistakenly believe that jihadists have no inherent violent tendencies.[23] This position is contradicted by radical Islamist theorist defenses for jihad and global conquest. Jihadist struggles predate Western ascendance.

Muslim assimilation of Western influences, however, does play a vital role in jihadist development. Within the context of the Ottoman Empires atrophy,

Napoleon's expeditionary forces in Egypt invited an intense debate in the Muslim World.[24] Most Muslim intellectuals sought to incorporate Western influence and some promoted cultural adjustment to facilitate modernization. With its close juxtaposition to Europe, the Turks were leaders in this regard. Acculturation to Western values increased during the final stages of the Ottoman Empire and accelerated dramatically under Kemal Ataturk post-WWI secularization campaign and abolition of the caliphate. Jihadists consider Ataturk's abolition of the caliphate in 1924 as the epitome of evil.

Assimilation and incorporation of Western influence was not universal. The nineteenth-century Mahdist revolt in Sudan expressed jihadist rage against the Colonial period. Sudanese Sufi mystic Mohammad Ahmad launched a rebellion against the British supported Ottoman-Egyptian occupation. Proclaiming himself Mahdi, he sought to liberate the Sudan of apostates and foreigners.

Driven by Messianic desires to create an authentic Islamic community, the Mahdi achieved some success with the conquest of Khartoum and the death of the British General "Chinese" Gordon. His jihadist state, however, was short lived. The Mahdi's successors would be defeated by British imperial forces that reimposed Turkish-Egyptian rule over the Sudan. Over a century later Sudanese leader Hussan al-Turabi sought to recreate the Mahdi's dreams of a regional caliphate. His regime provided bin Laden's terror network sanctuary in the early 1990s that proved critical in al-Qaeda's development.

The Mahdist rebellion proved ephemeral. It would be displaced by a quieter but profoundly revolutionary philosophical resistance to European dominance. This philosophical rebellion against foreign penetration of Muslim lands and Muslim acculturation to Western influence reaches its highest development in the work of two scholars who span the geographical canvass that is Islam.

Both reacted negatively to Western dominance and especially opposed Ataturk's policies whose separation of the political and religious realms was considered a villainous betrayal of Islam. Their work plays a formidable role in the development of the modern jihadist movement.

Maududi and Qutb

Harking back to a mythological past, Pakistani Abul Ala Maududi spoke of the twin perils of foreign influence and aggression.[25] Like the Karijites and the

Mahdi, Maududi urged resistance to Western acculturation and domination through armed rebellions and Islamic purity.[26]

Maududi reasoned that Muslim regression was a consequence to Western assimilation that could best be combated by recreating the cultural and religious context of authentic seventh-century Islam. Once the *ummah* was purified, Muslim capabilities to ward off foreign dominance could be fortified.

Maududi believed that the *ummah*'s religious-cultural purification would allow Muslims to rebuild a global caliphate to spread Allah's divine will across the globe. At its core, Maududi's work reflects an insecure fear of individual freedom and pluralism typical of all totalitarian ideologies that exalt a mythic past and seek total personal conformity. His texts *The Meaning of the Quran* and *Jihad and Society* are unapologetic in their defense of a totalitarian Islamic state and global conquest.[27]

The Pakistani believed that the Enlightenment's emphasis on personal autonomy and its separation of Church and State was a weakening, corrupting influence. Maududi argued European colonialism's export of Enlightenment freedoms and democracy was part of an insidious design to destroy Islam and break the *ummah*'s communal bounds.

Maududi's reaction represents a symbiosis between cultural-religious conservatism and anti-imperialist revulsion to European conquest. Maududi's ideas, however, pale in comparison to his Egyptian fellow traveler Sayyid Qutb who is the most revered and influential Islamist ideologue. Qutb's writings have inspired and been perverted by OBL and Ayman al-Zawahiri.[28]

Qutb's dominance among Islamist theorists is widely acknowledged. His *Milestones* is unequaled in its holistic rejection of all foreign influence and its exaltation of a mythic Islamic past that demands to be redeemed by violent agitation. Borrowing from Hassan al Banna critique of Western influence, Qutb joined the Egyptian Muslim Brotherhood and played a formidable role in the party's ideological development in the 1960s. Qutb's ideas also paved the way for the Brotherhood's most aggressive opponents who rejected their 1970's policy of accommodation to the Egyptian state. His most notorious acolyte Ayman al-Zawahiri saw the Brotherhoods informal deals with the Sadat and Mubarak regimes as a betrayal of Qutbian principles.

Qutb argued that years of European influence had produced ignorance (*jahiliyya*) of Allah's will.[29] He believed that *jahiliyya* was abetted by Muslim apostate rulers and Islamic religious revisionists who sought to make Islam congruent with modern (Western) society. Qutb argued that no genuine Islamic society could exist without a state tied to the Quran. He was especially critical of the traditional clergy of Al-Azhar University who he viewed as providing religious sanction for impious rulers.

While an early supporter of Nasser's Pan-Arabist movement, Qutb later rejected Nasser as an apostate ruler. As Paul Berman's argues, Qutb's rejection of secularism was based on its separation of religious and political authority that for Qutb creates a spiritual crisis in the Muslim World.[30] Qutb saw post-Christian Europe as a center of decadence intent on exporting hedonism and moral corruption to Islamic lands. Accordingly, Muslim political and cultural adjustment to European modernity weakened the moral foundations of the *ummah* and if unchecked would destroy Islam.

Qutb argued that Nasser's secularization policies denied Muslims the fulfillment of Allah's will that reached its zenith under Muhammad and his immediate successors. Because the seventh-century *ummah* made no separation between politics and religion, any deviation from Muhammad's Medina model is to be rejected. By separating religion from the state, Qutb reasoned, Nasser and Ataturk were guilty of apostasy for they conspired with the West to destroy Islam. Under such circumstances, jihad against such rulers was an affirmative obligation.

Qutb argued that *jahiliyya* had affected most of Muslim society and was reminiscent of Arabia's pre-Islamic period. Like the Prophet, Qutb argued this age of ignorance needed to be destroyed. Since *jahiliyya* was so profound, Qutb argued that only a small enlightened group had remained faithful to Allah's original vision. This group, Qutb argued, would lead an Islamic rebellion.[31]

Like Muhammad's early community, Qutb's vanguard would preach the true message and transform the society. Once most Muslims had restored traditional Islamic principles they would rebel against impious rulers. Only when this state of ignorance is destroyed can Islam achieve dominance that invariably leads to world domination and total conquest. Like the Italian communist leader Antonio Gramci, Qutb believed cultural transformation preconditions political transformation.

This worldview espouses a doctrine of aggressive jihad and rejects confining religious struggle to the realm of private belief. Qutb's jihadist views espouse a totalistic conception of Islam that fuses politics, personal morality, and religion in which no facet of human behavior would be relegated to the private self.[32]

His ideas depart significantly from many Sunni religious traditionalists that historically have given deference to political leaders or Muslim liberals who have advocated more assimilationist approaches.³³ The Egyptian jihadist was very critical of religious scholars associated with Cairo's Al-Azhar University. Qutb's *Milestones* belie the notion of jihad as only a consequence of external aggression.

Qutb's response to Western modernity and domination in the Muslim world is fraught with contradictions and a paradoxical reliance on Marxist-Leninist influences.³⁴ Echoing the early Bolsheviks, Qutb's revolution is guided by vanguard elites committed to the destruction of the old order. His infusion of Western totalitarian constructs for some corrupts the original Islamic foundations of his thought. It also may have propelled his progressive radicalization.

Qutb's ideas are grounded in a fascist and communist perspective that rejects Western liberalism and individualism as a corrupting bourgeois influence.³⁵ At the same time, Qutb's distinctiveness as an Islamic scholar cannot be questioned and his praxis of fascistic-communist thought with Islam is a potent combination.³⁶ The Egyptian's jihadist worldview achieves greater legitimacy through Quranic sanction that gives his ideas a quality unlike any secular totalitarian worldview. It has inspired a generation of devoted believers.

Qutb's progression toward totalitarianism was not immediate and it represents a culmination of internal reflection, egoism, and Nasserite repression. As John Calvert work speaks tellingly, Qutb emerged a radical as a product of 30-year evolution from secular nationalist and Islamic liberal to Jihadist totalitarian.³⁷ His long imprisonment and torture by Nasser's regime radicalized him. Only in the final decade of his life, did Qutb morph into a Manichean world separated by Islamic purity and Satan. Between these two worlds there could be no compromise. With its promise of universal justice and the eradication of evil one can understand the appeals of his ideas.

Qutb's blending of Lenin and Islam is not completely unique among Islamic radicals. The intersection of Marxism and Islam is represented in Shi'ite radicalism.³⁸ Some Iranian clerics connected Shia persecution with the exploitation of Marx's working class to justify their revolt against the Shah's regime. Iran's 1979 revolutionary discourse had sweeping anticapitalist rhetoric and policies that expropriated private capital. Like the Bolsheviks, Iranian radicals ruthlessly destroyed all opposition to their rule. Their revolutionary courts dispensed the same type of justice that Stalin had some 40 years earlier.

Leninism permeates radical Islamist thought with jihadists championing violent populist rebellions. Like Lenin's two-stage revolution, the Islamic rebellions would commence in the periphery against impious Muslim rulers and end in the advanced core countries with a final war of annihilation against the West. It would represent the culmination of Allah's divine will to create universal Islamic rule.

Qutb borrows heavily from fascist thought that exalts a mythic past and sees revolution as a form of national purification.[39] *Milestones Judeophobia* is eerily reminiscent of Mein Kampf and Qutb makes much of the Jews betrayal of Muhammad. Qutb, moreover, believed in the authenticity of the *Protocols of the Elders of Zion* and its portrayal of insidious Jewish financial conspiracy to control the planet. The *Protocols* have become a standard reference for many modern Islamic radicals like Abu Musab Suri, Abu Bakr Naji, and Ayman al-Zawahiri.[40]

Like some of his communist precursors Qutb is driven by egoistic pretensions devoid of human contact. His *Milestones* is a totalitarian worldview to recreate a mystical ideal past and avenge past injustice. Qutb's reported virginity and inability to find a suitable spouse is but one aspect of his egoistic behavior. So too were his aspirations toward martyrdom that would be achieved when Nasser's regime hanged him in 1966 for insurrection. His death explains his appeal for radicals out to avenge his death and carry forth his ideas.

Qutb *martyrdom* has inspired many followers some of whom have perverted and exploited his original message. *Milestones* does not lead to al-Qaeda's brand of Jihadism that while inspired by Qutb's writings repudiates many of his premises.[41] Despite his contempt for the West, Qutb's work centers on intra-Muslim conflict and not the Western *far enemy*. It is highly doubtful he would have approved of the 9/11 attacks.

Some suggest that Qutb's philosophy is largely nonviolent and he sought revolutionary transformation through preaching and conversion to transcend *jahiliyya*.[42] According to this view Qutbs sought violence against only recalcitrant rulers once most Muslims had reconnected with their faith. Qutb's revolution thus would be fairly bloodless.

Qutb's organization of violent revolutionary cells resulting in his 1964 arrest and his execution two years later belie this interpretation. Like many of his totalitarian fellow travelers, Qutb's was convinced that moral suasion amplified by violence could convince others of the righteous path and sweep away past injustice. The Khmer Rouge who killed millions of Cambodians were similarly under such illusions.

Qutb ideas contributed to the spread of revolutionary jihadist groups in Egypt. One of his followers Muhammad Faraj was a key leader in *Islamic Jihad* who sought to expand upon his mentor's legacy.[43] His political tract *The*

Neglected Duty elevated jihad to a central pillar of Islam and stressed the urgency of attacking the *near* rather than the *far enemy*.[44] Like Qutb, Faraj sought to link ideas with action. Faraj was hanged by the Mubarak regime for his complicity in the organization role in Sadat's assassination. His death added to the culture of martyrdom that most jihadists profess to aspire.

Under Qutb's grand vision, the consolidation of power in the *ummah* leads to a caliphate and Islam's global expansion. Qutb's followers are smitten with the same self-righteous egoism that propels many Marxist-Leninist revolutionaries. Despite their admiration for Qutb, many jihadists have not been dogmatic in their adherence to Qutbian principles.

Qutb's ideological descendants take the war to the far enemy as frustration begets desperation

Qutb's most important ideological heirs Abdullah Azzam, OBL, and Ayman al-Zawahiri have reinterpreted his message. They reversed Qutb's order of conflict by first targeting foreign powers, as an opening salvo in a final larger war against the Muslim apostates.[45] Their reinterpretation of Qutb is a consequence of Islamist frustration and failure to overthrow the apostate *near enemy*.[46]

Modern Sunni jihadists have failed to transform their societies through violent agitation. The Muslim Brotherhood's failed insurrections of the 1950s and 1960s and the collapse of the Algerian jihad in the late 1990s are testimony to the inability of jihadists to transform their societies. Only in weak or nonexistent states like Afghanistan and the Sudan in the 1990s did Sunni Islamic militants seize power.

Wars against foreign powers, however, were viewed as a resounding success, with the Afghan jihad as an impetus for revising Qutb's revolutionary scheme. The Palestinian Abdullah Azzam preached that the defense of the *ummah* against foreign aggression was an affirmative duty. Jihad thus formed a central place in Muslim individual life and his concept contributed to the jihadist reconfiguration of Qutb's message.[47]

As a theorist with a doctorate in Islamic religious studies and as a recruiter of Arab Afghans during the Soviet occupation of Afghanistan, Azzam unified Islamist thought with action. Indeed he is exceptional outlier among jihadists most of whom lack religious and social science training.

Azzam's personal connections to bin Laden and Zawahiri during the Afghan jihad insured his significance.[48] The Palestinian argued that glory through combat against foreign aggressors is a guarantor of martyrdom. Azzam lectures on jihad at Jeddah's King Abdulazziz University apparently riveted bin Laden during his student days.

Bin Laden was recruited in Pakistan as part of Azzam's support network for Arab fighters resisting the Soviet occupation of Afghanistan. While Azzam's doctrine of resistance was defensive and centered against foreign occupiers of Muslim land, it was a stepping stone for more aggressive version of jihad that paved the way for 9/11.

Assisted by generous US, Pakistani, and Saudi financial support, Afghan holy warriors and their Arab allies were successful in ending Soviet occupation. Despite the euphoria of victory against foreign aggressors, the immediate response of Arab jihadists was more faithful to Qutb's vision. Returning home after the Afghan jihad, these fighters refocused the struggle against the *near enemy.*

Islamic rebellions reached their bloodiest apogee in 1990's Algeria. The military's nullification of the 1991 elections denied the victorious Islamist National Salvation Front from forming a government and engendered an Islamist rebellion. Formed from the ranks of ex-Arab Afghans, the GIA led a jihadist insurrection against the government. The GIA insurgent campaign and the government's brutal counterterror policy resulted in vicious carnage leading to the deaths of hundreds of thousands

The GIA's *takfir* doctrine denounced opponents including Muslim civilians as apostates. The group's cells slaughtered villages and ritualistically beheaded opponents. Their nihilistic violence against civilians would be recreated by AQI after Saddam's overthrow by US forces. Takfiri doctrines can be seen in the brief Islamist rule in northern Mali where the Sufi populations were brutalized and their shines desecrated. Al-Qaeda's Somali affiliate al-Shabaab similarly has repressed the Sufi population in its quest to achieve Islamic purity.

Though Qutb rejected takfir doctrines, it does not take a dramatic leap to conclude that a society of nonbelievers who refuse to submit to the dictates of Islamic purity would be on the receiving end of revolutionary repression. Irrespective of Qutb's espousal of limited violence against apostate leaders, the GIA viewed itself as a Qutbian vanguard.[49]

The GIA's merciless campaign soon backfired. By the late 1990s the GIA's offensive capability was eroded by government's counterterror policy, internal divisions, and an erosion of public support. Jihadist tendencies toward extreme counterproductive violence, factionalism, and ideological extremism would be repeated in Iraq, Somalia, and Mali.[50]

Qutb's ideas inspired revolutionary agitation in his home country a generation after his death. Egyptian Islamic Jihad failed to ignite a popular rebellion against the Mubarak regime in the 1990s and its killing of civilians ignited a wave of popular revulsion that the group could not surmount. The group's high-profile terror attacks against foreign tourists at Luxor and Red Sea resorts had negative economic consequences that evaporated popular support.

Islamists groups elsewhere were no more successful than their Algerian and Egyptian comrades. The revolt of the Libyan Islamic Fighting Group (LIFG) in the 1990s was similarly repressed and unsuccessful. Like Hafez Assad's crushing of the Muslim Brotherhoods insurrection in Hama in 1982, Qaddafi's dictatorial regime ruthlessly dispatched the Islamist militants. Brutal government repression and little public support at home denied the jihadists a path to political power. Driven by frustration and disappointment, Islamists investigated why these jihadist struggles had failed.

Relying on conspiratorial explanations, Islamists saw a nefarious Zionist-Crusader alliance with the Muslim apostate rulers.[51] US financial, technical, and military assistance to Saudi Arabian, Jordanian, Moroccan, and Egyptian governments enhanced their ability to resist Islamist forces. Egypt's turn toward the United States during the Sadat regime and its subsequent signing of the Camp David Peace treaty with Israel in 1979 for jihadists exemplifies the impious nature of Sadat's government.

The advocates of war against the Western *far enemy* believed that attacks on the West could be a catalyst for ending US support for apostate regimes leaving their impious rulers vulnerable to Islamic rebellions. Faced with a wave of brutal terror attacks striking at its homeland, a weak post-Vietnam America would capitulate and disengage from the region. Heroic mujahidin would *vex* and *exhaust* the American superpower defeating its military on diverse fronts and imposing huge financial burdens.

Developed by OBL and Ayman al-Zawahiri, the *far enemy* doctrine reaches its climatic "triumph" in the 9/11 attacks. Unlike the long evolutionary struggle against the *near enemy*, the war against the *far enemy* is a recent development driven by the endurance of the *near enemy*. It is very much of a minority current in the jihadi world.

The *far enemy* strategy reverses the order of Qutb's revolutionary doctrine that viewed the struggle against the Western *far enemy* as peripheral. Despite their doctrinal deviations, bin Laden and Zawahiri are very much under Qutb's spell. Bin Laden met his brother Muhammad at King Abdulazziz University. Muhammad Qutb is a respected Islamic theorist that has spent much of his scholarly life preserving, embellishing upon, and defending his brother's legacy.[52]

Qutb's impact radiates in their personal life histories and their commitment to his legacy cannot be doubted. Hearing of Qutb's hanging by Nasser's regime, then 16-year-old Ayman al-Zawahiri committed himself to Islamist revolution. Zawahiri's *Knights under the Prophet's Banner* and *Bitter Harvest* speak glowingly of Qutb's martyrdom and ideals.[53] He longs to be in Qutb's mythic shadow.

Political events also inspired doctrinal deviations. The 1991 Gulf War introduced hundreds of thousands of US troops to protect the Saudi kingdom and expel Saddam Hussein's forces from Kuwait. Bin Laden viewed their *crusader* presence as violating Mohammad's prohibition of foreign troops in the lands of the twin sanctuaries of Mecca and Medina. The large scale US presence reinforced the praxis of Western support for impious apostate regimes so central to Islamist radical discourse. The Kingdom had betrayed Islam and defiled its honor.

Bin Laden looked in horror as infidel forces entered Saudi Arabia and an equally repulsed Zawahiri saw an Egyptian regime underwritten by American financial and military support crush Egyptian Islamic Jihad. Zawahiri was arrested by the Mubarak regime for his alleged complicity in the assassination of Anwar al-Sadat in 1981 whose signing of a peace treaty with Israel was considered by Egyptian jihadists the quintessence of villainy. He was later released and joined the Afghan jihad. He and bin Laden became exiles joining forces in Afghanistan and the Sudan. They eventually unified their organizations in Taliban protected Afghanistan.

Throughout the 1990s, events reinforced jihadist sentiments of anti-Islamic global complot. Brutal repression of the Bosnian and Chechen Muslim insurgencies intensified perceptions of an external conspiracy against Islam. The Israeli-Palestinian dispute and US support for Israel factor heavily in the saliency of conspiratorial theories in Islamist radical thought. America's status as the lone superpower in the post-Cold War era made it a convenient target for Islamist rage.

The political trajectory of 1990s lent itself to a narrative of a Zionist-Crusader conspiracy to plunder Muslim peoples, destroy their culture, and exploit their resources. Israel's usurpation of Muslim land and its oppressive policies vis-à-vis the Palestinians is one facet of a larger plot to wage war against the *ummah*.

Bin Laden's Wahhabist hostility toward foreign influences and his desire to hasten a return to the ideals of the original Muslim community contributes to the *far enemy* strategy.[54] Wahhabism was a Saudi eighteenth-century religious revivalist movement led by theologian Muhammad ibn Abd al-Wahhab who preached a return to early Islamic principles uncontaminated by foreign influences and based exclusively on the Quran and Hadith. Once the House of Saud had centralized sate power in the 1930s, Wahhabi doctrine became a state religion displacing more pluralistic Islamic traditions. Al-Qaeda's synthesis of Qutbian radicalism and Wahhabi traditionalism is a potent combination that alters the progression of jihadist strategy. Bin Laden and Zawahiri's reconfiguration of the jihadist message is an aberration that lashes out against the West and fantasizes about the *ummah*'s unification. It dreams of heroic mujahidin victories against a weak and corrupt West and revolutionary fever that revitalizes the ummah. Bin Laden-Zawahiri narrative of an impending victory over America is predicated upon the myth that Arab mujahidin had defeated the Soviets in Afghanistan.

Al-Qaeda's war against the United States involves a search for a successful strategy that had eluded Islamist revolutionaries. The failure of radical Islamism in Algeria, Egypt, and Libya in the 1990s weighed heavily on jihadists who needed some explanation for their inability to dislodge apostate regimes. Bin Laden's *far enemy* strategy was an audacious effort to topple Muslim impious rulers by bringing the war to their American protectors. Al-Qaeda's formation in Afghanistan was a consequence of long torturous process shaped by the jihadist movement's failures against the *near enemy*. It is to this issue that we now turn.

2

Al-Qaeda's Formation and Its *Far Enemy* Strategy

Introduction

My Muslim brothers of the world: Your brothers in Palestine and the land of the two holy places are calling upon your help, and asking you to take part of the fighting against the enemy—your enemy and their enemy—the Americans and the Israelis—they ask you to do whatever you can, with your own means and ability to expel the enemy, humiliated and defeated out of the sanctities of Islam.

Osama bin Laden[1]

Al-Qaeda's *far enemy* strategy desires to reignite the jihadist movement. Perplexed by Islamist failures in Algeria, Libya, and Egypt jihadists needed a new path to victory. The *far enemy* approach to jihadi revitalization emerged from struggles between contending jihadist visions. This chapter analyzes Abdullah Azzam's defensive jihad doctrine and how it morphed into al-Qaeda's attack policy against the US homeland. Bin Laden's displacement of Azzam as al-Qaeda's top leader catalyzed the organization's development into an international jihadist force that sought confrontation with America.

Azzam's 1989 assassination in Pakistan allowed the bin Laden-Zawahiri faction within al-Qaeda to pursue a maximalist version of holy war against Muslim and foreign adversaries. The organization's ambitious jihadist vision was given a major impetus by Sudanese and Taliban patronage. State support was decisive in laying the basis for the organization's development and implementation of *far enemy* strategy.

Al-Qaeda's progenitor: Abdullah Azzam and his defensive jihad doctrine

The Soviet Union in 1988 announced that it planned to retire its forces after a bloody occupation that cost the Russians 15,000 fatalities and left over a million Afghans dead.[2] Despite the marginal contribution of Arab fighters to the war, the mujahidin viewed their role as decisive.[3] Tens of thousands remained in Afghanistan tied to jihadist organizations or Afghan warlords.

One cannot overemphasize the importance of the Afghan jihad and its impact on the Arab mujahidin psyche. The trauma of colonialism, bitter jihadist failures at home, and humiliating defeats of national armies by Israel was lessoned by the Arab contribution to Afghan jihad. Success in Afghanistan and the mujahidin *defeat* of the Soviets reinvigorated the Arab fighting spirit that jihadists believed would be a catalyst for future victories. While more mythological than real, the *heroic* exploits of the Arab mujahidin against the Soviet infidel will embolden these *lions of Afghanistan* to test their fighting skill and valor against other enemies including the United States.[4]

Jihadists interpret the 1991 collapse of the Soviet Empire as a consequence of foreign fighter participation in the Afghan jihad and as an expression of Allah's divine will. Al-Qaeda texts frequently refer to the Afghan jihad as a model for successful resistance to the Zionist-Crusader alliance and imply that it foreshadows Islam's conquest of the world. Abu Musab Suri and Abu Bakr Naji use the mujahidin struggle in Afghanistan as the model for defeating the US and Israeli nemesis that has plagued the Islamic world. They frequently juxtapose *heroic* mujahidin with the cowardly decadent Western soldier. Without question the foreign fighter experience against the Soviets impelled aggressive impulses against the Satanic Zionist-Crusader alliance. The Afghan jihad set the stage for 9/11 and the subsequent *war on terror*.

Postwar Afghanistan posed a serious problem for the remaining Arab mujahidin. As political exiles they faced an uncertain precarious existence. Many like Abu Musab Suri had contributed to failed jihadist revolts in their home countries and were targeted by security services. Having assisted in the defeat of Soviet forces in Afghanistan, these fighters had five options: (1) they could remain in Afghanistan and contribute to the development of an Islamic state; (2) they could go to another battlefield in the defense of Muslim brothers; (3) they could return home and continue jihad against apostate regimes; (4) they could seek political asylum in Europe; or (5) they could join a Pan-Islamic jihadist movement committed to wage global jihad. Like Suri's experience many traveled back and forth between European asylum and diverse jihadist battlefields across the Muslim world. London's Finsbury Park, Milan's Islamic Cultural Center, Hamburg's al-Quds Mosque and Madrid's M-30 Mosque were key gathering places for jihadist groups to recruit and indoctrinate prospective mujahidin. Al-Qaeda's European network played a key role in its financial and organizational development. Without a key battlefield to engage the enemy, this recruitment network could not be sustained.

Also at risk was the infrastructure of Gulf State financial patrons that gave money to the Afghan mujahidin struggle. Referred to as the "golden chain" by the *9–11 Report* the network of Gulf contributors, Islamic charities, and supporting states financed and recruited Arab jihadists.[5] Diaspora communities in North America and Europe had generously contributed to the Afghan jihad and they possessed considerable financial resources that could be used for future causes. Having been successful in the defense of Afghan brothers, might this network be used for a grander jihadist purpose?

Within this context, al-Qaeda was born. Abdullah Azzam's vision of an International jihadist force to recover and defend Muslim territory in Kashmir and Palestine offered these fighters an attractive opportunity. In his *Defense of Muslim Lands* Azzam calls jihad an individual and collective responsibility. His jihadist vision was anything but traditional.[6] Classical jurists conceived jihad not an individual duty but as a collective responsibility of the ummah to violently engage foreigners in *Dar al Harb* or House of War. With Allah's will victory will be guaranteed even against the most powerful nemesis.

Azzam's conception of jihad allowed for private networks to combat foreign aggression against "Allah's domain." Under his vision al-Qaeda ("The Base") was formed in 1988 to train, recruit, and send jihadists to liberate Muslim territory. The creation of an international recruitment and training network devoted to jihad must have been a godsend for radical Islamists seeking battlefield glory. Emboldened by the success of their Afghan jihad, these militants hope to achieve similar victories in Kashmir and Palestine.[7] Many prospective jihadists also sought assistance to wage jihad at home against apostate regimes.

Azzam's pivotal role in al-Qaeda's development did not endure. The Palestinian's *defensive jihad* doctrine invited many interpretations. How might one define "Allah's domain" or the territorial reach of *Dar al Islam*? Historically, Islam's expanse stretched from Spain to South East Asia. Most of this territory was and is governed by what jihadists consider infidel regimes. Azzam's vision put a premium in responding to acts of foreign aggression against Muslim land and peoples and this greatly limited the scope of the jihadist battlefield.

Bin Laden and Zawahiri wanted a more expansionist view that permitted struggles against apostate Muslim regimes.[8] Their jihadist vision endorsed *takfir* or the right to declare other Muslims apostates. Bin Laden-Zawahiri's version of jihad was unacceptable to Azzam who rejected any intra-Muslim conflict or struggle against the *near enemy*. Azzam repeatedly denounced takfiri ideas as un-Islamic. Their differences on interpreting the scope of jihad led to a power struggle and eventual bin Laden's dominance over the organization. OBL's charisma and his immense fortune captured the attention of al-Qaeda's Shura or advisory council that in August 1988 elected Osama as emir of the organizations. Osama was also able to exploit his largely imaginary battlefield exploits against the Soviets to reinforce his mujahidin valor.

The bin Laden-Azzam rivalry has invited much discussion and controversy.[9] It is thought bin Laden's break with his former mentor was driven by Zawahiri who sought to use Osama's wealth to secure control over the fractured Egyptian jihadist movement. Zawahiri in Lawrence Wright's *Looming Tower* is presented as a Machiavellian figure whose ideological disagreement with Azzam and his desire to exploit bin Laden's finances explain the breach.[10] After Osama was officially named emir, Azzam's role in the organization was peripheral. The Palestinian scholar, however, commanded legions of followers. He is still revered in many jihadist circles. His opposition to Osama represented a threat to the Saudi's capacity to direct the international jihadist movement.

Under OBL and Zawahiri, al-Qaeda trained groups to be dispatched to multiple fronts. They organized committees governing military, media, and financial affairs. Al-Qaeda's totalistic jihadist conception included liberating Muslim territory from foreign aggression, fighting Muslim apostate regimes, and attacking US interests. Transcending the sectarian divide, al-Qaeda secured a relationship with Shi'ite Hezbollah whose bomb-making skills and culture of martyrdom they greatly admired.[11] Table 2.1 compares Azzam's original design of jihad with the more aggressive and expansive bin Laden and Zawahiri formulation.

Azzam's November 1989 death accelerated al-Qaeda's expansionist trajectory.[12] His car bomb assassination outside a Pakistani Mosque raised a number of issues such as who killed him and how his death affected al-Qaeda's progression? Whether Osama was responsible or not, Azzam's death allowed

Table 2.1 Comparison of Azzam's Defensive Jihad and bin Laden-Zawahiri's Offensive Jihad

Jihadist Vision	Target the Far or Near Enemy?	Takfir Doctrine
Azzam's Defensive Jihad	Individual and communal duty to protect *Dar al Islam* against foreign occupation. Limited war against the Far Enemy in zones of contention like Palestine and Kashmir. Al-Qaeda to be used as international jihadist force to liberate Muslim land from foreign occupation.	Rejection of all intra-Muslim conflict and takfir doctrine.
Bin Laden-Zawahiri Offensive Jihad	Wages struggles on multiple fronts against both *far* and *near enemies*. *Far enemy* to be targeted in zones of contention (Kashmir and Palestine) and outside the Muslim world. Endorses attacks on far enemy homelands.	Support for takfir doctrine and mujahidin struggles against apostate Muslims.

al-Qaeda to pursue a maximalist jihadist agenda that inexorably lead to attacks against the United States. Lawrence Wright believes that Zawahiri and his Egyptian followers in al-Qaeda were responsible for Azzam's death for it freed them to chart the organizations development.

The first Gulf War and the far enemy strategy

Bin Laden returned to Saudi Arabia to commit jihad against the Marxist regime in South Yemen. His Yemeni heritage, personal ambitions, and his antipathy toward communism cojoined compelling him to pursue violent agitation against the enemies of Islam. His relationship with the Saudi Royal family continued during his Yemeni jihad. During the Afghan war Osama worked with Saudi intelligence chief Prince Turki and the economic weight of the bin Laden economic group commanded considerable respect in the Kingdom.[13] Bin Laden's late father had considerable connections with the Saudi regime and had made his vast fortune off of lucrative government contracts. Indeed, Prince Turki had provided considerable financial support for bin Laden's group that acted independently of Pakistani and CIA support. It is not until the first Gulf War that Osama would oppose the Kingdom's rule.

Iraq's 1990 invasion of Kuwait changed bin Laden's relationship with the Saudi Kingdom dramatically. Once Saddam forces had annexed Kuwait to secure a direct link to the Persian Gulf, hundreds of thousands of Iraqi troops stood poised to strike Saudi Arabia. Inflated by his Afghan war experience, Osama presented a plan to use Arab mujahidin to liberate Kuwait to Prince Turki. Fanciful in its design, the plan was rejected by the royal family as naïve and unworkable. By 1990 Iraq had the fifth largest military force in the world making bin Laden's impractical.

Bin Laden saw the Kingdom's rejection of his plan as an ideological and personal affront.[14] The House of Saud's use of American troops was seen by bin Laden as violating Muhammad's prohibition of infidels in the *land of the twin sanctuaries*. For Osama, there could be no more dramatic evidence of the Kingdom's apostate nature. OBL's antipathy toward the regime was reinforced by the clerical establishment's theological justification for the international presence.[15] The Saudi Arabian regime and its corrupt clergy, accordingly, had become part of a broader Crusader-Zionist alliance to exploit Islamic land and its people.

Osama's vocal criticism of the Kingdom and the US military presence made him a pariah. His passport was revoked in 1994 and his assets were frozen by the regime. With the assistance of important Saudi families and a clandestine network of radical sympathizers, Bin Laden left Saudi Arabia for Pakistan a year after the Gulf War terminated.[16] He would describe his departure from his homeland by referencing the Prophet's flight from Mecca to Medina.

OBL's fixation on Muhammad's life and his belief that his struggle against the Kingdom parallels the prophet's fight against Mecca's polytheists has precedents.[17] Many past jihadist leaders felt impelled to wage war against impious Muslims because they desired to recreate the Prophet's Medina experience. What makes Osama distinct is his belief in the existence of a diabolical global conspiracy seeking to destroy Islam, contaminate its religion, capture its territory, and exploit its resources.[18]

Osama's conspiratorial worldview is predicated upon Leninist theories of a Western capitalist plot to control Third World resources. Within this framework, America's military presence in Saudi Arabia secures its domination over the country's oil fields that are vital for the global capitalist system. Gulf States' acceptance of foreign military forces is testimony to their betrayal of national interests that, in his theological worldview, violates Allah's will. Bin Laden seems to have Islamized neo-Marxist dependency theories that see an exploitive capitalist core extracting wealth from an impoverished and exploited periphery. This is very much in line with ideas developed by al-Qaeda theorists Abu Musab Suri and Abu Bakr Naji who developed similar themes in their jihadist commentaries.

OBL's conceptualization of a Zionist-Crusader alliance has shades of the *Protocols of the Elders of Zion* and *Mein Kampf* in its depiction of a world dominated by Jewish finance.[19] Reinforced by rapacious Jewish lobbies in Washington, Osama viewed America's support for Israel as part of a nefarious complot to secure control over Persian Gulf oil and Middle East resources.

The presence of American military and economic assets in the land of the *two sanctuaries*, accordingly, rewards corrupt apostate Gulf Kingdoms and states across the region. Local rulers are in effect kept in power by "Zionist-Crusader" forces. Within this context, the brutal repression of Islamist movement and jihadist groups in the region is an effort by corrupt elites to maintain their role in insuring American-Israeli regional hegemony.[20] Given his religious worldview the American-Saudi alliance was part of a satanic plot.

Osama's *far enemy* doctrine reverses the traditional jihadist struggle by targeting the US homeland. OBL thought striking America would force the United States to disengage from the region unleashing jihadist forces to overthrow weakened local rulers.[21] Such a belief was predicated upon his view of a weak declining America that would capitulate before *heroic* mujahidin attacks. With victory preordained the United States would disengage from the region. Without US financial and military support, apostate regimes, he thought, would fall like dominoes.

Osama's exile from Saudi Arabia confronted him with an uncertain future in the Pakistani frontier city of Peshawar. Bin Laden was concerned that the Saudi-Pakistani relationship could give Islamabad an opportunity to deport him back to the Kingdom. Afghanistan, moreover, was not a secure base given the country's descent into civil war and chaos in the wake of the Soviet pullout.[22] The euphoria of the victorious brother's victory over the Soviet infidels was short lived and Afghanistan soon degenerated into warlord bloodletting.

Zawahiri's post-Afghan jihad experience mirrored bin Laden's exile life in Pakistan.[23] Following the Afghan war, the Egyptian physician struggled to recover his leadership role of the Jihad Group. Zawahiri is reported to have been sighted in Bosnia and Central Asia after the Soviet withdrew. During this period, he was experiencing severe financial strain and lived a vagabond's life.

Bin Laden and Zawahiri fortunes were changed dramatically by developments in the Sudan. The emergence of radical Islamist government in Khartoum offered an ideal refuge for Bin Laden and Zawahiri to mount their expansive vision of jihad.[24] They no doubt viewed the Sudanese offer as part of Allah's divine plan.

Husan al-Turabi and Sudanese patronage 1992–6

Sudanese Islamist army officers in 1989 seized power in Khartoum and formed a radical Islamic regime. Orchestrated by National Islamic Front leader Husan al-Turabi, the military government hoped to create a global jihadist movement that offered safe refuge for violent Islamists across the world.[25] Turabi had been a minister in previous governments and leader of a movement organized around Muslim Brotherhood principles. The Sudanese radical used his position to consolidate extremist factions in the army and the state apparatus throughout the 1980s. Predating the Taliban, Turabi's patient building of an Islamist microculture that pervaded the army and state bureaucracy resulted in the most radical regime in the Sunni Muslim world until the rise of Mullah Omar's group.[26]

Educated in France and England the charismatic Turabi envisioned using Sudan as a base for igniting revolutions across the Muslim world. Considered the power behind the throne, his following within the government was unchallenged.[27] He believed that Sudanese state patronage could support regional and global jihadist networks to fight against American and Israeli hegemony.

Inspired by Mahdist nineteenth-century insurrection against British colonial authorities and their Egyptian proxies, Turabi sought a regional caliphate uniting radical groups. Turabi's offer of asylum to bin Laden and Zawahiri acknowledges their roles in the Afghan campaign and OBL's prominence as a critic of the United States. By providing a secure refuge Turabi shielded al-Qaeda and the Egyptian Islamic Jihad from international prosecution and provided bin Laden a base to recruit and train jihadists. OBL's Sudanese 1992–6 refuge was a critical component in al-Qaeda's African cellular network that assaulted US interests in the late 1990s.[28] It also provided Zawahiri with a greater opportunity to wrestle control over Egypt's splintered jihadist movement. Given Sudan's proximity to his native land, Turabi's patronage gave Zawahiri the opportunity to impose order on the fractured Egyptian jihadist movement.

Lorenzo Vidino argues that OBL's relationship with Turabi's regime resulted in an economic symbiosis with the Bin Laden Group subsidizing the Sudanese economy in return for the government's concession of duty free imports for OBL's businesses.[29] Bin Laden's relocation of his industrial group eventually evolved into a complex set of holding companies in construction, housing, financial services, and agriculture enterprise. Osama reportedly lent the regime $80 million and undertook major highway infrastructure development projects to reward his Sudanese patron.[30]

OBL planned to use his economic resources to secure the recruitment of international jihadist groups to fight on diverse fronts. Secure in his Khartoum sanctuary, Osama hoped to implement his expansive vision of jihad to challenge the security of America and its apostate allies, Sudan's strategic geopolitical position, moreover, was a useful base to develop alliances with regional jihadist networks. Zawahiri's influence and the proximity of the Egyptian Islamist movement factored heavily in this calculation.

Sheik Abdul Rachman's Islamic Group and Zawahiri's Jihad Group were well represented in bin Laden's camps. Vidino reports some 5,000 Egyptians were trained by al-Qaeda during its Sudanese period.[31] It is no mere accident that the bin Laden's Sudanese era was characterized by a substantial rise in terror activities against Mubarak's state apparatus and Egypt's important tourist economy. By the mid-1990s, terrorism in Egypt had become a central worry for Mubarak's regime with potentially devastating economic effects on its tourism sector.

Sudanese patronage, moreover, gave al-Qaeda an opportunity to consolidate its relationship with Iran and its Hezbollah proxy.[32] Iranian and Lebanese militants were invited into al-Qaeda camps to share their bomb-making expertise. The Iranians reciprocated by allowing al-Qaeda agents to travel to Iran for training by the Revolutionary Guards. Indeed, al-Qaeda's future bombing tactics mirrored Hezbollah-Revolutionary Guard technological and operational designs.[33] Ironically many of al-Qaeda's appendages in Iraq and Syria would later embark on a war against Shia *apostates*.

Sudan also offered bin Laden a base to attack US troops in Somalia who were participating in food relief and security operations. OBL, furthermore, encouraged al-Qaeda's Saudi and Yemeni cells to attack US forces in the Kingdom. Al-Qaeda's connection to Somali groups that in 1993 engaged US forces in Mogadishu bringing down two Blackhawks helicopters and killing 19

US Special Forces was quite remote.³⁴ Beyond some training to Somali militants, al-Qaeda agents did not stay long in the war ravaged country. Bin Laden, however, did not hesitate to exploit the opportunity to promote his network prowess against the American empire. America's quick exit from Somalia a year later would fuel bin Laden's aggressive plans against US interests and further his view of American weakness.

Bin Laden claimed credit for terror attacks against US military installations in Saudi Arabia in 1995 and 1996; al-Qaeda's responsibility for these assaults is highly disputed. Most of al-Qaeda's links to these events are quite weak and nebulous. The 1996 Khobar Towers attack against an American airbase is widely seen as the work of Hezbollah militants in Saudi Arabia.³⁵

These bombings did allow bin Laden an opportunity to grandstand and court his reputation as an anti-American defender of the ummah. The attacks consequences, moreover, reinforced in Osama's mind an American lack of resolve.³⁶ The US military's hasty exodus from Somalia in 1994 was sadly reminiscent of the Reagan Administration's 1983 withdraw from Lebanon after Hezbollah attacked the US Embassy and Marine Corps barracks killing hundreds.

Bin Laden's Sudanese period and his relations with Turabi's regime were far from idyllic.³⁷ His organization's strong connection to Zawahiri's Jihad Group engendered Cairo's outrage. The Egyptian regime pressured the Sudanese government to sever its relationship with OBL. Egyptian hostility toward Khartoum's patronage of al-Qaeda intensified after Zawahiri's failed assassination attempt on President Mubarak's life at a June 1995 Organization of African States meeting in Ethiopia.³⁸

Turabi's patronage of OBL also raised American and Saudi opposition. The Sudanese regime's refusal to curb bin Laden's activities made Khartoum an international pariah state. Bin Laden's vocal support for attacks against the Kingdom and his links to the 1993 WTC bombing suspects aggravated an untenable situation. International pressure and UN economic sanctions culminated in Turabi eventually distancing his regime from OBL's group.

Other forces came into play. By late 1995 OBL's economic network had lost a vast amount of money and his capacity to subsidize the Sudanese economy had reached a limit.³⁹ Khartoum could not count on OBL infrastructure projects and willingness to forgo payment. With their shared love of horses and racing, OBL and Turabi's son were on very good terms. The same cannot be said for bin Laden and Turabi's personal relationship which began to sour.⁴⁰ Despite their common outlook, Turabi's defense of women's rights and ostentatious lifestyle irritated the Saudi puritan.

Osama was concerned that Sudanese government could turn him over to American or Saudi officials. He had already been named a person of interest in the 1993 WTC bombing criminal and legal investigations. Events in Afghanistan, however, promised to bring OBL some relief. The rise of the puritan and fanatical Taliban in that country offered OBL even greater opportunities to develop and implement his *far enemy* strategy.

Organizational and ideological foundations of the Taliban-al-Qaeda partnership 1996–2001

The emergence of a radical Pashtun fundamentalist movement formed by Afghan student-refugees in Pakistani madrassas caught many Central Asian experts by surprise.[41] Much of the movement's rank and file and leadership were nurtured by Saudi trained and financed clerics who successfully exploited Pashtun cultural and religious foundations to justify their misogynistic and homophobic views.[42] Much of the rank and file of the Taliban was formed by Afghan religious students and war refugees in Pakistan.

The Taliban's ascent was facilitated by Pakistani and Saudi financial, logistical, and military support.[43] Both countries wanted to promote a radical Islamic movement for different purposes. Since the early 1980s the Saudis had promoted Wahhabi Islamic traditions and they saw the Taliban as a protector and incubator of their version of Islam. They also viewed the promotion of Islam as a defense against radical at home that had been critical of the Royal Family's right to rule.

Pakistan had strategic motives to use the Taliban to blunt the projection of Indian power in Central Asia. Indo-Pakistani rivalries and conflicts were most intense in Afghanistan and Kashmir that emerged as key conflict zones. Ahmed Rashid, for example, argues Pakistan's policy of *strategic depth* uses proxy forces to engage India whose three wars with Islamabad over Kashmir and whose regional military dominance continue to haunt the Pakistani elite.[44] Not surprising most of Pakistan's army is positioned along the country's Kashmiri border. The ongoing *war on terror* has not altered significantly the deployment of Pakistan's army raising concerns in Washington regarding Islamabad's commitment to fight the Taliban and its al-Qaeda allies.

Driving Pakistani and Saudi intervention, moreover, was a desire to avoid Afghan national dismemberment. Soviet withdraw in 1989 had shattered mujahidin unity resulting in tribal civil war. By 1992 the national unity government brokered by the United Nations had disintegrated as Afghanistan descended into chaos. With 40 percent of Afghan's population Pashtun, Pakistan, and Saudi Arabia threw their support behind the nascent Taliban.

The group's ideology, Pashtun tribal cultural conservatism and religious fundamentalism drove it to extreme violence in which religious mandates justified the cruelest punishments not seen since the Khmer Rouge. By 1996 the Taliban consolidated their rule over much of the country. Pashtun fundamentalist rule was punctuated by brutal tribal and sectarian massacres and religious zealotry. Their brutalization of women, religious minorities, and homosexuals resulted in widespread international condemnation.

When Bin Laden returned to Afghanistan the Taliban victory was imminent and it was clear that his network wanted to regain a state partner allowing it a hegemonic position to guide the jihadist struggle.[45] Taliban control of Afghanistan allowed for such a development.

The al-Qaeda-Taliban partnership mirrors the strategic relationship that Bin Laden enjoyed in his Sudanese period where state patronage provides a secure refuge to recruit and train jihadist groups. Buttressed by a close friendship with Taliban's spiritual and military ruler Mullah Omar, bin Laden insured his network's survival. Omar became critical in securing bin Laden's safety shielding him from Taliban criticism and international prosecution.

The Taliban also reaped some substantial benefits. OBL's financial resources and construction expertise resulted in number of Afghan infrastructure projects.[46] His connections to foreign jihadists also played a role in the formation of Brigade 055 of foreign al-Qaeda fighters who merged into the Taliban's military structure. Based on a variety of reports, al-Qaeda forces helped to defeat the Taliban's Uzbek, Tajik and Hazara adversaries and acquitted themselves well on the battlefield.[47]

Under Taliban protection dozens of camps were organized directly by bin Laden or by affiliated groups. Each camp was dominated by a militant leader who had achieved some notoriety in the Afghan jihad or had been involved in clandestine groups in the Arab countries.[48] Future AQI leader Abu Musab Zarqawi had a camp in the town of Herat near the Iranian border. Most of these leaders swore allegiance or bayaat to bin Laden. The sanctuary allowed bin Laden and Zawahiri an opportunity to sponsor and train jihadist groups across the Muslim world. By some conservative estimates tens of thousands of jihadists were trained by al-Qaeda.[49]

This is not to suggest the relationship was devoid of trouble.[50] The Taliban regime had many factions some of whom were not committed to international jihad. Many commanders feared that hosting OBL would isolate the regime and bring international pressure to bear: a view that became more prominent with OBL's declarations of war against the United States in 1996 and 1998 and al-Qaeda's attacks against US interests.

The Taliban's relationship with al-Qaeda represented ideological, personal, and strategic calculations that proved impervious to Saudi, American, and international pressures that even after 9/11 and as the prospect of a decisive international military response proved unshakable.[51]

During its Taliban years al-Qaeda pursued a two-track strategy of using its training camps to facilitate contacts with jihadist groups and exploit its fundraising channels to raise money for its jihadist enterprise.[52] The strategic importance of the camps buttressed by ample financial backing cannot be underestimated and were vital in the group's *far enemy* approach.

The training camps allowed al-Qaeda to penetrate many groups across the Muslim world hoping to morph their agenda into Bin Laden's brand of international jihad. This was especially true in Africa and South East Asia where networks with local jihadist groups proved decisive in al-Qaeda's attacks against US interests.[53] By the late 1990s, al-Qaeda facilitated the development of training camps in South East Asia by partnering with JI whose jihadist network spanned Indonesia, Malaysia, and Singapore.[54] JI developed close relations with al-Qaeda protecting many of its agents. Many Indonesian militants fought in the Afghan jihad and trained in al-Qaeda's camps including Riduan Isamuddin better known as Hambali who would later develop close relations with Khalid Sheik Mohammad (KSM). Both would plot projected attacks across the region and JI assisted in the 9/11 attacks.[55]

Al-Qaeda's connections to Asian, African, and Middle Eastern jihadist groups allowed the organization's logistical ability to mount attacks in diverse regions of the world. Equally important was bin Laden's financial and recruitment efforts in Europe and North America. These activities proved invaluable in soliciting funds and recruiting potential jihadists from disaffected Muslim Diaspora communities. By the mid-1990s, London had emerged as a key financial and recruitment center for international jihad. The United Kingdom's liberal political asylum and immigration policies allowed many militants and Islamist leader's safe refuge and a supportive environment to raise money and recruit fighters.

Much of this financial infrastructure was a legacy of the Afghan jihad. The Afghan Services Bureau (Maktab al-Khidamat—MAK) operating in the United States and England exploited the permissive environment of Western democracies raising money for a variety of terror causes.[56] The London Bureau became a major funding and recruitment center for OBL operations. Al-Qaeda theorist Abu Musab Suri ran al-Qaeda's global media operations from London. During this time, charitable groups and generous Gulf financial patrons became the principal source of money for al-Qaeda after the loss of OBL's business empire in the Sudan.[57]

Al-Qaeda's war trajectory against the United States

The United Islamic Front and its declaration of war: February 1998–2001

OBL's war strategy against the United States was preconditioned upon securing a state sanctuary that allowed him to train jihadists, maintain extensive media and propaganda activities, and avoid international criminal prosecution. Given his personal ties with Mullah Omar and his strategic relationship with the Taliban, he had ample opportunity to plan and execute terror operations.

Prior to Taliban protection no major attacks against US interests in the 1990s had strong direct links to al-Qaeda.[58] Despite his personal relationship with Sheik Omar Abdul Rachman, bin Laden had little role in the first WTC bombing. Previous attacks in Saudi Arabia like the assault against US trainees at a Saudi National Guard complex in 1995 were carried out by local jihadist groups. Saudi Hezbollah, additionally, was responsible for the 1996 Khobar Towers air force base attack that killed 19 American servicemen. Undaunted by the evidence, bin Laden insinuated his group was responsible for these attacks. In 1996 bin Laden issued a statement exposing the crimes of the Zionist-Crusader conspiracy and declared war against the United States for the first time.

OBL's ideological animus toward the United States rested upon a set of illogically connected ideas. Bin Laden's statements reflect a contradictory view of a weak dominant America that rationally is difficult to sustain. His war strategy was driven by America's supposed malevolent domination of the world,

US support for apostate regimes, and a culturally supremacist position that the America was atrophying. Osama's juxtaposition of American hegemony and internal decay is hard to sustain.

How a corrupt, decaying, and weak nation could achieve such a preeminent position does not seem to be entirely conceptualized. OBL's determination to attack the America is reinforced by his group's February 1998 merger with Egyptian, Bangladeshi, and Pakistani militant organizations. Their joint statement rails against the United States for its occupation of Saudi Arabia, its exploitation of Muslim resources, its support for Israel, and the declaration implores Muslims to kill Americans as a religious mandate.[59] Al-Qaeda, in short, declared war against the United States in February 1998 for a second time.

The group's official name The World Islamic Front against Jews and Crusaders is vivid testimony to its ambitions that were enhanced by its contacts with regional jihadist groups. Al-Qaeda's connections with African jihadist branches and cells were critical in its early strikes against US interests.

The African network

Al-Qaeda's East African network was a consequence of its Sudanese period.[60] Under Turabi's patronage, Bin Laden developed contacts with many local and regional jihadist groups. Al-Qaeda's infrastructure of clandestine jihadist cells was facilitated by Saudi money that was transforming religious beliefs across the region. Tolerant native Sufi traditions were being transplanted by the spread of Wahhabi militancy that created a fertile ground for jihad in the region. Financed by Gulf Charities, African clerics facilitated the rise of East African fundamentalism.

OBL hoped to use his African network to attack US interests in the early 1990s. Al-Qaeda's top operatives were sent to train Somali militants fighting US peace keeping forces. Hoping to spot potential targets Egyptian Abu Ubaidah al Banshiri was dispatched to Africa in the mid-1990s.[61] His death in a ferry accident in Lake Victoria in 1996 only redoubled al-Qaeda interests in using the region as a springboard for attacks against the American nemesis. Undaunted by the challenges al-Qaeda meticulously developed a cellular regional network.

Attracted by the weakness of African security services and the growing zeal of Kenyan and Tanzanian militants, al-Qaeda planned its most ambitious attacks against US interests.[62] The August 1998 bombings of the US embassies in Kenya and Tanzania killed hundreds, wounded thousands, and represented meticulous planning by al-Qaeda operatives and local militants.

Al-Qaeda sent an advanced team of top explosive experts to fabricate bombs in safe houses secured by Kenyan and Tanzanian groups. Targets were selected after a detailed analysis of security obstacles. OBL was involved throughout the operation selecting targets and approving the attacks operatives and strategy. Al-Qaeda was positioned to match its words with decisive action.

With local jihadist group assistance bombs were mounted on trucks and driven to sites to inflict maximum damage during the early morning when streets were crowded with travelers and shoppers. The attacks were patterned after Hezbollah's operations against American targets in Lebanon where suicide bombers drove massive truck bombs into complexes. Like the Lebanese operations, the bombings were near simultaneous and were launched to inflict substantial human and material losses. The assaults severity and audaciousness caught Washington by surprise. Prior to the embassy bombings, OBL was more of an annoyance than a real threat.[63] The Clinton Administration discounted the United Islamic Front's declaration of war as a rhetorical display. Many in the Administration feared provocative action against bin Laden would raise his cult standing in the Muslim world. The Administration's excessive caution proved to be fatal and played a role in al-Qaeda's first real attack against American interests.

Washington's passivity toward OBL's network terminated after the attacks. Badly embarrassed by the assaults, the Clinton Administration launched dozens of cruise missiles against some al-Qaeda training camps in Afghanistan and destroyed a suspected chemical weapons plant in the Sudan that had previous ties to OBL's business network.

Based on soil samples taken years before the embassy attacks, the Agency mistakenly believed that the industrial complex was being used to produce chemical weapons. While the United States retaliated, the attacks were badly planned and based on faulty information. The CIA miscalculated on OBL's whereabouts (he was far from the camps) and the plant turned out to have no direct connection to al-Qaeda's network.[64]

Fired 14 days after the African embassy bombings, the missiles hit nearly empty camps killing a dozen militants. The American radical Noam Chomsky labeled the missile strike against the Sudanese pharmaceutical plant "genocide" because it condemned hundreds of thousands to death because of the lack of medicine in an impoverished country.[65]

After the attack OBL emerged as a hero in the Muslim world and the failed American retaliation increased the notoriety of his jihadist network. Perceived American impotence (there were no follow-up strikes) became an important al-Qaeda recruitment device and underscored OBL impression of American weakness and moral rot. Al-Qaeda emerged undeterred and eager to strike decisively at the American homeland.

The Millennium Plot and the USS Cole Bombing

After the 1998 attacks, the United States became more vigilant in safeguarding its security. Bin Laden's warning of an imminent strike against the American homeland and the dawning of a new millennium put the nation on high alert. Hoping to exploit America's vulnerable 3,000 mile long northern border, al-Qaeda sympathizer Ahmed Ressam hoped to attack the United States.

The Algerian was granted political asylum in Canada in 1994 and became a citizen years later. Ressam traveled to Afghanistan in the late 1990s and met with Abu Zubaydah al-Qaeda's chief of external operations.[66] During this period, he trained in al-Qaeda camps and actively worked with other jihadist groups like the Algerian GIA. Prior to the attacks Ressam attempted to get al-Qaeda financial and logistical assistance, but his efforts were unsuccessful.

While not a direct al-Qaeda operation, the Millennium Plot was clearly inspired by bin Laden's February 1998 declaration of war. Working with fellow Algerians whom he hoped to meet in the United States, Ressam wanted to attack the US homeland on New Year's Eve 1999.

Using a workroom in British Colombia motel, Ressam manufactured a bomb. He subsequently placed the explosive device in a car hoping to transport it by ferry to Seattle. Once in the United States the car would be sent by rail to Los Angeles. The Algerian hoped to bomb LAX airport as a presentment of a jihadist war against the United States in the beginning of the new millennium.

Ressam may have pulled off his plan had it not been for the alertness of a US ferry inspector who noticed him acting nervously; when she attempted to search his car, he immediately ran. Investigation of the car found massive amounts of explosive materials and timing devices. US intelligence had virtually no knowledge of the plot.

Al-Qaeda's planned attacks against transport networks transcended planes and airports and included targeting US warships refueling in Gulf ports. Attacking American naval assets and transport shipping was an al-Qaeda priority because the vessels were vital links in the international petroleum economy critical in the maintenance of the Crusader-Zionist hegemony.[67] It formed a pivotal component in al-Qaeda's terror campaign to inflict economic damage on the world financial system forcing the United States to disengage from the region and end its support for apostate regimes.

The destruction of a US warship represented an important symbolic victory for al-Qaeda and could serve as invaluable propaganda for the group. Al-Qaeda's choice of Yemeni harbors used by US ships as refueling and resupply stops made sense. The Yemeni network had many active al-Qaeda cells and committed recruits.[68] As in the African bombings, an advanced explosives work team was sent into Yemen, a safe house was secured, and bin Laden agents worked with local jihadists.

Al-Qaeda's first effort to destroy a US warship failed. The attack on the USS Sullivan in 2000 was aborted when the raft filled with explosives sank and failed to reach its target. Undeterred al-Qaeda was able to devise rafts capable of transporting heavy explosives and successfully struck the USS Cole. Driven by two jihadists the raft laden with explosives reached its target. The explosion ripped a hole in the warship killing 17 sailors. While the battleship did not sink, it was badly crippled.

Unlike the embassy bombings, the US government failed to militarily respond fearing an adverse outcome a month before the November 2000 presidential election.[69] The Cole bombing demonstrated American weakness to confront a determined al-Qaeda that was intent on launching devastating terror attacks. This reinforced al-Qaeda's worldview of a morally bankrupt and cowardly America.

Khalid Sheik Mohammad (KSM) and the origins of the 9/11 attacks

Al-Qaeda's perseverance and capacity to learn from mistakes is not limited to the USS Sullivan plot. The 9/11 attacks represent a gradual adaption of techniques that evolved from previous failed attacks.[70] Within this context the 1993 World Trade Center (WTC) bombing, Ramzi Yousef and his uncle KSM connect directly to the design and planning of the 9/11 attacks.

The first WTC bombing had little connection to OBL other than his association with Sheik Abdul Rachman.[71] Sheik Rachman established an Egyptian Islamic Group cell in Jersey City dedicated to raising funds for various jihadist projects.

Rachman had built a personality cult through his commitment to the Afghan jihad. Meeting Bin Laden and Abdullah Azzam in Peshawar during the 1980s, Sheik Rachman played a critical role in soliciting funds for Afghan and Arab fighters.[72] Having lost his sight due to diabetes, Sheik Rachman was revered for his religious piety and zealous defense of jihad by many militants.

So impressed was bin Laden with the Sheik that he appointed him head of the Afghan Services Bureau after Azzam's death.[73] It is through these efforts that he comes into contact with explosives expert Ramzi Yousef and they join forces to plan a number of New York City (NYC) attacks. Among these conspiracies included bombings of the Holland Tunnel, the United Nations Building, and commissioning the first WTC attack. Had Rachman's group been able to succeed in all of these attacks tens of thousands could have been killed.

Sheik Rachman's group bought explosives, secured a bomb-making workshop, and rented a van to transport the bomb. Skilled in bomb making during his Afghan jihad years, Yousef fabricated an immense explosives device and put it inside a van that was driven to a WTC underground parking garage. Yousef left the United States shortly before the attack and went to South East Asia that had been home to a number of fundamentalist groups committed to jihad.

The 1993 WTC attacks failed to meet Yousef's expectations.[74] While the bomb ripped a hole in several floors of the WTC, killed six people, and wounded thousands, the structure stood. Many of the plotters (including Sheik Rachman) would have been rounded up by US authorities and been tried and convicted on terrorism charges.

The Justice Department took pride in its successful criminal prosecution of the 1993 WTC bombers, consciously omitting the use of the death penalty to deny the terrorists their martyrdom dreams.[75] This tactic did little to deter jihadist ambitions to attack the US homeland and succeeded in only making Sheik Rachman a cause celeb in many radical circles. Jihadist groups continue to demand his release.

Once in the Philippines and under the protection of local jihadists, Yousef used his JI connections to plan a series of attacks that included assassination plots against Bill Clinton and Pope John Paul II during their planned trips to the Philippines.[76] Yousef was assisted by his uncle KSM in Manila to carry out these and even more ambitious projects. Both Yousef and KSM were Kuwaiti nationals of Pakistani extraction. Multilingual they easily traveled between Central Asian and Arab jihadist groups and their mastery of English allowed them to converse with a great number of extremists across the globe. Their commitment to international jihad involved a number of Islamist causes of which the Palestinian struggle seemed preeminent.[77] America, for them, was the apotheosis of evil. Disappointed with the impact of the 1993 WTC bombing they conspired to launch an unprecedented and devastating attack against America.

The genesis for 9/11 was planned in the Philippines in 1995 in a plot named Operation Bojinka by local investigators.[78] Conceived by Yousef and KSM it involved midair bombings of a dozen American transpacific flights that could have killed tens of thousands. Based on trips that had multiple stops, terrorists would board the flights, implant bombs with timers, and depart after the planes first stop. The passenger jets would then explode in midair over the Pacific Ocean before they reached their final destination on the US West Coast.

Yousef staged a trial run of his project on a Philippines airliner that managed to land after the bomb exploded killing one passenger. He had secured a Manila workshop and fabricated numerous chemical based bombs. During one of his bomb-making activities a fire in the workshop forced him to hurriedly leave the premises. Police search of the workshop found computer hard drives with the operational details of the plot. Yousef was subsequently caught in Pakistan and extradited for trial in the United States. US officials again refused to try him on capital charges.[79] His conviction was hailed as model to fight the war on terror that did little to deter al-Qaeda war trajectory. Like Rachman, Yousef is a hero for jihadists who demand his release from his federal high security prison.

KSM no doubt wanted to avenge his nephew and make good on Yousef's grand ambition to strike at America in spectacular and grand fashion. KSM is very much an outlier in the jihadist world, his cosmopolitan outlook, sexual promiscuity, and alcoholic tendencies do not fit the typical behavior of al-Qaeda agents.[80] KSM spent much of his life as international businessman and world traveler raising money for jihadist causes.

Despite his licentious lifestyle he was able to make contact with al-Qaeda agents in Pakistan who in 1996 led him to Bin Laden in Taliban controlled Afghanistan. When KSM met with bin Laden and al-Qaeda director of military operations Mohammad Atef, he disclosed a grandiose version of Operation Bojinka involving numerous air based attacks on the US East and West Coasts.[81]

Al-Qaeda liked KSM's plans but felt that the design needed to be developed further. KSM and al-Qaeda took years to flesh out various attack options with the final approval not achieved until early 1999.[82] KSM's initial plans involved ten planes and two different terrorist squadrons. The first group would launch attacks against symbolic centers of US economic-military power that included the WTC buildings, the Pentagon, and what the *9–11 Report* believes to be either the Capitol Building or the White House. Planes would be hijacked and a flown into targets.

Operational planning for the East Coast attacks involved two subteams: one group trained in flight schools based in Europe or North America to commandeer the jets and the second group trained to subdue and control passengers allowing the pilots the time to travel toward the designated targets. The student pilots would also serve as an advanced team of leaders who would coordinate with an al-Qaeda central organizer to plan and execute attacks on their designated targets. Financial and logistical support would come from a master organizer and operational details would be adjusted depending upon conditions. Once the details of the respective operations were worked out and the pilots trained, the second team would accompany their team leaders when the attacks were to commence. The passenger jet flights selected would be tightly scheduled to make the attacks on the different locations almost simultaneous to enhance their shock value. This follows closely the Hezbollah model that al-Qaeda historically has sought to emulate.

Mohammad planned the West Coast attacks to mirror Operation Bojinka blueprint with midair explosions of US bound transpacific flights. In sum, the operation involved ten planes: four on the East Coast acting as weapons of mass destruction and six on the West Coast with a tenth plane commandeered by KSM. Mohammad was to land the plane on American soil and personally kill all of its male passengers. Once the plane was on land, KSM planned to arrange a press conference reading an al-Qaeda manifesto replete with demands for US disengagement from the Middle East.

KSM's ambitious project triggered some reservations. OBL and Atef scaled his original design down to the East Coast attacks.[83] Atef and OBL picked a Saudi-Yemeni team based in Asia to mount the operation. OBL's personal connections to this group and the need for complete secrecy were deciding factors. This group would serve as an advanced team that would be trained in American flight schools and once the pilots were ready they would be met by the second group.

Al-Qaeda's operational network and cells in North America would provide support facilities and assistance. Despite OBL confidence in his handpicked team the operation did not get off to a good start. Entering the United States in early 2000, Khalid al-Midhar and Nawaf al-Hazim had difficulty with English and performed badly in the flight school training. Given such problems, al-Qaeda sought an alternative team to mount the operation.[84]

The Hamburg cell and the 9/11 attacks

Much has been written about the radicalization of Muslim Diaspora populations living in the West.[85] Most of these studies have been written in the post-9/11 era. Known as the Hamburg cell 9/11 terrorists Mohammad Atta, Ramzi Bin al-Shibh, Ziad Jarrah, and Marwan al Shehhi catalyzed this burgeoning field of social studies. They have become the standard referent point for scholarly investigation of Islamic homegrown terrorism in the West.

Born in wealthy families, multilingual, and well educated, these young men opted to study in Europe because of the lack of opportunity in their home counties. Prior to their emigration to Germany to study at various universities, none were radical and Jarrah was not especially religious. Only slowly did their commitment to jihad emerge.[86]

Marc Sageman explains their radicalization as part of a group bonding process where alienated, lonely young men develop a new collective identity.[87] Meeting at a local mosque and at student associations these young men were indoctrinated by jihadist recruiters and subjected to relentless anti-Western propaganda, martyrdom videos, and pseudo-religious justification for jihad.

The radicalization process was not immediate but unfolded over years. While each may have their own distinct motives for jihadist adventure, it is clear that group dynamics and intense personal relations were important. With the exception of Jarrah, they shared a common apartment. By acting together on a transcendent quest for martyrdom they filled an emotional void.[88] They would inspire many young Muslim men in Europe and North America to travel down a similar road.

The Hamburg cell's connection to al-Qaeda occurred accidently. The young men sought to join the Chechen jihad but they encountered visa problems. While in Germany they became acquainted with al-Qaeda affiliated agents who led them to the network's Afghan camps.[89] Their commitment and intelligence impressed al-Qaeda trainers and excited Mohammad Atef who recognized their utility as team leaders for the 9/11 operation.

Recruited by Mohammad Atef and approved by OBL, the Hamburg team applied for US student visas. Atta, Jarrah, and Shehhi were accepted for flight pilot training in American schools and easily obtained visa approval for travel to the United States. Bin al-Shibh failed to get a US Visa and he remained in Europe and Middle East to coordinate and support the operation.⁹⁰ Given the Cole attack his Yemeni origins complicated his visa application.

Atef's inclinations about the Hamburg team proved prescient and each performed dutifully: getting the necessary training. They were accompanied by a Saudi West coast operative Nawaf al-Hazim who became fourth team leader. Targets and dates would be approved by al-Qaeda central headquarters. OBL and Atef were kept informed about the team's progress by KSM who coordinated planning with Bin al-Shibh.

The 9/11 operation gained a sense of urgency when al-Qaeda agent Zarcarius Moussaoui was apprehended by the FBI. His arrest was based on concerns by a flight instructor in the school that he had ulterior motives for pilot training. Envisioned as a backup pilot for the 9/11 operation, Moussaoui had some information that could jeopardize the attacks. Held by US authorities in August 2001 on visa violations, al-Qaeda feared that Moussaoui would provide clues to the FBI about the operation.

This is not the only time the FBI heard complaints about Arab students taking flight lessons. FBI agents in Arizona tried to convince their Regional Office in Colorado to commence an investigation but bureaucratic and legal obstacles impeded any effective action.⁹¹

With their grand project endangered, OBL moved the operation ahead of schedule. KSM's scaled down ambitions were almost fully realized. Three of the jumbo jet planes reached their targets with devastating impact. Tons of jet fuel eviscerated the Twin Towers killing thousands and partially destroyed the Pentagon.

The archetypal symbols of US financial and military power were brutally assaulted and close to three thousand of its citizens killed. Al-Qaeda's lone mistake was the failure of Jarrah's commandeered plane to hit its designated target. Why it took the Jarrah team so long to take over the cockpit is a great mystery. The *9–11 Report* provides virtually no clues.⁹²

What we do know is that Jarrah faced a passenger led rebellion that forced him to crash land in a field in Western Pennsylvania. It was the only really effective thing that Americans did to blunt al-Qaeda's grand project.

Watching the operation on satellite television from his Afghan sanctuary OBL and his inner circle of comrades rejoiced. 9/11 or what they described as "Holy Tuesday" was the culmination of their dreams of delivering a decisive death blow to the *Zionist-Crusader alliance*. They fully expected some US retaliation but doubted the will of a weak America to sustain a military effort against them. It was the beginning of a series of miscalculations by al-Qaeda's central leadership.

The 9/11 attacks demonstrated huge failures in aviation security and exposed the weaknesses in CIA and FBI intelligence operations. Successive Administrations consistently underestimated the terror networks will and capacity to launch catastrophic attacks against the American homeland.

While some individuals in the CIA and the National Security Council urged more aggressive action against al-Qaeda, terrorism was given a relatively low priority and America relied heavily on a law enforcement model that was poorly suited to combat al-Qaeda and its allies. The fear, caution, and reluctance to take dramatic action by the US government came to an end after 9/11 attacks. The long *war on terror* was about to begin.

3

Al-Qaeda's Post-9/11 Strategy and Organizational Devolution

Introduction

If the number of Americans killed is one-tenth of the numbers of Russians killed in Afghanistan and Chechnya, they will flee heedless of all else. That is because the current structure of the American or Western military is not the same as the structure of their military during the era of colonialism. They reached a stage of effeminancy which made them unable to sustain battles for long periods of time and they compensate for this with a deceptive media halo.

Abu Bakr Naji[1]

Al-Qaeda's post-9/11 capability is intensely debated in academic and intelligence communities. The controversy has taken a very personal edge in the dispute between terror experts Bruce Hoffman and Marc Sageman.[2] Al-Qaeda's operational ability after 9/11 is a very difficult issue to resolve given the organization's secrecy and clandestine status.

The Sageman-Hoffman dispute centers on the collapse of al-Qaeda's Afghan sanctuary and its impact on the network's ability to launch attacks. Sageman argues that al-Qaeda is reduced to an ideological movement that can inspire lone wolfs or homegrown terrorists. Accordingly, it has no real operational, financial, or logistical capability to mount operations.

Bruce Hoffman argues that al-Qaeda was hurt by the American campaign after 9/11 but has regrouped under Pakistani tribal protection and recovered its offensive capability. The organization has, additionally, branched out globally making it a more difficult organization to combat. Hoffman argues al-Qaeda is now posed to mount a multiplicity of attacks against Western interests at home and abroad. In essence it is a hydra-headed menace.

These perspectives have elements of truth but both are incapable of capturing the al-Qaeda's complex post-9/11 mutation. Subsequent chapters will deal with the deficiencies of these perspectives. The next chapter, for example, critiques Sageman's homegrown theory as it pertains to the Madrid and London bombings, while the final chapter, examines the Predator drone program's devastating impact on al-Qaeda's central hierarchy and its Taliban allies. These attacks and the 2011 killing of OBL in a daring Special Forces on his Abbottabad compound have blunted al-Qaeda's resurgence.

While Hoffman may be right about al-Qaeda's resurgence in its Pakistani Taliban Waziristan sanctuary from 2005-9, the organization has recently been weakened.³ Pakistani military operations in South Waziristan against al-Qaeda's Taliban allies have also limited the terror network's regeneration. This is verified by bin Laden's Abbottabad correspondence that contemplates moving al-Qaeda operations to Yemen.⁴ Osama was horrified by the number of al-Qaeda associates that had fallen victim to the drone program.

Especially critical in damaging al-Qaeda's position has been the weakening of TTP. Consolidating some 40 militant groups in Waziristan, the TTP aligned with al-Qaeda in 2007 and embarked on a terror campaign that struck at Islamabad and Western interests.⁵ TTP leader Baitullah Mehsud was enraged by Islamabad's alliance with the United States and the Pakistani military's campaign in the region to weaken al-Qaeda. He and his successor Hakimullah were killed by CIA directed drone strikes.

TTP's terror campaign against the Pakistani state and its civil society killed thousand including former Prime Minister Benazir Bhutto in an audacious attack during one of her campaign rallies. The groups' suicide bombs, cell phone triggered attacks, and improvised explosive devices bear al-Qaeda's hallmark. They repeat the pattern of al-Shabaab, AQIM, and AQAP attacks after their affiliation with al-Qaeda Central. Mehsud's daring strategy was unprecedented, never had a jihadist terror group mounted a systemic effort to overthrow the Pakistani regime.⁶ The Taliban's 2009 violation of a truce agreement with Islamabad in Swat Valley, moreover, forced the military and security services to retaliate. Given the ferocity of the TTP terror campaign, public support for Islamabad's efforts to drive its forces out of Waziristan has grown.

What is clear is that al-Qaeda after 9/11 did not have centralized operations capable of independently financing and mounting terror operations. It, however, has played a role in post-9/11 operations like Bali, Madrid, and London.[7] Al-Qaeda was able to financially, technically, and operationally assist regional and local militant organizations to attack its adversaries. Its al-Sahab media operations, moreover, continues to stir jihadist sentiment and passions. Established shortly after 9/11 the al-Sahab Institute for Media Productions is the networks main production company. Its production rate of attack videos, al-Qaeda leadership statements, documentaries, and training manuals is a vital component in bin Laden's propaganda machine. Al-Sahab released some 97 videos in 2007 alone.

Al-Qaeda's cyber jihad operations are its vital connection to disaffected Muslims and aligned organizations across the world. They are invaluable sources for recruitment of fighters to key battle zones and provide assistance to disaffected Diaspora Muslims interested in attacking the Western homeland. Al-Qaeda affiliates in the Maghreb, Somalia and Iraq have developed media production companies that interface with al-Sahab and are released through bin Laden's main distribution outlet Global Islamic Media Front. Bin Laden before his death had hoped to centralize communication strategy al-Qaeda affiliate under his media production and design companies.

It is quite evident that the rise of associates and affiliates tied to al-Qaeda are a vital component in the parent organizations strategy to defeat the West. The Sageman-Hoffman debate is overly didactic and it understates the importance of affiliated and associated groups. These groups have important relations with al-Qaeda. Fernando Reinares argues, for example, that al-Qaeda's network is more polymorphous than either camp recognizes.[8] It is a multifaceted threat that operated in many theaters.

Al-Qaeda's interfaces with multiple groups: some of whom are affiliated, aligned, and independent. Accordingly, al-Qaeda's most significant post-9/11 operations are characterized by multiple linkages between different groups and individuals with no single actor completely responsible. These relationships frequently mutate and shift over time.

Many experts have analyzed al-Qaeda's post-9/11 evolution and arrived at dramatically different conclusions.[9] Evolution is, however, not the right word. *Devolution* is a more accurate characterization. Since 9/11 al-Qaeda has mutated into a *decentralized*, *fragmented* and *dispersed* organization that relies on aligned and affiliated groups to implement its strategic vision. Al-Qaeda, moreover, has become progressively weaker in the last years and increasingly dependent upon these networks. Its capacity to control the jihadist movement has greatly diminished over time. Many of these affiliated and associated groups have acted counter to al-Qaeda's strategic design to attack America.

Al-Qaeda's *devolution* has occurred on two basic levels. First, its emirs in Iraq, Somalia, Yemen, and the Maghreb have joined with local jihadists to create new regional branches. Deprived of funds from cash-strapped al-Qaeda Central these affiliated organizations have diversified into criminal activity with some of its members more attracted to financial incentives than the network's ideological cause. Second, al-Qaeda's broad alliance with autonomous local groups has conflated the *near* and *far enemy* doctrine complicating the parent organization's overall strategy. Managing this complex set of loosely connected autonomous actors presents a myriad of organizational and ideological challenges for al-Qaeda Central in its effort to craft a response to the US *war on terror*.

This chapter develops a conceptual framework to explain al-Qaeda's multifaceted response that does not correspond to either Hoffman's or Sageman's post-9/11 theories. The organization's mutation and relations with affiliates, associates, insurgent groups, and lone wolf terrorists after the 9/11 attacks is sketched. Later case studies will explore these associations and how they evolved in Europe, Iraq, Somalia, Yemen, and the Maghreb. Concluding chapters will look at the al-Qaeda's future prospects in West Africa, its organizational unraveling, the decimation of its senior and midlevel leaders, and its ability to exploit the turmoil of the Arab Spring. Unable to launch devastating strikes against the American homeland since 9/11, al-Qaeda's long-term future the book concludes is grim.

Al-Qaeda's control over activity conducted by affiliated and aligned groups and individuals varies dramatically. This chapter is organized into four key sections. The first section examines the Taliban's overthrow and the impact on al-Qaeda's organization and operational ability. Secondly, it is followed by an analysis of al-Qaeda s foremost theorists Abu Musab Suri and Abu Bakr Naji, and their influence on the organization's post-9/11 strategy. The third section analyzes al-Qaeda's *devolution* from a centralized hierarchical organization into a network of alliances and affiliations and it discusses al-Qaeda's partnership with JI an Indonesian terror network responsible for the 2002 Bali bombings. It is argued that from the Bali's bombings begin al-Qaeda's post-9/11 strategy that is repeated in terror attacks in Madrid, London, Iraq, Yemen, Somalia, and the Maghreb. Al-Qaeda's terror war, moreover, is part of an orchestrated military campaign designed to weaken Western resolve to conduct antiterror operations.

The destruction of the Taliban sanctuary and al-Qaeda's predicament

The Bush Administration and US intelligence community were surprised and embarrassed by the scale of 9/11 attacks. The WTC and Pentagon assaults killed close to 3,000 people. Al-Qaeda's Holy Tuesday operation hit the symbolic foundation of American financial and military power. Such devastation was physically and psychologically unnerving. In the resulting chaos the Administration was confused as to who was responsible for the 9/11 attacks. Some members of the Administration reportedly blamed Saddam Hussein's regime for the attacks and were eager to prepare military retaliation against Iraq.[10]

Al-Qaeda authorship of the attacks, however, became quickly apparent and the Administration had to forge a military retaliation strategy. Given the gravity of the attacks, it became abundantly clear that a traditional law and order approach had failed. Repeated criminal prosecutions and grand jury indictments had not shielded the country from al-Qaeda's wrath. The Clinton Administration's legalistic approach, paradoxically, made Sheik Rachman and Ramzi Yousef celebrities in the jihadist world. Some jihadists groups pledged to attack America in order to secure Yousef and Rachman's release.[11] Remarkably this approach still has die-hard adherents.

Despite its necessity there was a great deal of anxiety about military intervention in Afghanistan. The Russians and British had failed to quell Afghan rebels and were forced to retreat after experiencing heavy losses.[12] Fearing the consequences of military involvement, the Administration negotiated with the Taliban to hand over bin Laden obviating the need for a military response.

This initiative was bound to fail. The Clinton Administration tried to convince Mullah Omar to hand over bin Laden, but to no avail. The friendship and ideological ties between the Taliban leader and Bin Laden were impervious to the most severe threats and sanctions.[13] Mullah Omar had married one of bin Laden's daughters and lived in a house that the Saudi leader had built. Afghan cultural norms of not betraying honored guests played an important role in insuring bin Laden's safety. The month-long negotiations between the Bush Administration and Omar's regime allowed al-Qaeda's top leadership time to plan an escape to the Pakistani frontier. It was a very costly mistake.

Despite the delayed American military response, al-Qaeda and the Taliban forces were unprepared. The Taliban and al-Qaeda leaders were also surprised by the depth of the America retaliation. Planning for the WTC and Pentagon attacks was confined to senior al-Qaeda leaders. Many al-Qaeda and the Taliban cadres were critical of the 9/11 attacks but were forced by necessity to endorse al-Qaeda's strategy.[14] The prospect of an American counterstrike was a sufficient catalyst for unity. This solidarity was no substitute for an effective strategy to resist the American onslaught.

In mid-October 2001 the Administration employed an unconventional military campaign using CIA paramilitaries, Special Forces teams, and Afghan Northern Alliance (NA) ground forces. The NA was an anti-Taliban coalition of Tajik, Uzbek, and Hazara warlords that had opposed the regime's extremism and pro-Pashtun policy. They had been fighting the Taliban since their 1994 ascension. Their leader the legendary Tajik warlord Ahmed Mehsud had been assassinated by al-Qaeda agents masquerading as reporters a day before the 9/11 attacks.[15] Al-Qaeda feared that Mehsud knew something about the "Holy Tuesday" operation.

American air power and laser guided munitions were directed by CIA-Special Forces teams to hit Taliban and al-Qaeda troop formations, convoys, and military assets. The results were devastating. In the resulting Taliban and al-Qaeda losses, NA ground forces were able to mount a ground offensive that quickly yielded results. Within a month ground fighting and laser guided air strikes killed thousands of al-Qaeda and Taliban. Abu Musab Suri estimated that al-Qaeda had lost 80 percent of its fighters in the American led campaign (including senior military commander Mohammed Atef) and that American technological superiority on the battlefield made open confrontations with US forces suicidal.[16] Al-Qaeda's vaunted Brigade 055 was decimated by American airstrikes and had very few survivors. Pakistani analyst Ahmed Rashid, furthermore, determined that the Taliban had been routed losing one-fifth of its military forces.[17] Especially devastated were the thousands of Pakistani tribal warriors who volunteered to assist the Afghan Taliban who fell to US airborne and Special Forces attacks. Coalition losses, on the other hand, were negligible.

Al-Qaeda and their Taliban allies were poorly prepared for the American military response that they believed would involve massive air attacks and a

Soviet style conventional campaign that they believed they could easily defeat. The CIA-Special Forces asymmetrical responses shattered their expectations and it is clear that al-Qaeda had no real response other than faith that Allah would guide them to victory.

Predictions of an early American quagmire were not realized. By November, NA troops and their international allies entered Kabul and by mid-December al-Qaeda and the Taliban had retreated to the Hindu Kush Mountains and the Afghanistan-Pakistan border. US forces believed that they had bin Laden trapped in his Tora Bora cave complex along the frontier and a massive bombing campaign could kill him.

The US intervention was, however, not a complete success. Senior al-Qaeda and Taliban leaders including OBL, Ayman Zawahiri, and Mullah Omar survived and many fighters were able to seek refuge in Pakistan. The small number of combat troops deployed prevented US forces from achieving complete elimination of al-Qaeda. Driven by a Vietnam syndrome and a fear that substantial losses could sap public will the Administration attacked quite late and with insufficient military capability.

The battle of Tora Bora symbolized the Administration's fears and caution. Despite repeated pleas by CIA operatives to deploy the tenth Mountain division stationed in Uzbekistan to seal off the border, the Administration was content to rely on local tribal allies and a mass bombing campaign.[18] The assault that featured 25,000-pound Daisy Cutter bombs did not prevent the bulk of bin Laden's forces from retreating into Pakistan.

The American led campaign was also hindered by the ambiguous role of Pakistan that despite its support for the US campaign against al-Qaeda continued to provide clandestine Taliban assistance. Having trapped large numbers of al-Qaeda and Taliban forces in Konduz the Bush Administration temporarily ceased military operations to permit the withdraw of Pakistani Inter-Services Intelligence and military personnel who left in a poorly supervised airlift.[19] Konduz became a terrible augury of future relations. Little is known about the numbers of Taliban or possibly al-Qaeda Pakistani military and Inter-Services Intelligence officers took with them on this airlift.

Faced with heavy losses and possible destruction Taliban and al-Qaeda forces retreated to the Pakistani frontier. With their senior leadership intact they prepared for a guerilla war against US and coalitional troops. Their withdraw to the Pakistani frontier was made practical by the country's long porous border and supporting Wazir tribes whom had contributed thousands in the defense of the Afghan Taliban brothers. These regions are where the Pakistani state is weak and fundamentalist regional warlords dominate.

Regrouping along the Pakistan frontier around Pashtun tribal belts of North West Frontier Province (NWFP) and Federally Administered Tribal Areas (FATA) was, for al-Qaeda, logical given tribal support for past jihadist struggles.[20] Dominated by warlords Mullah Nazir and Nek Mohammad, Wazir tribes offered bin Laden and Zawahiri shelter and support.[21]

These regions had provided refuge for many foreign fighters some of whom married with local women. Thousands of militant fighters from the Islamic Movement of Uzbekistan (IMU) whom had settled in South Waziristan were welcomed by their Afghan and Arab jihadist brothers. Al-Qaeda, the IMU, and Afghan war lords Jalaluddin Haqqani and Gullbuddin Hekmatyar hoped to regenerate the Taliban insurgency from their Pakistani sanctuaries.[22] Both Haqqani and Hekmatyar had past connections to the Pakistani Inter-Services Intelligence during the Afghan jihad and Taliban periods and by all accounts continue to receive state financial and technical assistance.[23] The FATA and NWFP sanctuaries continue to be critical to the Taliban insurgency against coalition forces in Afghanistan.

The dozens of radical groups along the frontier is a legacy of past Pakistani support for a variety of jihadist causes. Al-Qaeda and the Haqqani network, for example, have had strong organizational and ideological connections dating back to the Afghan jihad. Indeed, some analysts consider Pakistan to be a leading state sponsor of jihadist groups in Central Asia.[24] Without question, the Inter-Services Intelligence has been a financer and coordinator of jihadist groups in Afghanistan and Kashmir. Its history of support for the Taliban and a variety of Kashmir jihadist groups is driven by a desire to counter Indian interests in the region. Billions of US military and economic support for Pakistan have not changed the strategic direction of Pakistani foreign policy. The bulk of Pakistan's army continues to be deployed in the Kashmir border region.

Despite preserving its top leadership, the military campaign badly hurt al-Qaeda. The terror group's command and control to mount operations was degraded and disrupted, and the loss of its camps damaged its recruitment and training ability.[25] Al-Qaeda security became dependent upon networks that often were not able to secure the safety of its leaders.

Al-Qaeda was most vulnerable in Pakistan's frontier cities where Ramzi Bin al-Sheeb, Abu Zubaydah, Abu Musab Suri, and KSM were detained in 2003 and 2005 antiterror operations. Bin Laden's networks in Europe, North America, and the Middle East were disrupted with many agents rounded up and cells destroyed. In addition, al-Qaeda's financial sources became depleted as charities associated with the group had their bank accounts frozen worldwide. Al-Qaeda's operational infrastructure had been damaged by the Afghan military campaign and the global disruption of its regional networks.

The death or imprisonment of midlevel leaders and operatives forced al-Qaeda to search for new strategy to counter Washington's Global War on Terror (GWOT). While it is difficult to ascertain decision making of a secret shadowy clandestine network, the analyst can examine al-Qaeda statements and actions to infer organizational direction and strategy. Fortunately, al-Qaeda's propaganda outlets and theorists have been quite active allowing for some informed speculation.

Since 9/11 al-Qaeda's communications network al-Sahab Media Productions has produced hundreds of videos and statements.[26] They represent a vast wealth of information that al-Qaeda hopes to communicate to enemies and supporters.

Al-Qaeda's post-9/11 strategy: The jihadist doctrines of Abu Musab Suri and Abu Bakr Naji

Many analysts have tried to ascertain al-Qaeda's post-9/11 strategy and operational capability.[27] The movement's dispersion, furthermore, has been a catalyst for academic discussion. This search for a post-9/11 strategy has led many to the work of Syrian jihadist Abu Musab Suri. For some observers, Suri is the architect of al-Qaeda's efforts to defeat the West after 9/11.[28]

There are many valid justifications for this conclusion. The prominence of Suri's writings, lectures, and video tapes in jihadist websites and the popularity of his ideas is unmatched by any other theorist. No other modern jihadist has written so clearly or extensively. Suri's 1,600 page book *The Call for a Global Islamic Resistance* is considered by many jihadists as the blueprint to defeat the West in the Global War on Terror.[29] So influential was Suri that at the time of his 2005 arrest in Pakistan the FBI had assigned a $5 million reward for information leading to his capture.

Suri's book emphasizes a decentralized jihad of uncoordinated small groups attacking Western interests. Al-Qaeda's dispersion seems consistent with homegrown terrorist threats popular in press and academic circles.[30] The spread of homegrown terrorism supposedly responsible for the Madrid and London bombings has no doubt stimulated academic attention to Suri's ideas. The sheer volume of his work that includes many books, articles, and taped lectures commands attention. *The Call for a Global Islamic Resistance* conclusions were based on life of activism in the Syrian, Algerian, and Afghan jihads and over decades of intellectual reflection on the history of guerilla insurgencies. Suri had taken part in the failed Muslim Brotherhood revolt of the 1980s against the secular-socialist Baathist regime of Hafez al Assad. The regime's destruction of the Brothers insurgency at Hama in 1982 made an indelible impression upon him about the dangers of hierarchically organized revolutionary movements.

His role in al-Qaeda and other jihadist organizations, moreover, is uncontested. Suri was an important figure in al-Qaeda Spanish network. Having spent many years living in Spain, he had strong personal and organizational relationship with the Spanish network's leader Abu Dadah who played a role in facilitating a 9/11 planning conference in Taragona Spain.[31] His Spanish wife continues to defend him denying all allegations that he is a terrorist. He is wanted by Spanish courts for his al-Qaeda involvement in Spain.

Suri was also a GIA and al-Qaeda media representative in London during the 1990s. He was a passionate defender of the GIA until almost the end of its barbaric insurgency that even he could not defend. Most famously the red-haired Syrian was the conduit for Bin Laden's meeting with Peter Bergen in 1998 in Afghanistan shortly after the African Embassy bombings and bin Laden's declaration of war against the United States for a second time.

Suri's devotion to al-Qaeda's leaders, however, is suspect. During his years in Afghanistan in the 1980s and 1990s he frequently clashed with bin Laden over ideological and strategic issues.[32] When he ran his own camp during the Taliban period, Suri did not swear fidelity to bin Laden. Their contrasting personalities, furthermore, found bin Laden angered by Suri's volatility and brashness.

The Syrian later criticized Osama when the Saudi leader refused to follow Taliban orders and moderate his offensive campaign against America. Suri was a great admirer of Mullah Omar and he ran the Taliban's media operations. He viewed Taliban rule as an ideal to be emulated by Muslims. Suri and bin Laden clashed over relations with the Taliban with the Syrian supporting Omar's decision to be in charge of the supervision of all training camps in the country. He was appalled by Osama's lack of respect for the Taliban and his unwillingness to coordinate policy with Mullah Omar's government. Suri, moreover, criticized al-Qaeda's hierarchical structure which left it vulnerable to American military retaliation after 9/11. By his account, al-Qaeda lost 80 percent of its Afghan force after 9/11 with al-Qaeda's vaunted Brigade 055 decimated by US air strikes.[33]

Published online in 2004 Suri's *The Call for a Global Islamic Resistance* is a sweeping critique of jihadist organizations failures in Syria, Algeria, and Egypt. In his book the Syrian jihadists warn that hierarchical structures are vulnerable to police penetration and disruption. Suri is especially critical of Zawahiri's Egyptian Islamic Jihad (EIJ) whose organization played a pivotal role in al-Qaeda's development. He describes the EIJ's terror campaign in the 1980s and 1990s as a "total failure."[34] Having been a passionate supporter of the Algerian GIA he later condemned the group's excesses and mistakes. Given such failures, it was clear a new jihadist path was needed.

Instead of central direction Suri advocated an alternative strategy that he called tanzim or *system not organization*.[35] Borrowing from Che Guevara's "el foco" theory, Suri's doctrine involves a decentralized jihad conducted by small spontaneous and uncoordinated bands of attackers. The fragmented structure of the jihadist insurgency had numerous advantages. Among these decentralized attack formations were less vulnerable to government retaliation since each cell was independent. Even if police and intelligence forces were able to penetrate and destroy one cell its damaging impact would be minimal on the jihadist movement. Unable to effectively retaliate, the enemy would be drawn into multiple fronts characterized by repeated strikes by small groups.

Suri expected that the United States and its allies would be unable to fend off such groups whose growth would be exponential with each victory. The exhausted Americans would soon disengage from the Middle East leaving their apostate allies vulnerable to Islamist revolts. For Suri, the Afghan jihad against the Soviets and the victory of mujahidin forces could be repeated against the West.

The Call for a Global Islamic Resistance sees the United States as the architect of an imperial grand design to control the Middle East, exploit its resources, and destroy Islam through military occupation and globalization. Suri argues that the 1991 Gulf War was an opening salvo by the West to control Mideast oil and reinforce apostate rule in the region. The spread of global capitalism, moreover, was a form of cultural pollution to destroy Muslim society. Islam, he reckons, has a retributive right to attack the American homeland, kill its civilians, and employ mass casualty attacks.[36] Suri is unrepentant in his defense of extreme violence against Islam's enemies.

Parts of Suri's book outline the use of weapons of mass destruction to weaken, punish, and terrorize the West. The success of Suri's *system, not organization* strategy is preconditioned upon mass ideological conversion and the excitation of communitarian passions. His basic theory is that American military campaigns in Islamic lands would inspire transnational Muslim unity unleashing global religious passions. Small bands would rise to fight American forces across the globe. Decentralized jihadist cells would harass Western forces and each violent encounter would inspire a contagion of volunteers and combatants. Victory over the diabolical West would be insured by small bands of heroic mujahidin.

Sections of *The Call for a Global Islamic Resistance* are overly idealistic and unworkable. Suri's romanticism about the capacity of vanguard elites to stir up mass religious passions seems dependent upon mystical forces. These sentiments belie his reputation as a realist but it is typical of jihadist thinkers whose faith in divine guidance is unshakeable. They fervently believe that the slumbering ummah can be awoken from its jahilli ignorance by heroic battlefield exploits and martyred jihadists.

Suri who clings to takfir doctrine and arguments of jahilli ignorance seems reluctant to follow the logical consequences of his ideas. Indeed, takfiri doctrine impedes mass mobilization reifying vanguard elites committed to the true path of Islamic liberation. Power struggles between elites committed to ideological purity are inevitable. The history of the jihadist movement is replete with division and fragmentation caused by Islamist infighting and internecine power struggles.[37] Muslim masses in the Sunni Islamic world have not responded in sufficient numbers to evoke the transformation envisioned by Suri's book. The movement remains elitist and divided.

Like many jihadist thinkers Suri adopts Marxist-Leninist and Maoist doctrines of neocolonial exploitation and guerilla wars in the capitalist periphery to develop his theory. His endorsement of Che's *el foco* strategy ignores the Argentine's failures in the Congo and Bolivia. Che's defeat in Bolivia was a consequence of his inability to arouse proletarian consciousness among the rural Indian peasantry. Violence and insurrection cannot be easily manufactured by elites who seek to stir popular passions and cleanse society of impurity and injustice.[38]

Tactically Suri's decentralized jihad has profound limitations. Small groups who attack spontaneously tend to be inexperienced amateurs whose assaults frequently fail. Joseph Jay Carafano's study of 50 averted attacks in the United States since 2001 found most were conducted by small groups who lacked training and organizational connections.[39] Such bands can cause at best limited damage and their repeated failures reduce the appeal of the jihadist cause.

Mass indoctrination of jihadist passions requires central orchestration and hierarchical direction. How else could the strictures of jahilli ignorance be transcended? Suri assumes that the internet and social media could stimulate the ummah's revolutionary awakening. Yet the *jihadesphere* is so immense, *so* fractured and so quarrelsome that such unity is unlikely. Only a strong bureaucratic entity capable of mounting a concerted propaganda campaign could direct the masses toward the desired path.[40]

Despite his prodigious work and popularity among younger jihadists, it is unlikely that Suri had much influence on al-Qaeda strategy after 9/11. Bin Laden disliked him and his outsider role limited his leverage within the network. Significantly, Suri's work has never been officially endorsed by al-Qaeda Central. Near the end of his life, moreover, bin Laden wanted to centralize media operations among al-Qaeda's regional franchises to ensure a more uniform, coherent message.[41] This is counter to Suri's decentralized jihad vision.

After Suri was arrested by Pakistani and FBI authorities in 2005 he was reportedly sent to the US Diego Garcia naval base and later on to Guantanamo where we believe he was extradited to Syria for his jihadist activities on behalf of the Muslim Brotherhood. If American intelligence believed Suri was influential in al-Qaeda it is highly doubtful that they would have sent him to Syria. He is rumored to have escaped in a jailbreak during the popular revolt against Bashar al-Assad's regime and he may be with jihadist forces in the revolutionary movement. His exact status is unknown. American officials do not appear to be overly concerned about his current activities.

While Suri may be the most prominent jihadist thinker in the post-9/11 era, his influence in al-Qaeda is eclipsed by Abu Bakr Naji whose e-treatise *The Management of Savagery: The Most Critical Phase in Which the Ummah Will Pass* has been officially endorsed by al Qaeda media operations.[42] As an al-Qaeda ideologue and tactician his ideas seem better aligned with al-Qaeda strategic behavior after 9/11. Referred to as "Al-Qaeda's playbook" by analysts, Naji's e-treatise was published in 2004 by an al-Qaeda e-media outlet.[43]

The *Management of Savagery* outlines a policy of *vexation* and *exhaustion* consistent with al-Qaeda's actual attacks in Europe and its assaults against coalition troops in Afghanistan and Iraq.[44] Naji writes of a multifaceted campaign designed to weaken the West's resolve and forces its disengagement from the Middle East. His goal is to cripple al-Qaeda's *far* and *near enemies*.

Naji outlines al-Qaeda's strategy in the following passage taken from the *Management of Savagery*:

The primary goal for the stage of the power of *vexation* and *exhaustion* is:

1. —exhaust the forces of the enemy and the regimes collaborating with them, disperse their efforts, and working to make them unable to catch their breath by ways of operations of the choice states, primary or otherwise. Even if the operations are small in size and effect . . .
2. —attract new youth to the jihadi work by undertaking qualitative operations . . . by qualitative operations . . . like the operations in Bali . . . and the large operations in Iraq.[45]

The al-Qaeda strategist emphasizes the targeting of civilians, transport infrastructure, and economic institutions.[46] His strategy is impelled by al-Qaeda's desire to inflict immense economic, psychological, military, and political pain upon the West. The targeting of *soft* targets and civilians is designed to sway public opinion and put pressure on Western policy makers to end antiterror measures. No type of attack is excluded and Naji especially emphasizes the use of nuclear, chemical, and biological weapons against civilian populations. Al-Qaeda's enemies shall not be accorded any mercy.

He, moreover, endorses attacks against any regime that cooperates with Washington's war against al-Qaeda. This includes assaults against "apostate" regimes in the Muslim world. Like Suri's *The Call for a Global Resistance*, Naji's uses takfiri doctrine to justify the most brutal attacks against impious Muslims. He assumes that American troops are weak, frequently comparing them unfavorably to Soviet forces.[47] Accordingly, the West is too soft, effeminate, and decadent to stand up to the *brave* and *heroic* mujahidin. Naji's *Management of Savagery* repeatedly juxtaposes Islamic bravery and strength with Western cowardice and weakness.

Naji's views history as a series of Western colonial aggressions against the Muslim World. His review of the Modern Middle East begins with the Franco-British Sykes-Picot treaty to colonize much of North Africa and the Arab Middle East.[48] Naji concludes that Europe's goal was to weaken the Ottoman caliphate and implant a Jewish state in Palestine. The collapse of the Turkish caliphate in 1919 paved the way for complete colonization of the region. *The Management of Savagery* argues that the end of Franco-British imperial control after WWII did not eliminate Western aggression. Instead, decolonization led the French, British, and Americans to support Pan-Arabist and monarchial *apostate* regimes who brutally repressed Islamist movements. Israel's creation in 1948, moreover, continued a European colonial presence aided and abetted by global Jewish finance and American patronage.

Naji argues that the Soviet Union's collapse and the Cold War's end ushered a new wave of American-Israeli imperial aggression against the Muslim World. He interprets the Gulf War as an insidious American bid to appropriate Muslim land and resources.[49] Continued American support for Israel and its policies in the occupied territories is offered as proof of an international Jewish conspiracy to destroy Islam and reinforce apostate rule. The Saudi monarchy is, accordingly, the handmaiden of American influence and power in the region. Its rulers must be overthrown.

The Management of Savagery outlines alliances with organized groups in a diverse number of battlefields or "open fronts." Naji puts much premium on the failed states in Yemen and the Maghreb. Citing Paul Kennedy's work on the collapse of European empires and the dangers of imperial overextension, Naji believes American military forces can be drawn into Afghanistan, Iraq, and other battle zones and they will suffer crippling human and financial losses similar to the 1980s Soviet experience.[50]

He believes that al-Qaeda and associated group's attacks in North America and Europe could fracture the international coalitions will to fight and sway public opinion against military intervention.[51] Naji's doctrine of *vexation* and *exhaustion* puts an emphasis on propaganda and central direction of the mujahidin struggle against the Crusader-Zionist alliance. He believes al-Qaeda must be the catalyst to direct associated and affiliated organizations in a systemic campaign of terror and psychological intimidation. Only a centralized organization with a well-orchestrated propaganda campaign could facilitate this kind of long-term policy to weaken the West and its apostate allies.

Success on the battlefield, therefore, is preconditioned upon a concerted media and propaganda strategy.[52] The purpose of this communication's strategy would be twofold. First, dramatization of mujahidin victories against Western troops and terror strikes in North America and Europe would arouse Muslim passions to join jihadist forces and weaken al-Qaeda's enemies. Second, mujahidin victories and exploits could be used to cajole and sway public opinion in Western countries to pressure their governments to disengage their forces from Islamic battlefields.

Al-Qaeda media operations after 9/11 are consistent with this Naji's vision. Established shortly after the American invasion of Afghanistan, al-Sahab Institute for Media Productions turns out documentaries, explosives fabrication manuals, leadership statements, and warnings to Crusader states designed to encourage broad Muslim resistance and Western disengagement from the Muslim world. It is a vital link to unify jihadist efforts to defeat the West and rally mujahidin forces.

Al-Sahab has steadily increased its production rate of videos releasing hundreds of original works. Jeremy White reports that there are 50 al-Qaeda affiliated websites in nine different languages devoted to training, recruitment, indoctrination, and propaganda.[53] Al-Sahab has featured 20 videos of bin Laden and 40 from Ayman al-Zawahiri since 9/11 urging resistance to Crusader-Zionist and *apostate* forces. Al-Qaeda's media advisor American Adam Gadahn has played an important role in increasing the English language materials and has improved the overall technical and visual quality of al-Sahab videos.[54]

The Management of Savagery's grand aim is to create Islamic enclaves in power vacuums created by Western disengagement and overthrow the West's apostate Muslim allies. Citing Taliban rule in Afghanistan as a model for mujahidin forces, Naji discusses the imposition of Islamic structures in these territories.[55] He advocates stern measures for those who resist these Talibanesque microstates.

Al-Qaeda's fight against the West and their apostate supporters is part of a larger struggle to restore the caliphate. Naji's merger of the *near* and *far enemy* allows him to advocate alliances with multiple networks some of whom have had a generation of struggle against Muslim regimes. Against such states there can be no mercy. Naji speaks favorably of Islamic Jihad's targeting of the Egyptian tourist industry in the 1990s and the importance of launching crippling economic strikes.[56] No target is off limit.

Naji's endorsement of multiple front attacks orchestrated by a central network with numerous alliances, branches, and cells sets the ideological and organizational context for al-Qaeda's post-9/11 strategy. It is a far more accurate depiction of al-Qaeda behavior than Suri's Global Resistance Call. Directed by a hierarchical command center, the damage that these organized networks can inflict is far greater than Suri's decentralized jihad.

Brynjar Lia's analysis of al-Qaeda's post-9/11 media strategy and its hundreds of publications, videos, and audio tapes by the terror provides supporting evidence for Naji's *vexation* and *exhaustion* strategy.[57] Lia argues that al-Qaeda propaganda from the period 2001–9 has emphasized the value of striking America, Europe, and Muslim apostate regimes. Al-Qaeda media outlets have endorsed crippling economic strikes, attacking civilians, and urged the brutalization of enemy troops. He argues that al-Qaeda's list of enemies has grown and the group's support for extremist violence has inhibited its ability to become a mass movement.[58]

Al-Qaeda's inability to trigger a mass movement may be due to its elitist and extremist takfiri ideology. Naji assumes that extreme violence against the West and her allies will trigger popular sentiment in the Muslim world to join jihadist forces and solidify the eventual Western defeat. Such an extremist and nihilistic worldview is limited to a select population whose elitist tendencies militate against the development of popular movements. Such violence, in fact, has alienated many more Muslims than it has attracted.

This ideological conundrum may explain al-Qaeda's alliance strategy in the post-9/11 era. Given the difficulty of engineering a mass conversion in the Muslim world to the jihadist cause, al-Qaeda needed partners to share their ideological sympathies. The terror organization's emphasis on combating apostates who side with America was an effort to forge alliances with diverse jihadist groups.[59] In addition, this merger was driven by strategic necessity to cooperate against common enemies and pool organizational and financial resources.

Al-Qaeda's post-9/11 strategy of *vexation* and *exhaustion*: The critical role of insurgents, associates, and affiliates

With its central command structure and capacity for autonomous action degraded, al-Qaeda was too badly weakened to conduct independent operations. Fortunately for al-Qaeda past associations with aligned networks could be relied on to mount a retaliatory policy of *vexation* and *exhaustion*. These collaborative efforts involved al-Qaeda providing technical, financial, ideological support for groups willing to operate within its overarching strategy. The implementation of the policy, however, became dependent on the operational capability of aligned groups, insurgents, and networks.

Many factors explain why aligned and affiliated groups agreed to cooperate with al-Qaeda. Regional jihadists were desperate to regenerate their movements. Many of these groups had stalled or stagnated under government pressure and internal divisions. The imprimatur of al-Qaeda support raised the ideological profile of aligned groups lending it prestige and enhancing its recruitment appeal. These partnerships were, moreover, convenient given common enemies. Both groups benefited; aligned networks received, advanced training, bomb-making expertise, and in some cases financial support while al-Qaeda Central got to enlarge its retaliatory capability that was badly damaged by the early phases of the Global War on Terror.

Such a policy was a risky strategy given the enlargement of enemies and the inevitable responses of threatened international, regional, and local actors. Al-Qaeda's post-9/11 strategy and its merger of the *near* and *far enemy* is a generic trend within the jihadi community. Thomas Hegghammer, for example, argues that jihadist groups are increasingly coalescing and that these shifting ideological agendas are driven by frustration, desperation, and failure.[60] They like al-Qaeda are in an existential search for a successful strategy to defeat their enemies. Each partner sees these mergers as compensating for some of their organizational, financial, and technological deficiencies.

Alliances between international, national, and local jihadist networks tend not to endure with groups splintering over ideological and leadership disputes. Numerous examples abound. The Egyptian and Algerian jihadist movements eventually splintered into rival groups badly damaging their terror campaigns.[61] Metamergers among jihadists do have powerful short-term advantages allowing for multiple attacks in diverse corners of the world. Al-Qaeda was able to capitalize on these partnerships that set the stage for the Bali, Madrid, and London attacks and the Iraq insurgency.

Al-Qaeda's alliance policy allowed it multiple venues to implement its strategy of *vexation* and *exhaustion*. One way to envision the terror organizational *devolution* is to construct a typology of groups that vary in the degree of al-Qaeda's direction and the scope of their territorial field of operation. Al-Qaeda is similar to a diverse network of diffuse actors held together by overarching if transient mutual benefits where central control and coordination are problematic. Table 3.1 examines levels of al-Qaeda control over its allies and the local/regional threats posed by such groups. These alliances offer al-Qaeda Central many opportunities to strike at multiple opponents. What follows is a brief description of each group type and its benefits to al-Qaeda. The case studies in the following chapters will develop further al-Qaeda's relationship with these different networks.

Cell A involves groups that maintain autonomous and distinct organizations and leadership structures from al-Qaeda. They do, however, cooperate with al-Qaeda because of a common ideological agenda and similar enemies. They coordinate actions, share financial, technical, logistical expertise, and sponsor joint projects. Their partnership or associations is on an ad hoc basis and they agree to exploit targets of opportunity and cooperate when it jointly serves their

Table 3.1 Levels of al-Qaeda control

	Regional Threat	Local-National Threat
Distant Organizational Connection to Al-Qaeda	Cell A (Associates): Autonomous Islamists Groups cooperating with al-Qaeda (JI, Lashkar e-Taiba, TTP, Haqqani Network, MICG), Bali and Madrid attacks. Attacks by Haqqani network against US forces and the Afghan government in post-Taliban era.	Cell B (Lone Wolf/Homegrown Terrorists) small groups or individuals inspired by al-Qaeda (Major Nidal Hassan and Mohammad Moreh).
Close Organizational Connection to Al-Qaeda	Cell C (Affiliates): These groups are regional and sworn fidelity to al-Qaeda (AQIM/AQAP). Attacks on apostate regimes and Western interests in Yemen and Maghreb.	Cell D (Insurgents): Group of fighters connected to al-Qaeda (al-Shabaab/AQI) committed to overthrow apostate regimes supported by international troops. Zarqawi campaign of terror in Iraq 2003–6.

interest. This very much reflects al-Qaeda's pre 9/11 relationship with the jihadist community.

There are numerous examples of this type of alignment al-Qaeda has coordinated actions with the Indonesian JI, the MICG, Pakistani TTP, and the Haqqani network to attack Western interests and US allies. JI and al-Qaeda engineered the October 2002 Bali bombings while MICG with al-Qaeda assistance was responsible for the 2003 Casablanca and 2004 Madrid bombings.[62] The Bali terror attack is discussed later in this chapter while the Madrid attack is analyzed in the next chapter. All three attacks were part of a strategy to weaken coalitional partners of the United States and fracture the international coalition in the war on terror. These assaults were often either warned or commented upon by al-Qaeda press and media operations.

In Pakistan, al-Qaeda's alignment strategy after 9/11 was buttressed by the 2007 formation of the TTP. Created by the late South Waziristan warlord Baitullah Mehsud to unify 40 local jihadist and tribal groups, the TTP adopted al-Qaeda's international agenda. Mehsud wanted to present a unified front against the Pakistani state. Enraged by Islamabad's military incursions into FATA at the behest of Washington's war on terror, the TTP sought to disrupt the

Pakistani-American antiterror alliance. Analysts believe that al-Qaeda's Pakistan strategy hinges on the TTP's ability to force Islamabad to end its cooperation in the American led war on terror and preserve Waziristan's jihadist sanctuary.[63]

The TTP's creation is a departure for Pakistani jihadist groups that had never before mounted operations against Islamabad. Utilizing advanced al-Qaeda explosives techniques TTP launched hundreds of suicide bombings against Pakistani military and civilian targets killing thousands.[64] TTP is thought to be the author of former Prime Minister Benazir Bhutto's 2009 assassination. Reflecting its alignment with al-Qaeda was TTP's international agenda that featured the aborted plots to bomb the Barcelona subway system in 2008 and a failed Times Square bombing in NYC in 2010. Bin Laden's declassified Abbottabad letters speaks of a strong association with Mehsud's group.[65]

TTP and al-Qaeda operations are closely coordinated and their military wings are frequently integrated. Al-Qaeda's formation of Lashkar al-Zil or Shadow Army was conceived as a mobile guerrilla force to replace Brigade 055 that was shattered in late 2001 by the US military retaliation after the 9/11 attacks.[66] Composed of hundreds of Arab and Central Asian jihadists the Shadow Army has joined the TTP military campaign against Pakistani forces in North Waziristan and actively cooperates with the Haqqani network in terror and guerrilla operations against Coalition forces in South Waziristan.

Al-Qaeda has a long association with the Haqqani network. Dating back to the 1980's Afghan jihad the ideological, personal, and organizational ties between the al-Qaeda and Haqqani networks have endured. The network's patriarch Jalaluddin Haqqani is an important tribal warlord whose power base straddles the Afghanistan-Pakistan border. During his 30-plus-year rule over the organization Jalaluddin supported numerous jihadist causes providing Uzbek, Arab, Afghan, Indonesian, and Pakistani fighters training facilities, funds, and access to battlefields in Afghanistan and Kashmir.

Pakistan has used the Haqqani network as a proxy to attack Russian, American, and Indian troops operating in the region. The Inter-Services Intelligence and the Haqqani have a strategic relationship for over 30 years with Islamabad providing key financial and military support. The network has substantial links to international and regional jihadists groups. Jalaluddin provided sanctuary for Arab mujahidin during the 1980's Afghan jihad including Abdullah Azzam and bin Laden. His personal connections to a generation of Arab and Central Asian mujahidin and his battlefield exploits against the Soviets are legendary in jihadist circles. The Haqqani family has erected a vast criminal-business-terror enterprise that actively recruits funds and fighters from Arab Gulf States. Its diverse contacts and financial sources guarantee its independence from both Islamabad and the Taliban.

Don Rassler and Valhid Brown of West Points Combating Terrorism Center argue that the Haqqani network funds and logistical assistance were pivotal to al-Qaeda's formation in the 1980s and 1990s and its preservation after the 9/11 attacks.[67] Jalaluddin's patronage of bin Laden's organization enabled al-Qaeda to erect training camps along Haqqani supply routes in North Waziristan and Loya Paktia. Bin Laden and Haqqani mounted joint operations against Soviet troops setting the stage for their attacks against US and Afghan forces in the post-9/11 period.

The relationship matured after the Soviet disengagement with the Haqqani family providing an important nexus for al-Qaeda's Taliban association. During the 1990s, Jalaluddin and his sons shielded al-Qaeda form Mullah Omar's efforts to restrain bin Laden's international jihadist activities. Significantly, bin Laden and Zawahiri 1998 fatwa declaring war against the United States was issued from Haqqani controlled territory and the family helped secure escape routes for al-Qaeda leadership after the 9/11 attacks.

Bin Laden's network was able to partially regenerate under the Haqqani's network protection in its North Waziristan sanctuary. The family's ties to the Inter-Services Intelligence and Pakistani military insure that Islamabad will not mount military operations in Haqqani controlled territories. Today the organization is led by Sirahuddin Haqqani who has erected a vast business empire built on arms smuggling, kidnapping, money laundering, extortion, and drugs.[68] The movement's pivotal position as a nexus linking al-Qaeda, the Taliban, Uzbek and Kashmiri jihadist organizations and its immense financial base allows it to field tens of thousands of guerrilla fighters.

US military and intelligence officials believe that the Haqqani network has played a key role coordinating and assisting the Taliban insurgency and actively cooperated with al-Qaeda to attack coalition forces. The Haqqanis have been linked with high-profile 2008 attacks against the Indian embassy in Kabul and facilitated the 2009 TTP attack against the Camp Chapman CIA base in Khost Afghanistan that killed seven of the Agency's personnel. Al-Qaeda and the Haqqani continue to mount joint operations against US and Afghan forces. The Haqqani network, however, has little presence in Western countries for which al-Qaeda must depend on disaffected Muslim immigrants to wage jihad on European and North American soil.

Cell B of the matrix represents Suri's decentralized jihad theory that features small autonomous bands or lone wolf terrorists. While ideologically inspired by al-Qaeda's call for global jihad these small groups of fighters and individuals have no organizational, logistical, and financial relationship with al-Qaeda Central. They operate independently, choose their own targets, and are self-financing. They are influenced mainly by al-Qaeda's media operations, fidelity to bin Laden's far enemy doctrine, and their own individual agendas.

Popularized by Marc Sageman work on homegrown terrorist bands many analysts mistakenly believed these groups were responsible for the Madrid and London bombings. We now understand that these attacks involved complex sets of actors and networks that include al-Qaeda Central direction, formal and informal links, and partial sponsorship.[69] Chapter 4 analyzes the Madrid and London public transport attacks and provides evidence of strong and substantial al-Qaeda connections to these bombings.

This does not mean that homegrown or lone wolf terrorism poses no security threat to Western interests. Of the 50 aborted plots to attack the US homeland since 9/11, the vast majority have involved small groups or individuals with only tangential links with al-Qaeda Central or its affiliates. Chapter 8 will examine al-Qaeda's efforts to recruit jihadists to strike the American homeland. This type of terrorism is illustrated by Colonel Nidal Hassan's 2009 shooting rampage in Fort Hood, Texas killing 13 fellow servicemen and Farouk Abdulmutallab's aborted Christmas Day 2010 bombing on board a Detroit bound plane. Both jihadists had contact with departed AQAP leader Anwar al-Awlaki who played an instrumental role in encouraging their radicalization. Hassan awaits a military trial for murder while Abdulmutallab has pled guilty to terrorism charges and has been sentenced to life imprisonment in a high security federal prison.

Cell C involves jihadist organizations that swear loyalty to al-Qaeda's central leadership and become a territorial extension or affiliate of al-Qaeda. Unlike associated groups who cooperate with al-Qaeda when it suits their interest, affiliates *pledge* to further the goals of al-Qaeda's central hierarchy. They have sworn loyalty to al-Qaeda's Shura Council and they seek to align their policy with its central direction.[70]

It would be a great mistake to conclude that groups like AQAP and AQIM are mere territorial appendages of al-Qaeda's central leadership. They vary dramatically in obedience to al-Qaeda and each network has retained its organizational and operational freedom. Here bin Laden's Abbottabad correspondence is illustrative.[71]

Bin Laden's letters express frustration and dismay over the behavior of al-Qaeda affiliates. He especially opposed their strategy of confrontation with local adversaries and killing of Muslims. Even his most loyal affiliate AQAP that has a far enemy strategy comes under blistering criticism for its independent medial operations and its insurgency against the central government. Bin Laden was especially wary of AQAP leader Anwar al-Awlaki and refused to give the Yemeni-American his blessing as a regional emir. Prior to bin Laden's death he sought to recentralize al-Qaeda control over his affiliates and align their strategy with his *far enemy* doctrine.

Cell D of Table 3.1 involves national insurgent groups that have adopted the al-Qaeda brand name. Examples of this relationship include most notably AQI and al-Shabaab in Somalia. Both have fought local governments supported by international troops. There are operational independent from the al-Qaeda central leadership but pledge to follow its direction. The exigencies of battlefield conditions and the salience of the near enemy for these groups impel them behave autonomous of al-Qaeda's Central direction. The independence of these groups often produces strains and conflicts with al-Qaeda central leadership. Both al-Shabaab and AQI have been heavily criticized by bin Laden and Zawahiri for sectarian polices and indiscriminate killings of Muslims.[72]

Chapter 5 will explore AQI's anti-Shi'ite policy and targeting of civilians that so dismays Ayman al-Zawahiri in his 2005 letter to AQI leader Musab al-Zarqawi while Chapter 6 will outline al-Qaeda grievances with al-Shabaab's targeting of Sufi Muslims and the Somali group's draconian imposition of Sharia law.[73] Significantly, bin Laden's Abbottabad letters suggest that his endorsement of Zarqawi's group was a huge mistake that it badly hurt al-Qaeda's image in the Muslim world.

The four groups identified (associates, lone wolves, affiliates, and insurgents) are broad categories and many of al-Qaeda's post-9/11 attacks involve many cells that span across networks. The Madrid and London bombings involved homegrown terrorists, al-Qaeda direction, and associated networks. Irrespective of their degree of responsibility for the attack, all acted with common objectives and coordinated their actions to facilitate al-Qaeda's *vexation* and *exhaustion* strategy.

Al-Qaeda's grand design was to attack multiple enemies in diverse settings across the world to break the international coalition's capacity to wage the war against terror. To accomplish this end al-Qaeda had to rely on allies that had organizational and financial capability to mount attacks. One such partner was the Indonesian jihadist network JI. The groups October 2002 attack in Bali represents al-Qaeda's first real effort to implement its *vexation* and *exhaustion* strategy.

The al-Qaeda-JI partnership and the Bali attacks

South East Asia was ideal canvass for al-Qaeda to launch attacks against US interests and allies after the 9/11 attacks. Radical movements in Indonesia and Malaysia and Muslim secessionist groups in Philippines and Thailand offered a fertile context for jihadist mobilization. The region, moreover, had witnessed a growth in fundamentalism that was supplanting more tolerant Sufi traditions. Indonesia and Malaysia, additionally, failed to actively repress violent jihadist groups after 9/11.[74] The region's lax post-9/11 security environment offered al-Qaeda and aligned networks opportunities to mount operations.

In the late 1980s and early 1990s, al-Qaeda developed strong relationships with Philippine and Indonesian Islamists groups like Abu Sayyaf Groups (ASG), the Moro Islamic Liberation Front (MILF), and JI. Many of these group's militants had either fought in the Afghan jihad or had been trained in camps in Afghanistan and Pakistan. By the late 1990s, al-Qaeda assisted these regional jihadist groups in the formation of training camps in remote Philippine and Indonesian islands.[75]

Al-Qaeda used the Philippines as a major base of operations in the mid-1990s. Ramzi Yousef and his uncle KSM planned numerous operations. Among them were plots to kill the Pope John Paul II, President Bill Clinton, and the infamous Operation Bojinka that becomes the basis for the 9/11 attacks. Yousef's plan to blow up 11 transpacific flights to America was averted when a fire engulfed his workshop after a failed bomb-making experiment. Local officials were able to decode Yousef's computer hard drive that detailed the operation. Having its Manila based network disrupted, al-Qaeda shifted attention to Indonesia and Malaysia and its JI alliance.[76] The reluctance of the Indonesian government to uproot Islamist networks facilitated terror planning and operations.

JI's origins lie in a 1970's educational and religious movement called al-Mukmin that focused on the theological instruction of Muslim youth.[77] Created by Indonesian preachers Abu Bakr Bashir, Abdullah Sungkar, and Shahrul Nizim, al-Mukmin's madrassa education network developed a political party and movement. As Rohan Gunaratna has pointed out, JI's leaders have

Arab lineages that allowed them to secure Gulf State donors facilitating the growth of its madrassa network.[78] By the early 1980s, JI flush with Gulf donor contributions financed a regional Islamist movement.

Repressed under the Suharto regime, many of al-Mukmin's leaders were imprisoned. When released in 1987 they moved to more secure Malaysia. With an accommodating government and a lax security environment, Bashir and Sungkar created JI in 1991, the movement's platform called for a regional Islamic caliphate in Indonesia, Malaysia, Singapore, and the Philippines. Openly espousing jihad, JI began to coordinate activity with ASG, MILF, and al-Qaeda.

When democracy returned to Indonesia in the late 1990s, JI's leaders ended their exile and mobilized a very strong and extensive network. Responsible for al-Qaeda's South Asian sphere of operations, Omar al-Faruk developed ties to local jihadist networks.[79] Bashir volunteered JI personnel and resources to Farouk in the service of al-Qaeda's goals in Southeast Asia. Al-Qaeda's relations with JI were facilitated by Riduan Isamuddin (a. k. a. Hambali) an Indonesian JI militant who had met bin Laden in the late 1980s during the Afghan jihad.

Hambali had extensive al-Qaeda connections and was involved in its regional planning and operations in the 1990s.[80] He had established a front company to finance Operation Bojinka and at KSM's behest formed a cell composed of Indonesian militants to hijack planes. Those individuals recruited (Basyir "Lilie" bin Lap and Mohammad Farik bin Amin) played pivotal roles in the Bali bombings.[81] Given his status as the only non-Arab in al-Qaeda's Shura council, Hambali's prominence in the organization cannot be questioned.

Hambali and the JI network, furthermore, have direct connections to the 9/11 attacks.[82] Among these are providing a Malaysian safe house for Zarcarias Moussaoui and sponsoring an al-Qaeda planning conference featuring two 9/11 bombers and the planners of the USS Cole attack. A year before 9/11, JI worked with al-Qaeda in an aborted plot to attack US servicemen in Singapore and a number of other joint ventures.

Al-Qaeda's relationship with JI continued well after the 2001 WTC and Pentagon attacks. Working with al-Qaeda, JI launched its most deadly assault. On October 12, 2002 the organization attacked the Indonesian Island of Bali killing 202 people (mostly Australian tourists) and wounding over 200 others. JI terrorists targeted a night club, a bar, and the US consulate building. Using a suicide bomber, a massive car bomb, and cell phone triggered explosives, Bali had the character of a sophisticated al-Qaeda operation.

Like the Madrid and London attacks, local police and intelligence officials thought that there was little link to al-Qaeda. Subsequent investigation and the confessions of key JI terrorists, however, revealed substantial al-Qaeda involvement. Indeed, al-Qaeda provided $30,000 for the operation and some of the operatives involved in the Bali bombings had deep connections to bin Laden's organization.[83] The attacks sought to punish Australia for its cooperation with Washington's war on terror and cripple the Indonesian tourist trade. Bali will set the stage for future attacks.

JI and al-Qaeda have a common agenda to rid Indonesia of Western influence and construct as Islamic emirate that could serve as an al-Qaeda state sanctuary. Throughout the 1990s al-Qaeda and JI had established training camps in remote Indonesian islands which they hoped could spearhead operations across the region. Consistent with al-Qaeda's vision, JI hoped to create a caliphate spanning Indonesia, Malaysia, Singapore, Thailand, and the Philippines.

Captured by police in Indonesia and Thailand in 2003, key Bali bombing suspects Imam Samudra and Hambali confessed to substantial al-Qaeda involvement in the attacks. Indeed, two cell members Lilie and Amin were recruited by Hambali to be at the service of KSM in an aborted airplane hijacking plan. Samudra justified the attacks arguing that Bali symbolized the cultural pollution of drug taking, sexual promiscuity, and alcohol that the West had hoisted upon Indonesia.[84] He, furthermore, sought to punish America and kill Americans on behalf of bin Laden's organization. By 2002 it is clear that JI had adopted al-Qaeda's *far enemy* doctrine. Shortly after the Bali attacks, al-Qaeda praised the assaults. JI would later go on to launch attacks in Bali again in 2005 and attack the Marriot Hotel in Jakarta in 2007.

The Bali attacks were al-Qaeda's opening salvo in its *vexation* and *exhaustion* strategy. Working with Turkish agents al-Qaeda followed up the Bali attacks with bombings of two synagogues, a British bank headquarters, and the United Kingdom's consulate in Istanbul in November 2003 killing over sixty people and wounding hundreds.[85] The combined impact of the two attacks is known as the Turkish 9/11. Al-Qaeda's assistance to aligned, insurgent, and affiliated groups committed to its campaign against the West is repeated in the Madrid and London attacks and in terror campaigns in Afghanistan and Iraq. Throughout 2002 and 2003, bin Laden's organization warned Washington's European allies that al-Qaeda strikes would punish them for their participation in Afghanistan and Iraq wars. It is to this issue that we now turn.

4

Al-Qaeda's Role in the Madrid and London Bombings

Introduction

I ask honest peoples especially the ulema, preachers and merchants to form a permanent committee to enlighten European peoples of the justice of our cause. . . . I also offer a reconciliation initiative to them to stop operations against every country that commits itself to not attacking Muslims or interfering in their affairs including the U.S. conspiracy against the Muslim world. . . . The reconciliation will start with the departure of the last soldier from our country. . . . For those who reject reconciliation and want war, we are ready.

Osama bin Laden[1]

Homegrown terrorism is an important topic in academic discussion about Islamic radicalism in the West. Small cells of Muslim extremists committing or planning terror attacks in Western countries abound in academic accounts.[2] Among examples most commonly cited are the Madrid and London bombings. Both attacks initially were viewed as being free of al-Qaeda connections.

Marc Sageman's work has been in the forefront of the homegrown terrorism theories.[3] His research presents a post-9/11 al-Qaeda that is unable to operationally launch attacks but continues to be a source of ideological inspiration for alienated Western Muslims. With its Afghan terror sanctuary destroyed after 9/11, al-Qaeda depends on Diaspora Muslim extremists to take action against the West. The threat of al-Qaeda inspired terror attacks is especially pronounced in Europe whose Muslim immigrant ghettoes are a fertile base of jihadist recruitment and mobilization.

Sageman argues the 2004 Madrid Train bombings and the 2005 London Subway bombings were the work of first and second generation Muslims attacking Western countries for their support of the Iraq war. Sageman concludes both attacks were locally organized, planned, and executed with little or no al-Qaeda organizational and logistical connection. His research is seconded by many studies arguing that homegrown terrorism is the premier danger facing Western societies.[4]

Homegrown terrorism theorists argue that the Madrid and London bombings were the work of a discontented *bunch of guys*. Seeking fame and glory through jihadist actions, these young men forge friendships and social networks oriented around extremist Islamic causes. The war in Iraq, therefore, has been a catalyst for disaffected Muslims leading them to join radical movements. Sageman argues that the Iraq war has catalyzed a new Jihadist wave of fighters who seek to wage an internal war against European and North American society.

Sageman argues that al-Qaeda's ideological appeal for Islamic immigrants is driven by counterproductive policies. The Iraq war and European labor market discrimination against Muslim immigrants have combined to produce jihadist recruits seeking vengeance and religious glory. Ending these policies, he concludes, will take the fire out of the latest wave of jihadist terrorism.

Madrid and London, therefore, are part of a larger pattern: a common narrative connecting efforts by young Muslims to bring down transatlantic flights, to attack the London subway system, and ignite car bombs in Piccadilly Circus. Sagemen tells us these plots are exclusively the work of first and second generation Muslims enraged by the Iraq war. It should, however, be obvious even to the most casual observer that the end of the Iraq war and foreign occupation has not greatly diminished the global Islamist terror threat.

This chapter debunks the homegrown terrorism thesis by examining al-Qaeda involvement in the Madrid and London attacks. It uses a comparative case study of the two bombings and subsequent plots in Spain and England to demonstrate substantial al-Qaeda involvement. Al-Qaeda worked with regional jihadist networks, alienated individuals, and local cells to pull off both attacks. The terror network, moreover, has been connected to repeated efforts to attack Spanish and English interests. Spain's disengagement of its forces from Iraq after the Madrid attacks has not contrary to Sageman's prediction diminished the jihadist threat to Spanish security.

The Sageman-Hoffman debate

Sageman's thesis of a weakened al-Qaeda and a predominately internal jihadist threat has prompted criticism. Bruce Riedel warned as early as 2007 that al-Qaeda's death was greatly exaggerated and that the terror organization has been reconstituted in remote tribal areas in North West Pakistan.[5] Bruce Hoffman furthermore has critiqued Sageman's work and its empirical foundations.[6] Having reconstituted its logistical capabilities under the protection of the Pakistani Taliban, Hoffman argues, that al-Qaeda remains a potent external threat. The sprouting of Taliban-al-Qaeda terror training camps in Waziristan and their connection to extremist Pakistani Diaspora terror cells operating in Europe and North America can be seen in the London bombings of July 7, 2005 and the failed July 21st London subway attacks. Disrupted by the British police and American authorities the August 2006 conspiracy to down ten transatlantic flights by igniting liquid explosives involved al-Qaeda working with British nationals of Pakistani descent. Spanish authorities similarly disrupted TTP 2007 plan to attack the Barcelona subway system. Each of these cases involves immigrants tied to external al-Qaeda Pakistani training.

Hoffman's argument of a reenergized al-Qaeda Central may be overstated. The growth of al-Qaeda affiliated terror networks after 2001 is not so much a reconstitution of al-Qaeda Central, as it is a partnership between international and regional networks.[7] These networks, not locally organized groups, may be the most dangerous threat to Western security. This is especially true in Spain and France that in the early 1990s it became home to a jihadist infrastructure of extremist groups, radicalized Imams, and clandestine criminal activities designed to support terrorist actions.[8] The Algerian GIA, its numerous successors and the GICMs had extensive European fundraising and recruitment operations during this period.

Pakistani networks tied to al-Qaeda have penetrated segments of the Muslim Diaspora community in England and were vital in the training of suicide bombers involved in the successful July 7th attacks and the failed July 21st attack. Labeled *Londinstan* by its critics, the English capital has been for decades a receptive home for Muslim radicals and extremist organizations.[9] Aided and abetted by the United Kingdom's generous immigration, civil liberties, asylum and welfare policies the country was viewed as an ideal sanctuary for extremists to plan foreign jihad against "apostate" Muslim governments.

With the loss of its Taliban sanctuary after 9/11 al-Qaeda became dependent on regional and local affiliates for operational capability. Al-Qaeda affiliates in Iraq, Pakistan, the Maghreb, Yemen, and Somalia reflect an alliance between international and regional jihadists born by mutual failure. Bin Laden's and Zawahiri's alignment with Maghreb jihadists in 2006, for example, enhances al-Qaeda's capability to strike North Africa and Europe, while allowing Algerian, Moroccan, and Tunisian Islamists to attain ideological credibility, enhanced training, global reach, and religious legitimacy.

Formed in 2006, AQIM has historical antecedents. Al-Qaeda frequently acted through regional proxies in the 1990s. Muslim Diaspora communities in Europe have been linked to terrorist recruitment and finance for international and regional jihadist groups. For many years Spain, England, and France have been a logistical, financial, and recruitment center for many Maghreb networks.

The Algerian Islamic Combat Group (GIA) launched attacks in France in the 1990s has a strong history of cooperation with al-Qaeda. The GICM and Maghreb based Salafist Group for Preaching and Combat (GSPC) similarly have partnered with bin Laden. This alignment can be seen in the 2003 Casablanca and 2004 Madrid attacks.

Contrary to Sageman's "bunch of guys" thesis, the Madrid bombings suggest strong al-Qaeda, GIA, and GICM penetration. Similarly, al-Qaeda in Pakistan and its affiliates were connected to the July 7, 2005 London subway and double decker bus bombings carried out by disgruntled British born Muslims of Pakistani descent. Both attacks were part of an al-Qaeda campaign to punish European allies of the Bush Administration's "war on terror" and a critical pillar of their *vexation* and *exhaustion* strategy.

Far from a local attack by Moroccan immigrants seeking vengeance against Spain for its Iraq war participation, 3/11 reflects a complex web of terror networks working in tandem to achieve long-term objectives. The London bombings similarly were carried out by al-Qaeda trained terrorists who became radicalized in Britain. What follows is an analysis of al-Qaeda's role in the Madrid attacks and the London bombings.

The "bunch of guys" theory fails to explain 3/11

The Madrid 2004 commuter train attacks are well known, but bear a brief review. In the morning of March 11, 2004, 10 of 13 cell phone triggered bombs exploded on 4 commuter trains just outside Madrid's Atocha train station. Timed to inflict maximum damage on thousands of rush hour suburban train passengers, the 10 explosions left 191 people dead and another 1,800 wounded.

The terror attacks occurred just before the Spanish elections in which the government's response and the subsequent police investigation had far reaching political consequences. The governing conservative Popular Party hastily blamed the Basque terrorist movement ETA (Basque Unity and Homeland) for the attacks: a view contradicted by the law enforcement investigation that traced the attacks to an Islamist network.

Muslim extremist responsibility for the attacks was confirmed by the police who connected three unexploded cell phones bombs to a Moroccan immigrant with well-known al-Qaeda contacts. Additional evidence (Koranic audio tapes and explosive detonators) found in two stolen cars left abandoned in suburban stations close to where a dozen terrorists boarded different trains contradicted government claims of Basque authorship.

Al-Qaeda claims of authorship based on e-mails to an Arab language newspaper in London on March 11 and an anonymous call to Spanish authorities on March 13 claimed that attacks were revenge for Spain's role in the Iraq war. The gravity of the attacks and disconnect between the evidence found and the governments public claim of ETA responsibility soon had profound consequences.

The governing party's "disingenuous" campaign was denounced by the opposition Socialists Party whose campaign rhetoric blamed the government's Iraq war policy for Continental Europe's worse terror attack. The Spanish public agreed giving the Socialists an unexpected elector victory, allowing them to implement their promise to withdraw Spanish troops from Iraq.

Police investigations linked the 3/11 attacks to a network of 27 Arab immigrants and criminals. Of this group, 7, believed to have been the group responsible for planting the cell phone triggered bombs, committed suicide on April 3 when cornered by police in their Madrid apartment building. The remaining terrorists would have been tried by the Spanish, Italian, and Moroccan courts years later and sentenced to maximum jail terms.

The parliamentary and judicial commissions investigating the attacks have found that the network was largely self-financing and organized, composed of local cells of Moroccan immigrants enraged by Spain's Iraq war participation.[10] While complex and laborious, these inquiries did not find significant ETA or al-Qaeda sponsorship and largely reinforce the views of Marc Sageman and

Spanish terror expert Javier Jordán that the 3/11 was an example of homegrown terrorism.

This conventional view has been vigorously attacked. Fernando Reinares, Michael Radu, and Lorenzo Vidino have maintained that al-Qaeda Central and its regional affiliates played leading roles in the 3/11 attacks and that the conventional view is contradicted by substantial empirical evidence.[11] The government's 3/11 investigations, moreover, emphasized the Iraq war's responsibility suggesting that the attack was an isolated event. The persistence of the jihadist threat in post 3/11 Spain, however, with seven aborted attacks challenge homegrown terrorism explanations. Spanish withdraw from Iraq has not, contrary to the expectations of homegrown terror analysts, saved the country from Islamic terrorism.

What follows is a critique of the homegrown terror theory as it applies to the 3/11 attacks. The argument proceeds on several levels. Among these are (1) al-Qaeda's' integration of Moroccan and Algerian affiliates in Europe; (2) sustained al-Qaeda contacts with and penetration of the 3/11 network; (3) a chain of events linking an al-Qaeda inspired meeting in Istanbul to the Casablanca and Madrid attacks; and (4) the durability of the Islamist network in Spain after 3/11 that continues to target Spain and use its territory for terrorist financing and recruitment.

Al-Qaeda's Moroccan and Algerian associates

Moroccan and Algerian Islamist terror networks in Europe predate the development of al-Qaeda's European infrastructure. Liberal European immigration and asylum laws attracted large number of Muslims escaping political persecution and economic stagnation. Starting in the 1950s, Muslim migrations to the continent would reach substantial levels by the 1990s with a total population oscillating between 15 and 20 million.

Repression of Islamist groups in the 1980s and 1990s across North Africa and Arabia and their failure to defeat home governments resulted in extremists migrating to Europe. Operating from the security of their European benefactors, Islamists found their capability to wage war against their near enemies reenergized. Particularly prominent in the development of a renewed jihad struggle against the near enemy were the Algerian GIA and GICM; a struggle that would eventually morph into attacks against the far enemy of the West.

The GIA has struggled against Western and North African governments. Formed by Algerian jihadists who fought the Soviets in Afghanistan and from radical factions within the National Salvation Front (FIS), whose election victory in the 1991 elections was nullified by the Algerian military, the GIA transplanted some of its operations to France.

Enraged by France's support for the Algerian government and its repression of the FIS, the GIA attacked the Paris subway system in 1995 and used the country to raise financial support and recruit fighters for their beleaguered Algerian comrades.

The GIA's brutal insurgency against the Algerian regime would soon backfire and split the Islamist movement, spawning groups like the GSPC who also used Europe to finance terror operations and recruit European Muslims to fight for jihadist causes.

The development of a European criminal infrastructure involving drugs, illegal immigrants, passport, and credit fraud tied to Islamist terror networks allowed the GIA, GSPC, and GICM to use clandestine enterprise to mount terror operations, co-opt illegal immigrants, and train terror recruits.

Immigration flows from North Africa, Arabia, and South West Asia and the relative isolation of Islamic Diaspora communities would further the aims of jihadist recruiters. Faced with wars raging in 1990's Bosnia, Chechnya, Kashmir, and Algeria, Islamists could mount wars against Far Western and Near Eastern adversaries.

These jihadist wars, however, paled in comparison with the struggle against the United States whose policies of support for the Islamists enemies in North Africa and Arabia deserved a dramatic response. Formed by Afghan-Arab jihadists of the Soviet war and protected by Islamist Somali and Afghan governments, al-Qaeda would establish connections to Maghreb terror networks operating in Europe.

Rohan Gunaratna argues that al-Qaeda had achieved a partial integration of the Moroccan and Algerian European networks by the late 1990s.[12] United in their hostility toward the United States, these groups partnered resources, training, recruitment, finances, and personnel.

By the end of the twentieth century, Europe became a breeding ground for future jihad waged on multiple fronts. Al-Qaeda's Hamburg, London, and Madrid cells played vital roles in 9/11 attacks. Especially critical was a July 2001 meeting between Mohammad Atta and Ramzi Binalshibh in Tarragona, Spain:

a meeting that GIA operatives had facilitated, and which finalized the operation details of the WTC and the Pentagon attacks.[13]

Al-Qaeda's dependence on Algerian and Moroccan networks accelerated after the destruction of Bin Laden's Afghan sanctuary and the disruption of his European command and control system. This relationship can be seen in the organizational structure of the 3/11 network, whose Madrid bombing would occur, not so coincidently, 911 days after the WTC attack.

The 3/11 network: International and regional Jihadist connections

Studies of the 3/11 network indicate the strong presence of al-Qaeda, GIA, and GICM operatives in the planning, organization, and execution of the Madrid attack.[14] Among the most important of Spain's al-Qaeda elite who had contacts with the 3/11 terrorists were Syrian Abu Dadah and Moroccan Amir Azizi. Considered al-Qaeda's leader in Spain, Abu Dadah recruited key 3/11 bomber Jamal Zougam into the organization in the 1990s. Working with Amir Azizi (who would later die in a CIA Predator drone attack in 2005 in Waziristan) Dadah successfully established a bridge to Maghreb based jihadist organizations, developing an operational synchronicity across the European-North African divide.

Spain's role in 9/11's planning produced a sharp police crackdown. By November 2001 dozens of al-Qaeda's Spanish operatives had been arrested or had fled. Abu Dadah would eventually be captured by Syrian authorities in 2002 and turned over to Spanish authorities, who tried and convicted him for the 9/11 attacks.

Recruited into al-Qaeda in the mid-1990s Amir Azizi traveled between Spain and Taliban Afghanistan with the key task of recruiting Moroccan fighters. Under Azizi's guidance, many of these fighters received training in the use of cell phone triggered explosives in Afghanistan.

Fleeing Spain in 2002, Azizi became an al-Qaeda and GICM liaison and an architect of the Islamist post-9/11 response to the American led *war* on *terror*. Critical in this respect was Azizi's orchestration of a February 2002 Istanbul meeting where representatives from Maghrebi jihadist organizations pledged fidelity to al-Qaeda, complete with plans to attack European and North African countries aligned with the US war in Afghanistan.

Furthering the connection between al-Qaeda, the GICM and the 3/11 networks was Mustafa al Maymouni. The brother-in-aw of one of the 3/11 bombers, Maymouni coordinated al-Qaeda-GMIC operations. His frequent travels between Spain and Morocco were characterized by contacts with bombers responsible for the May 2003 Casablanca and March 2004 Madrid attacks.

The May 16, 2003 Casablanca attacks targeted a Spanish restaurant and cultural center featured 14 suicide bombs that killed dozens including 4 Spaniards. Al Maymouni participation in the attacks is reinforced by his arrest by Moroccan authorities, an unexpected development that changed the leadership direction of the 3/11 Network. His arrest forced his bother-in-law (Tunisian Sermane Ben Abbdelmajid Fakhet) to take charge of one of the Madrid cells.

GICM's penetration of the 3/11 Network is also strengthened by Abenabi Kounja, who was one of the 3/11 bombers who committed suicide a month after the attacks. Having immigrated to Spain in the 1990s from Morocco, Abenabi traveled between Spain and Morocco communicating with key GICM operatives including Fakhet and al Maymouni.

Al-Qaeda and GICM operations played instrumental roles in the cellular organization of the attacks. The 3/11 network of bombers and conspirators involved three main groups: one centered in Madrid's Levapies neighborhood led by al-Qaeda operative Jamal Zougam; one based around Madrid's Villaverde mosque directed by drug dealer Jamal Ahmad; and one led by GMIC operative Fakhet.

Analysts believe that Fakhet took charge of al Maymouni cell after his arrest for the Casablanca attacks, effectively establishing a GMIC linkage.[15] Given that two of the cells were linked to al-Qaeda-GICM operations and the connections between the Casablanca and Madrid attackers, the 3/11 plot goes beyond a predominately local conspiracy. This conclusion is reinforced by al-Qaeda-GICM activity prior and immediately after the Madrid attacks.

Al-Qaeda post-9/11 plan: From Istanbul to Casablanca to Madrid to London

The Madrid attacks took place precisely 911 days after the NYC and Washington DC attacks. Having lost its operational capacity after the Taliban's fall, al-Qaeda's post-9/11 operations depended on Moroccan, Algerian, and Pakistani affiliates to strike back at Western interests. Al-Qaeda's post-9/11 adaptation elevated the role of its Maghreb operatives like Amir Azizi. During the 1990s, Azizi formed associations with Moroccan, Algerian, Tunisian, and Libyan jihadist groups. These connections allowed Azizi to send North African operatives in Afghan camps to learn about, develop, and use cell phone triggered explosives.

The Moroccan organized a February 2002 Istanbul meeting in which Maghreb based organizations pledged fidelity to al-Qaeda, charting a common strategy to attack Western interests. Based on Spanish and Moroccan police investigations of the e-mail and phone traffic of key Casablanca and Madrid bombers, Azizi had sustained contact with GIA and GICM networks.[16]

Azizi's prominence in al-Qaeda cannot be doubted. As chief lieutenant for al-Qaeda's director of external operations Hamza Rabia, Azizi helped craft the organization's post-9/11 *vexation* and *exhaustion* strategy. Rabia and Azizi died in a CIA drone attack in 2005 in Taliban controlled Waziristan confirming that the Moroccan had penetrated al-Qaeda Central and was heavily involved in the planning of external operations.

Captured eight days before the Madrid attacks by Belgian police, al-Qaeda-GICM operative Youssef Beljad possessed two cell phones purchased with phony birth dates that coincide with the dates (May 16 and March 11) of the Casablanca and Madrid attacks. The phones were purchased during a period coinciding with OBL's October 2003 audio tape threat against "Crusader Spain." Beljad's, additionally, had spent a month in Spain contacting members of the 3/11 network and was known as a key link between GICM and al-Qaeda Central whose remnants had escaped to Taliban controlled areas of Pakistan.[17]

Al-Qaeda's influence on the Madrid attacks can also be seen in its pre- and post-3/11 pronouncements. In addition to bin Laden's October 2003 warning, al-Qaeda published two December 2003 documents posted on jihadist websites titled "Jihad in Iraq: Hopes and Dreams" calling on Muslims to attack European countries involved in the Iraq war and in bin Laden's "A Message to the Spanish People" hinting of the possibility of an al-Qaeda attack in Spain.[18]

These publications suggest a common strategy to target weaker European states whose electorates support for the Iraq war were at sharp variance with their government's commitment. The terror organization's communiqués on 3/11 (claiming responsibility) and its subsequent pronouncement congratulating the Spanish people for electing the opposition Socialists suggest a strategy consistent with the 2002 Istanbul meeting. Combined with al-Qaeda's connections to the GICM and to the 3/11 bombers, these pronouncements cannot be idly dismissed as mere opportunist propaganda.

Al-Qaeda's threats against Spain after its Iraq withdraw, as well as the large number of planned attacks aborted by Spanish police since 3/11, indicate an organized Islamist assault.[19] These threats and the thwarted attacks are inconsistent with Sageman's autonomous "bunch of guys" seeking vengeance for Iraq theory. It is to this issue that we now turn.

Al-Qaeda's network in post-3/11 Spain: The omnipresent Jihadist threat

Spain's withdraw from Iraq has not removed from being a target of Islamic terrorism. Al-Qaeda's fixation on Spain predates the Iraq war. As Fernando Renaires notes, the 3/11 plot was constructed well before the Iraq invasion and had complex motivations and roots.[20] While incendiary for the 3/11 bombers, Iraq became a convenient pretext to justify the train attacks.

Al-Qaeda's aims in Spain are ideological, situational, and logistical. Ayman al-Zawahiri's threats against "Crusader Spain" after 3/11 reference Spain's 700-year Islamic past and the need to recover the lost Muslim lands of Al Andaluz. This suggests, at a minimum, a desire to punish Spain for its defeat of the Muslim Iberian caliphate and a historic grievance exacerbated by Spain's possession of North African enclaves Ceuta and Melilla.

The final testaments and videotapes left by the seven terrorists that immolated themselves in a fiery explosion when cornered by police also emphasize the historic grievance argument. Nor did they intend 3/11 to be an isolated event; a desire underscored by their botched attack (the explosives failed to detonate) on the Madrid-Seville train line and their plans to assault Jewish and British interests in Spain.

Al-Qaeda, furthermore, seeks retaliation for Spain's prosecution of its 9/11 and 3/11 networks. Among its most notable effort have been a failed 2004 plot to bomb Spain's National Court where records of the 9/11 and 3/11 investigations are contained.

Al-Qaeda affiliates have not stopped there. Spanish authorities are concerned that Pakistani extremists based in Barcelona have formed a partnership with Taliban-al-Qaeda network in Waziristan. Pakistani militants have been linked to attempts to blow up Barcelona's equivalent of the Twin Towers in 2006 and to a disrupted 2008 plot to attack that city's subway system.

The planned subway bombing has been connected to late Pakistani warlord and the late al-Qaeda protector Baitullah Mehsud, whose organization took credit for the failed plot.

Javier Jordan notes that six of seven post-3/11 attempts to attack Spain have been linked to either Pakistani or Maghreb jihadist organizations tied to al-Qaeda.[21] This is contrary to Sageman's arguments that the principal threat to Western security comes from alienated second and third generation North American and European Muslims. In Spain, the principal Islamist security threat comes from recent immigrants linked to external regional and international terror organizations.

Spain territorial connection to North Africa including Spanish citizenship for Muslim populations in its Moroccan Ceuta and Melilla enclaves makes it an ideal smuggling route for drugs, immigrants, money laundering, and identity fraud, that traditionally have been cash cows for Islamist terror networks. Spanish and Moroccan authorities have documented jihadist connection to and penetration of North African mafias that have dominated the hashish and illegal immigrant trade.[22]

Formed by Ayman al-Zawahiri, AQIM fused Algerian, Moroccan, Tunisian, and Mauritanian terror networks to coordinate efforts to bring down home governments and attack European interests. Al-Qaeda's integration of GIA, GSPC, and the GICM makes formal its tacit alliance consummated in the 2002 Istanbul meeting.

After bin Laden's killing by US Special Forces in May of 2011 Spain continues to be the target of al-Qaeda orchestrated or inspired plots. In August 2012 two Chechens and one Turk linked to al-Qaeda Central were involved in a plot to use remote control airplanes to explode over a sports stadium in Gibraltar. The three were arrested by authorities and they remain in detention awaiting a terrorism conspiracy trial.[23]

Al-Qaeda's Maghreb branch moreover has been linked to numerous attacks against the Spanish government and to kidnapping, ransoming, and killing of European tourists and workers. Operating in failed states like Mali, AQIM can recruit and train jihadists across North Africa and Europe. The recent war in Libya and the Qaddafi's downfall has unleashed an uncontrolled arms trade in the region had augmented AQIM's combat capability and undoubtedly contributed to its brief terror sanctuary in North Mali.

Spanish police in April 2013 arrested a Moroccan and Algerian who operated independently in Murcia and Zaragoza.[24] Both were linked to AQIM websites whose communications had been monitored by intelligence agents for over a year. One of the individuals unsuccessfully attempted to acquire terrorist training during the organization's brief West African sanctuary. Based on press reports, the two had praised the April 15th Boston Marathon bombings that killed three people and wounded hundreds.[25]

Fearing an impending attack against the scheduled Madrid Marathon authorities took no risks and arrested the two suspected AQIM sympathizers. AQIM's partnership with the al-Qaeda network reflects both weaknesses as autonomous and functioning organizations. Unable to defeat the *far enemy* and launch catastrophic post-9/11 attacks, al-Qaeda's union with North African regional networks enlarges its capability and allows it to give ideological legitimacy to regional organizations. This pattern can be seen in the July 7, 2005 attacks in London in which al-Qaeda and its Pakistani affiliates partnered with British Muslims to launch attacks against the Western *far enemy*.

"Londinstan" and the United Kingdom's Jihadist microculture

During the 1990s Britain incubated a jihadist microculture that amounted to a veritable safe haven for radical imams and ex-mujahidin who were intent on radicalizing British Muslims.[26] The United Kingdom's supportive milieu of civil liberties protections, liberal immigration, flexible asylum practices, and welfare policies prompted a migration of Islamic radicals escaping persecution in their own homeland. Many of these extremists fought in jihadist wars in Afghanistan, Kashmir, Chechnya, and Kashmir.

Labeled Londinstan by critics, England's capital became attracted many radicals seeking to pursue jihad against the *near* and *far* enemy. London's microclimate of Salafi-jihadist groups included the Algerian GIA, the Moroccan GSPC, the Pan-Islamic Hiz ut Tahrir (Islamic Party of Liberation), and a variety of Saudi and Egyptian extremist organizations.[27] These groups congregated around the city's mosques, Islamic community centers, and book stores hoping to raise funds and recruit fighters for jihadist causes.

London's Finsbury Park Mosque became the preeminent symbol of United Kingdom's radical Islamist culture and home to many extremist imams.[28] Egyptian preacher Abu Hamza's denounced England's treatment of Muslims and urged the United Kingdom's adoption of Shariah law before the Finsbury Mosque faithful. Hamza was an ex-mujahidin who used the mosque as an operations center for world jihad. Among the Mosque's attendees were Richard Reed the notorious shoe bomber, the 9/11 would-be twentieth bomber Zarcarias Moussaoui, and 7/7 bomber Jamaican born Jerome Lindsay.

Londinstan hosted Abu Qutada who is considered al-Qaeda's main European ideologue and paymaster.[29] The Palestinian worked with al-Qaeda theoretician Abu Musab Suri to form a financial and recruitment network for the GIA and the Algerian GSPC.[30] Qutada who has been in and out of British prisons since the July 2005 bombings is wanted by Jordanian and Spanish authorities on terrorism charges. British and European Community courts have repeatedly blocked his extradition and provided him with generous welfare payments. Recently the British government developed a protocol with the Jordanian government that seeks to provide Qutada with a fair trial in Jordanian courts forbidding any torture induced confessions. His case continues to be a source of controversy in British and European Community courts despite his recent deportation to Jordan.

Rounding out the city's vibrant Islamist infrastructure was Syrian Omar Bakri who formed the revolutionary Al Muhajiroun (Soldiers of Islam) designed to promote jihad among British Muslims.[31] Many of these clerics preached hatred of Britain while enjoying substantial welfare benefits and were repeatedly protected by an English system that prized the rule of wars and civil liberties protections. Britain's liberal political asylum laws where the "victim" simply had to have a "fear" of persecution resulted in very few asylum applications denied.

Once militants entered the United Kingdom, immigration officials either failed to implement deportation decrees or lost track of them whose concealment was enhanced by passport and identity fraud. Throughout the 1990s, England was repeatedly criticized by Arab and European countries for its incubation and protection of a militant jihadist infrastructure that contributed to the mobilization, recruitment, and financing of radicals committed to a terrorist agenda.

The United Kingdom's ethnic and economic tapestry where militants organized and preached could not be more hospitable. The dominance of South-Central Asians among Britain's 1.6 million Muslim immigrants and their descendants guaranteed a fertile breeding ground for radicalization and recruitment of fighters.[32] Britain's Pakistani Muslim Diaspora populations have deep ancestral ties with their homeland that features over 400,000 visits between the 2 countries.

Pakistani fundamentalism had been linked to growing Islamism in Britain's Muslim population. Within the past three decades, Pakistan's policy promoted jihadist causes in Afghanistan and Kashmir. The proliferation of Islamist parties and extremist organizations has spread beyond the nation's borders to its Diaspora communities.

Studies of the British Muslim community demonstrate less assimilation among South Asians than other ethnic groups.[33] British Muslim Pakistanis are more fundamentalist than most other coreligionists. The persistence of arranged marriages with Pakistani brides and religious based education within this community has aggravated fundamentalist attitudes.

Britain's Muslim population is clustered in urban communities and lag in most social indicators. Britain's policy of multiculturalism has exacerbated an intragroup cohesion that frequently is hostile to the nation.[34] This is especially true of Britain's native born Muslims whose feelings of social and economic isolation have produced an existential identity crisis.[35] Many native born British Muslims have turned to religious fundamentalism and Pan-Islamic causes to overcome alienation.

A supportive Jihadist microculture, social alienation, and Britain's support for the Afghan and Iraq wars have catalyzed extremism among some British Muslims. Islamic bookstores, internet cafes, social clubs, community organizations offer many venues for radicalization and mobilization.[36] The overrepresentation of Muslims in British prisons also is a fertile breeding ground for extremism including British converts to Islam.

Only after 9/11 did Britain recognize the gravity of the problem. Government reports after the attacks indicated the presence of some 2,000 al-Qaeda militants and a strong Islamist microculture to indoctrinate British Muslims.[37] Despite these concerns Londinstan continued paving the way for the 7/7 network and attacks.

The 7/7 network and the London attacks

The 7/7 cell of three British born nationals of Pakistani descent and one Jamaican born Muslim convert seemed at odd group to commit the worse terror attack on British soil. Ringleaders Sidique Khan (age 30) and Shizad Tanweer (age 22) born in the northern city of Leeds, both appeared well assimilated to British society. The progeny of a relatively prosperous middle-class Pakistani immigrant parents they exhibited no real alienation or radicalism. Khan and Tanweer grew up in the same area and struck a friendship based on common associations.[38]

The third British born bomber 18-year-old Hasib Mir Hussein a by-product of religious but not militant Pakistani working class family in Leeds and 19-year-old Jermaine Lindsey a Jamaican born convert to Islam, similarly, exhibited little radicalization. All four had exposure to some university education with Khan becoming a school counselor and mentor. While the factors behind their radicalization can never be really known, it appears that it was a confluence of forces.[39]

Based on family accounts Khan and Tanweer seemed to have been changed by their trips to Pakistan. Though they traveled to Pakistan on different occasions and under different pretexts Khan was to receive religious education and Tanweer was to visit family. Khan traveled twice in August 2003 and stayed in Pakistan between October 2004 and February 2005. His return to Britain greatly surprised his family.

At age 18 Hussein made a journey to Mecca that produced a life altering experience where the young roughneck foreswore alcohol and Western dress. He became a devotee of Finsbury Park where he may have met Jermaine Lindsay whose conversion to Islam followed his mother who converted when she married a Muslim. Jermaine was reportedly close to his stepfather.

The four came together as a consequence of mutual contacts at mosques, book stores, social clubs, and gymnasiums. Khan, Tanweer, and Hussein hanged out at an Islamic bookstore in Leeds and watched extremist videos dramatizing the West's attacks against Muslims and glorifying jihad. This social bonding reinforced their Islamist alienation. Sageman suggest that group dynamics play critical roles in terror organization and planning for attacks.[40]

The confluence of the Iraq war, external al-Qaeda training and self-radicalization appear to be the triggering point for the attacks. Using the training he received in Pakistan, Khan and Tanweer converted two rental flats into bomb-making factories that produced four hydrogen peroxide bombs. Khan provided the financing with a personal loan and maxed out credit cards for the operation. Once the attack date had been settled the bombs that had been cooled by commercial refrigerators were placed in knapsacks.

Traveling from diverse points, the four met at King Cross Station a major subway connecting center. Taped by the station's closed circuit camera Khan, Tanweer, and Lindsay got on three different lines which once the trains left the station were derailed by near simultaneous explosions. The attacks created widespread damage and produced mass panic.

Hussein failed to hop on one of the lines leaving the station. It appears that the battery that was to trigger the bomb was defective. Hussein went to a near but store to buy a new battery. Instead of going back to Kings Cross Station Hussein got on Tavistock Square double decker bus where he discharged his bomb on the top level.

The attacks killed 52 Britons and left over 700 wounded. Unlike the Madrid bombings, there was no confusion of the attacks authorship. No British investigator or politician suggested Irish Republican Army responsibility. Al-Qaeda had warned European allies of the United States in 2003 that attacks were imminent if they did not withdraw troops from Iraq and Afghanistan.

Once investigators uncovered the bombers identities there was shock and resignation. Despite ample warning of the presence of a violent jihadist British subculture, the British public seemed surprised that the attacks had been committed by three British natives who came from successful immigrant families. Investigators initially thought that July 7th attacks were committed by a homegrown cell with no al-Qaeda link. Subsequent analysis, however, proved substantial al-Qaeda connections.

Al-Qaeda involvement in July 7th attacks

Al-Qaeda links with the attacks are deep and varied. Among the most critical of the connections are Khan and Taweer travels to Pakistan. Both went to contact family or engage in Islamic studies but in reality they met with al-Qaeda and Taliban who transported them to Waziristan for bomb training.[41] Khan's August 2003 trip to Pakistan put him in contact with Omar Kayam who was later implicated in a fertilizer bomb plot disrupted by British police and MI5. Khan also met with Kayam in Britain during different stages in the planning for that operation.[42] British intelligence failures to connect Khan with Kayam's operation is widely blamed for its inability to foil the 7/7 attacks.

Before departing for Pakistan on November 2004, Khan filmed a martyrdom video. British investigators suspect that Khan in the video sought to go to Afghanistan to fight and die for the Taliban.[43] Once he arrived in Pakistan Khan stayed until February 2005, more than enough time to master the construction of hydrogen peroxide bombs. Despite his intent to fight American forces in Afghanistan, Khan's Pakistani and Arab handlers must have convinced him to return to England to attack the British heartland.[44]

The Pakistani and al-Qaeda connection to the 7/7 plot is furthered by Khan's many calls to a public phone in Pakistan. Apparently Khan believed he was being watched by British police and took extreme caution not to be caught. To avoid detection, the 7/7 plotters used 10 different cell phones. Based on police interviews with family members they spoke of a mysterious Mr "Khan" (not Sidique) who met with the 7/7 bombers in Britain and left shortly before the attacks. Sidique's father believes this man was instrumental in his son's radicalization.

Any doubts about al-Qaeda's connection to the 7/7 network were dispelled by subsequent events. Khan's martyrdom video released by an al-Qaeda media outlet after the attacks features an appearance by al-Qaeda leader Ayman al-Zawahiri praising the bombings. In the video, Zawahiri talks about the attacks as retaliation for the Iraq war and Britain's violation of the al-Qaeda truce offered to European allies. Released by al-Qaeda in 2006, a second video features Tanweer pledging fidelity to al-Qaeda and expressing his desire to wage jihad against the British state.

German authorities in 2011 arrested an al-Qaeda courier who had microchip files of the organizations attack plans. Described as a "treasure trove" of invaluable information, the files contain accounts of al-Qaeda's involvement in the London attacks. Based on news accounts of this evidence, al-Qaeda British operative Rachid Rauf documents his meetings with Khan and Tanweer in Pakistan and their bomb training in Taliban controlled camps.[45] The files also implicate Rauf in other al-Qaeda plots and attacks including the failed copycat subway attacks that occurred two weeks later in London.

The targeting of mass transport with the use of multiple simultaneous attacks by suicide bombers is consistent with al-Qaeda approach to inflict mass civilian casualties. The 7/7 attacks were not a sporadic attempt by homegrown terrorists. They instead reflect an al-Qaeda inspired and orchestrated effort to attack European states. Though the attacks were locally financed, the success of the attack was dependent upon al-Qaeda and Taliban directed training. This pattern appears in other UK plots and attacks. The 7/7 attacks demonstrate a systematic al-Qaeda effort to direct attacks within the context of an overall strategy.

Post-7/7 al-Qaeda plots and attacks in the United Kingdom

The 7/7 bombings were not an isolated event, but part of orchestrated plan to punish Great Britain for its foreign policy and post-9/11 crackdown on London's radical Salafi-jihadist microculture. After 9/11 the British state became less permissive and began to tackle radical organizations with the arrest of high-profile extremists. Despite these efforts, the British legal system and its asylum policies were not abruptly changed until the London attack and a failed copycat effort 14 days later.

Committed by East African extremists the July 21st attacks on the London Tube and a double decker bus provide more evidence of al-Qaeda orchestration.[46] The terrorists hoped to copy the 7/7 attacks but their rigged explosives failed to detonate. Subsequent investigations including the arrests and conviction of the four main terrorists and their network of conspirators indicate al-Qaeda connections. Ringleader Muktar Said Ibrahim was an extremist who received al-Qaeda training in Sudan and Pakistan.

The danger posed to the British public by the successful 7/7 attack and the failed 7/21 attacks pale in comparison with al-Qaeda effort to detonate ten liquid based explosions on transatlantic flights between the United States, Britain, and Canada. Once again the key organizer of the attack (Abdullah Ahmed) had links to Pakistani Taliban allies of al-Qaeda.[47]

The plot foiled by British police, MI5, and American authorities in August 2006 could have killed over 1,500 people. Based on a prior bin Laden effort (Operation Bojinka) to bring down 10 Anglo-American flights over the Pacific, the August 2006 conspiracy was timed to occur on the fifth anniversary of 9/11 and involved a network of British Pakistanis with links to extremist organization in Waziristan.

This August 2006 conspiracy by al-Qaeda was part of a centrally directed strategy to strike at British interests. MI5 Director Dame Eliza Manningham-Butler revealed in November 2006 that al-Qaeda affiliates in Pakistan had been linked with 30 known plots.[48] Fortunately none of them has been as successful as the London bombings. The August 2006 "planes operation" may represent the zenith of al-Qaeda control and command over its UK terror campaign.

Britain continues to be targeted by "homegrown" Islamic extremists that are either trained or ideologically inspired by al-Qaeda or its affiliates. Like the 50 or more plots foiled by US intelligence and police authorities, most of the UK based terror conspiracies have been conducted by amateur local jihadists with little or no formal training. Among some of the more notable failed terror attacks and plots since the aborted August 2006 conspiracy are as follows:[49]

- Botched effort by British-Pakistani physicians on June 29, 2007 to ignite car bombs in central London and to launch a suicide jihadist operation at the Glasgow airport. The car bombs failed to detonate properly and the *martyrdom* mission was scuttled by airport baggage handler who restrained one of the jihadists while the other inflicted mortal wounds upon himself when he attempted to ignite the car he had crashed into the airport with gasoline.

- Attempted May 22, 2008 bombing of an Exeter café by a disgruntled South Asian British national frustrated when the explosive device malfunctioned leaving his hands badly burned.
- Failed terrorist conspiracy by a British convert to bomb a shopping center in Bristol was foiled by an informer who informed police that the young man had numerous cuts and burns on his feet and hands. His injuries had been sustained by his experiments with HTMD explosives.

Not all of the post-2006 plots to strike at Britain have involved untrained novices. On February 21, 2013 a British jury at a Woolwich Crown Court found three South Asian British born Birmingham men guilty of planning and conspiring to carry out a terror campaign in Great Britain. The group had been trained by an al-Qaeda Pakistani affiliate in Waziristan in bomb making and they were in contact with Abu Zaid al-Kuwaiti, a senior al-Qaeda leader who would later die in a CIA Predator drone strike.

While the evidence is far from complete, the Birmingham cell's radicalization appears similar to the July 7, 2005 group. Born in Britain with remote links to their South Asian ancestral homeland, the three lower middle-class young men became alienated and frustrated with life in the United Kingdom. Faced with bleak economic prospects, the circle of young friends turned to religious extremism as a form of personal and group liberation.

Their commitment to a trans-Islamic jihadist identity was fortified by extremist websites, videos, and literature. The cell's leader Irfan Khan was a great admirer of the late Anwar al-Awlaki and a passionate devotee of AQAP's English language e-magazine *Inspire*. Al-Qaeda publications were found in the group's possession and their many recorded conversations praise the late cleric for his jihadist conviction and vision.

The three men sought to implant up to seven rucksack bombs at different locations in Birmingham that investigating officials claim could have killed more people that the July 7th bombings eight years earlier. It is considered by authorities to be the most serious plot in the United Kingdom since the aborted August 2006 effort by al-Qaeda agents to attack Anglo-American passenger jets traveling between the United Kingdom and the United States.

The plot was foiled by an extensive police surveillance operation named Pitsford that monitored the group's e-mail and phone conversations. Despite al-Qaeda's training of the Birmingham jihadists and its sponsorship of their martyrdom videos, this operation is remarkably different from the July 7, 2005 attacks. Terror analyst Raffaello Pantucci argues that al-Qaeda had little control over the scope of the 2013 Birmingham plot and has lost its capacity to select targets and maintain contact with is agents.[50] This contrasts sharply with its ability to remain in contact with Sidique Khan's jihadist cell responsible for the subway and double decker bus bombings.

Since 2009 al-Qaeda Central in Waziristan has been devastated by the CIA's drone assassination program with many senior leaders and midlevel cadres killed. Pakistani military incursions into the area have harassed al-Qaeda Pakistani affiliates forcing the closure of many terrorist camps. Based on police monitoring of the Birmingham cell's phone conversations and e-mail traffic, the three in Waziristan lived a nightmarish existence with constant fear of being a victim of the CIA directed campaign. They were reportedly trained in a clandestine safe house in bomb-making preparation and their al-Qaeda handlers wanted them to be proficient enough to teach British Muslims how to fabricate explosive devices.

Al-Qaeda operatives in Waziristan had warned the Birmingham cell that the frontier territory was not safe and that they should warn other British jihadists not to travel to the area. They should accordingly share their knowledge with other inspiring jihadist and stay home to attack the British *far enemy*. Given the incomplete control al-Qaeda exercised over the Birmingham group and the precarious nature of conducting training in Waziristan, the failure of the cell to carry forth its operation is not surprising.

Not all post-7/7 jihadist plots to kill British citizens in the United Kingdom have failed. On May 2013, two British born Islamists killed and beheaded soldier Lee Rigby in broad daylight in an East London street. After running over him with their car they decapitated him and surreally had conversations with bystanders. One of the young men a British citizen of Jamaican ancestry justified his actions as retaliation for British involvement in the Afghan and Iraq wars.

Based on preliminary police investigations there appears little organizational connection to al-Qaeda. They appear to be homegrown radicals that at most may have been inspired by al-Qaeda propaganda or local extremist imams. Lee Rigby's killing is reminiscent of Muhammad Moreh's 2012 assassinations of

French soldiers, a Rabbi, and three Jewish school children in Toulouse which were also *justified* as revenge for French military involvement in Afghanistan.

Madrid and London: Al-Qaeda's "zenith" in Europe

The Madrid and London attacks represent an al-Qaeda plan to use radicalized segments of Europe's Muslim Diaspora population to attack the West. Both attacks were the consequence of an orchestrated strategy outlined in an al-Qaeda 2003 Istanbul meeting to attack European allies. While both attacks are locally financed and implemented, al-Qaeda training, orchestration, and direction were vital to their success. These organizers of these attacks sought to further al-Qaeda's *vexation* and *exhaustion* strategy.

The parallels between the attacks are striking. Al-Qaeda used regional and local networks in Spain and England to augment its operational capability. Al-Qaeda's connections with the MICG were vital in pulling off the Madrid bombings and its Taliban allies in Pakistan working with British Muslims were instrumental in the London attacks.

The attacks had different political impacts resulting in the desired Spanish withdraw from Iraq but British resolve to press forward in the war on terror. Despite 3/11's "success," it should be noted that the Spanish case was only a partial victory for al-Qaeda for it did not end the Spanish presence in Afghanistan nor blunt the efforts of Spanish security services to dismantle Islamist networks.

The targeting of mass transport system and the use of synchronized attacks with timed explosions and suicide bombers are classic al-Qaeda techniques. Taliban training camps affiliated with al-Qaeda in Pakistan were vital to the success in the London attacks. High-profile al-Qaeda leaders Rachid Rauf and Ayman al-Zawahiri were connected to these attacks and Amir Azizi and members of Abu Dadah al-Qaeda Spanish cell were instrumental in the Madrid attacks.

Both 3/11 and 7/7, however, are not carbon copies of the 9/11 operation with cells formed and financed by al-Qaeda. Instead, the London and Madrid bombings represent a synergistic relationship between autonomously formed local and regional networks that operate with some al-Qaeda direction and training. Al-Qaeda's links to Madrid and London go beyond ideological exhortation and deviate from homegrown terrorism narrative.

While successful in an operational sense, al-Qaeda failed to fracture the Western coalition in the *war on terror*. The Madrid and London attacks hopefully represent the zenith of al-Qaeda's capability in Europe and its strategy to weaken Western resolve in the fight against Islamic extremism. The West's determination to continue this struggle against al-Qaeda and its network encountered its greatest test not in Europe but in Iraq.

5

Zarqawi: Al-Qaeda's Tragic Antihero and the Destructive Role of the Iraqi Jihad

The Mujahidin made a few mistakes in Iraq. The mistakes were committed because of hasty and poor decisions by some of the brothers. Those mistakes involved a number of military operations. If the Mujahidin had closely examined those military operations beforehand, the situation might have been better. Those in charge of the military operations had totally ignored anticipating the benefits or drawbacks those operations might generate.

Al-Qaeda internal communique[1]

From young hoodlum to "Arab Afghan"

Born Ahmed Fadihil al Khalayleh in the impoverished Jordanian town of Zarqa, Abu Musab Zarqawi's modest origins depart from al-Qaeda's wealthier and better educated founders. This disparity played some role in the personal and ideological disagreements with al-Qaeda throughout his bloody terrorist career.[2] One of nine children, Zarqawi showed little academic promise. His municipal clerk father and devout mother had a difficult time taming their impulsive son.

Not finishing his high school career Zarqawi became a street thug indulging in alcohol and deviant sexual behavior. Called the "green man" by his friends his body was adorned with emerald tattoos.[3] Despite his later religious piety, young Zarqawi eschewed religious services preferring Zarqa's mean streets. What little employment he had did not last.

Imprisoned in 1987 for assault Zarqawi stayed a few months in prison. Once released, his mother urged him to attend Al-Farah mosque. Known for its radical jihadist preachers, the mosque's sermons exerted a profound effect nurturing Zarqawi's religious commitment and political activism.[4]

Zarqawi's path from alcoholic deviant to religious fanatic is a road traveled by many zealots.[5] Studies of religious extremists suggest that many choose religious devotion as a form of personal renewal. By embracing the call for jihad, Zarqawi could purge an ugly past characterized by alcohol, crime, and sexual abuse.

His commitment to jihad and Islamic fundamentalism should be of no surprise because Zarqa was a hotbed of Islamic extremism. The town overwhelmingly supported Jordan's version of the Muslim Brotherhood in local and national elections.[6] The large Palestinian presence, similarly, was guarantor of anti-Western sentiment and hostility to King Hussein's government whose armed repression of the Palestinian Liberation Organization would not be forgiven.

Zarqawi commitment to Salafi-jihadist doctrine and his hostility toward the Jordanian monarchy grew in the 1980s. He joined the ranks of the "Arab Afghan" mujahidin relatively late in the Soviet occupation of Afghanistan. Arriving in a safe house just outside Peshawar in 1989, Zarqawi met many leading jihadist figures.[7]

By far the most influential on his own jihadist extremism was the Jordanian theorist and cleric Abu Mohammad al-Maqdisi.[8] Having studied in Kuwait, Iraq, and been a lecturer at Saudi Arabia's Abdullah Azziz University, Maqdisi was a preeminent ideologue in the global jihadist movement. His essays and books gained notoriety among jihadists animating them to rebel against apostate governments throughout the Muslim world.

Maqdisi's revolutionary writings developed the doctrine of *loyalty* and *renunciation* which called the Muslim faithful to rebel against any government not based on Shariah.[9] The Palestinian-Jordanian imam's denounced the Saudi royal family for their departure from Islamic law. Maqdisi revolutionary discourse greatly exceeded bin Laden's radicalism at the time. The imam soon became Zarqawi's spiritual mentor.

Zarqawi's journey to Pakistan led him to Palestinian Abdullah Azzam whose recruitment of Arab Afghans brought bin Laden to the Pakistan-Afghanistan border. Abdullah Azzam was interested in combating foreign aggressors violating Muslim land and peoples and did not share the Maqdisi's fixation on combating the *near enemy*.[10] Unlike Zarqawi, Azzam rejected the killing of Muslims for political purposes and repeatedly denounced takfiri doctrine un-Islamic.

From his Hayatabad safe house Zarqawi traveled to an Afghan training camp and joined the Haqqani group fighting anti-Islamist forces in the chaos of post-Soviet Afghanistan. His training at the Sada camp allowed him to make connections with many jihadists who would later join the Zarqawi network that spanned from Central Asia to Europe.[11] Zarqawi did little fighting in Afghanistan for the Soviets had withdrawn. Denied the opportunity to fight foreign infidels, Zarqawi dabbled in journalism for a Pakistani Islamist magazine and Afghanistan's ennui impelled him to leave for Jordan in 1993.

Zarqawi return to fight the *near enemy*

Zarqawi journey home to continue the jihadist struggle was emblematic of the foreign fighter experience. Returning mujahidin were instrumental in Islamist violence in Algeria, Libya, and Egypt inviting scrutiny by intelligence services and government repression.[12] Throughout the 1990s extremist violence against the *near enemy* spurred dramatically and reached almost apocalyptic level in Algeria where hundreds of thousands died. Typically these revolts ended in failure.

Despite efforts by his family and wife for him to lead a normal life, Zarqawi continued his revolutionary activities against the Jordanian monarchy. Maqdisi's return to Jordan furthered Zarqawi commitment to jihadist activism. Composed of ex-mujahidin and local Islamists, Zarqawi and Maqdisi formed a terror network called Bayat al Imam.[13]

They served as the organization's leadership and fulfilled very different roles: Maqdisi acted as chief ideologue while Zarqawi developed the terror network operational and financial capabilities. Given their connections to ex-mujahidin and local Islamists, they attracted many recruits and supporters. The prominence of Maqdisi's writings and his public call for King Hussein's overthrow invited attention of security services. Bayat al Imam was under constant surveillance by the Jordanian General Intelligence Department (GID) which had gained notoriety for being one of the most effective intelligence agencies in the region.[14]

The group's initial venture into terrorism was not promising. Zarqawi and Maqdisi planned to attack Israeli forces in the West Bank. The explosives obtained by Maqdisi ended up in a cemetery hiding place close to Zarqawi's family home. GID operatives succeeded in disrupting the plot in 1994 and arrested Zarqawi, Maqdisi, and the 15 recruits. Faced with rough interrogation techniques that invited numerous confessions, many pled guilty and were sentenced to 15 years.[15]

Zarqawi never broke before his Jordanian interrogators, proudly admitted his complicity in the terror plot, and was defiant before his military prosecutor's questioning accusing the monarchy of treason for its 1994 peace treaty with the Israeli government. These qualities of endurance and toughness served him well in Jordan's notorious and brutal prison system.

Jail was an ideal place for Zarqawi's talents. The prisons were full of radical Islamists seeking a leader and desiring a network to join. Given his propensity for violent agitation, Zarqawi earned the hostility of prison officials and the respect of fellow inmates. The "green man" hardened his body with a vigorous weightlifting routine and his charisma and brutal tactics created a huge following.

Despite the notoriety of his writings Maqdisi was easily overshadowed by his mentee. Zarqawi's hatred of apostates strengthened during his prison years. His Manichean zealotry reached a fever pitch with the Shi'ites whose apostasy he felt had to be punished. While not very sophisticated in his worldview, Zarqawi built a network of believers in prison that would serve him well in later terror exploits.[16]

Zarqawi liked the structure, brutality, and isolation of prison rarely communicating with his family and friends. Having trumped his spiritual mentor in prison, Zarqawi exaggerated his exploits as mujahidin. He spent his time memorizing the Koran, engaging in turf wars with fellow inmates, and quarreling with officials for refusing to wear a prescribed uniform.

Out of his original 15-year sentence Zarqawi served 5 years. The death of King Hussein in 1999 and the ascendance of his son Abdullah forced the new monarch to make the traditional gesture of an amnesty that resulted in the release of 3,000 Islamists. Seeking to court the parliamentary support of the Islamic Action Front (IAF), Abdullah pardoned the Islamist prisoners based on an IAF compiled list releasing Zarqawi and Maqdisi.[17]

The King later admitted that his 1999 pardon was a grievous mistake for it only increased the ranks of religious extremists committed to violent agitation against his regime.[18] Faced with the burdens of civil society, Zarqawi spent only a few months with his wife and family. True to form he failed to keep stable employment. Fearing GID repression, Zarqawi fled to Pakistan in June 1999 to join the al-Qaeda network in Afghanistan. Despite their friendship, Maqdisi failed to accompany his student opting to renew the struggle against the Jordanian regime: a decision that would result in repeated incarcerations.[19]

Early al-Qaeda connections and Zarqawi's Herat camp

Upon his arrival in Pakistan, Zarqawi sought integration into al-Qaeda's ranks. While known to al-Qaeda leadership as a committed jihadist, Zarqawi appeared too rough and unsophisticated to much of the organization's core leadership.[20] Both Ayman al-Zawahiri and bin Laden had severe reservations about the Jordanian roughneck. Had it not been for the intervention of al-Qaeda leader Abu Zubaydah, Zarqawi could have languished in obscurity.[21]

The Jordanian Zubaydah had followed Zarqawi exploits and admired his fierce activism against the Hashemite monarchy and Israel. He convinced al-Qaeda to finance a Zarqawi run camp in Herat that was not far from the Iranian border.[22] The location of the camp reflects al-Qaeda's ambivalence toward the young Jordanian that characterized their future relations. Zarqawi's suspicion of al-Qaeda leadership goals and his rejection of their *far enemy* strategy endured until the 9/11 attacks. Even his October 2001 statement of fidelity is questionable.[23]

The Herat camp was designed to recruit Jordanian jihadists. This was typical of al-Qaeda that had organized its complex of camps according to national groupings. Given his prominence in Islamist radical networks in the Hashemite Kingdom, Zarqawi was a logical choice. With an initial capitalization of $3,000 Zarqawi pursued this objective of recruiting prospective Jordanian jihadists and he used his Herat terror camp to build an organizational network that eventually stretched from Central Asia to Europe.[24]

Zarqawi's Herat camp included some 10 barracks and 3,000 recruits. His later success in Iraq was vitally connected to his Herat experience. There are numerous reasons for this outcome. First, the sheer number of trainees created a wealth of contacts in Jordan and in its European Diaspora community. The vital role of Syria and Turkey as transit points for Jordanian militants created links to radical networks that widened Zarqawi's operational range.

Despite al-Qaeda financing, Zarqawi's ambitions to strike at the Hashemite monarchy and the Israelis were rarely achieved. Zubaydah committed $35,000 for Zarqawi to attack Jordanian and Israeli interests.[25] With this money Zarqawi planned an operation in 2000 where suicide bombers would drive an explosive laden truck into Amman's Radisson Hotel that hosts numerous Western tourists. The plot was foiled by the GID security services badly embarrassing Zarqawi.[26]

While these associations are important, they are surpassed by Zarqawi's connections to Iraqi Kurdish Islamists.[27] Given its militant outlook, the Islamic Movement of Kurdistan (IMK) was a natural partner for al-Qaeda. IKI's Kurdish militants in Syria, Iran, and Europe enhanced its appeal for it permitted attacks that transcended national borders. Al-Qaeda Central wanted to use the Kurdish enclave in Iraq as an operating base for future terror operations.[28] Zarqawi had used Iranian Kurds to protect and transport Arab fighters to the Herat base. Zarqawi's Iranian contacts were connected to Kurdish brothers in Iraq and by extension to Mullah Krekar's group. Al-Qaeda's intent to use Iraqi Kurdistan as a terror sanctuary accelerated after 9/11 in order to open a new front to engage US forces.[29]

9/11 and escape to Iran

The 9/11 attacks caught many al-Qaeda militants by surprise. Some commanders and foot soldiers had severe reservations about a strategy that targeted the US *far enemy* diverting jihad from targeting Muslim *apostate* governments.[30] Among these critics was Abu Musab Zarqawi.

Despite his reservations about 9/11 Zarqawi pledged *bayaat* or allegiance to bin Laden in October 2001.[31] He engaged American forces when Washington retaliated. Hoping to draw the Americans into a protracted guerrilla struggle, the conflict defied the Islamists expectations.[32] Taliban forces and their al-Qaeda allies were easily routed by an American response that emphasized strategic air strikes, Special Force's operations, and anti-Taliban NA proxies.

The collapse of the Taliban-al-Qaeda terror sanctuary produced havoc within the Islamists ranks. Zarqawi was wounded when an American missile fell on his Afghan safe house and his escape to Iran was dependent on the financial largesse of his European network whose resources succeeded in transporting Zarqawi to secure locations in Iran.[33] Iran's degree of cooperation with al-Qaeda is intensely debated.[34] Bin Laden's Abbottabad correspondence presents a very murky but conflicted set of relationships.[35] Given their ideological differences, they are not natural allies.

Al-Qaeda, however, never shared Zarqawi's hostility toward the Shi'ites. The Shia-Sunni conflict has not been featured prominently in the group's literature until Zarqawi forms his Iraq terror network.[36] The Jordanians later sectarian campaign in Iraq targeting Shi'ites was repeatedly criticized by al-Qaeda Central's leadership and would become a source of strain. The current conflict raging in Syria with Sunni jihadist organizations like al-Nusra Front that has pledged its fidelity to al-Qaeda Central diverts Jihadism's path away from bin Laden's *far enemy* strategy.

Al-Qaeda and Iran have cooperated when it was to their mutual advantage. Two 9/11 bombers, for example, used Iran as a transit point for the attacks with Iranian authorities easing visa and documentation requirements. Iran and al-Qaeda's hostility toward the United States and their revolutionary ideologies have facilitated an ambiguous relationship that has swung between confrontation and cooperation.[37]

This complex relationship can be seen in Iran's dealings with Zarqawi when he was in the country recovering from his wounds. Zarqawi's convalescence was marked by periodic detention, release, and being able to travel to Syria and Iraq freely to plan for his group's alliance with Kurdish Islamists. During this period he was to facilitate the assassination of American diplomat Lawrence Foley in Amman. The October 28, 2002 killing of the American represents Zarqawi's first real success and began a brutal and nihilistic terror campaign that would convulse the entire region.[38]

Al-Qaeda and Ansar al Islam

Al-Qaeda's decision to use Iraqi Kurdistan as a rear base of operations increased dramatically after American efforts to topple Saddam Hussein's regime. Zarqawi's network had built a formidable relationship with Kurdish Islamists in Iraq and Europe that became a source of finance, jihadist recruitment, and the movement of prospective terrorists to training camps in Afghanistan. The loss of the Taliban safe haven after 9/11, made Iraqi Kurdistan invaluable to al-Qaeda.

Kurdish Islamists had operated in Iraq since the 1970s and their ranks expanded after the first Gulf War. Protected by an international no-fly zone that prevented entry to Saddam's forces, the Islamic Movement of Kurdistan, Hamas, Tawid, and the Second Sorah Unit was given a safe haven to develop.[39] Committed to an Islamic state these groups were receptive to al-Qaeda's worldview.

Zarqawi's relationship with Mullah Krekar unified these various groups and al-Qaeda finance facilitated the formation of Jund al Islam (Soldiers of Islam) in September 2001.[40] The Jordanian's Herat camp and his connections to Iranian Kurds extended his reach to Iraq and beyond. By late 2002 Zarqawi established a base of operations in Iraqi Kurdistan that culminated in an al-Qaeda union with Jund al Islam which became the organizational basis of Ansar al Islam (Soldiers of Islam).[41]

Zarqawi established terror camps to prepare foreign jihadists to resist the American invasion of Iraq. During this period al-Qaeda attacked the pro-American Patriotic Union of Kurdistan (PUK) who competed with the Islamists for the affections of Iraqi Kurds. Ansar al Islam was, however, not well prepared to withstand the American air and ground assault. Once again heroic mujahidin failed to live up to their grandiose expectations.

The March 2003 US attacks involving laser guided precision bombings, Special Force's operations, and PUK militias that killed 180 Ansar al Islam militants and resulted in 150 prisoners.[42] Zarqawi and his loyalists had sidestepped the American assault by relocating to Anbar Province planning a terror network with local Iraqi Sunni support. His "strategy" of confronting coalition forces evolved over time, relied heavily on improvisation, foreign fighters, media propaganda, and extreme brutality.

Zarqawi's strategy to defeat the Americans in post-Saddam Iraq

The US invasion of Iraq quickly dispatched Saddam's army and security forces prompting state implosion and an inability of coalition forces to maintain order. With the small size of the invasion force, the US military was bedeviled by armed insurgents in Iraq's cities and countryside. Instead of directly engaging US forces much of the Iraqi army "melted away" with its remnants forming part of a nascent Iraqi resistance campaign.[43] The defeated Baathists would join with Islamist forces. This coalition of insurgents would bedevil US occupation authorities during 2003–6 and Zarqawi's dynamic and nihilistic efforts almost succeeded in achieving al-Qaeda's *vexation* and *exhaustion* strategy.

Led by American Paul Bremer the newly formed Coalitional Provisional Authority (CPA) could not maintain order and its policies intensified the insurgency. The CPA's order to dissolve the Iraqi army, the state apparatus, and the Baathist Political Party that stripped military and political loyalists of their job was especially damaging.[44] This policy left 250,000 Sunnis unemployed and dispossessed of political and economic power. The CPA's policy of Iraqi democratization empowered the Shia majority (roughly 60 percent of Iraq's population) challenged Sunni dominance of Iraq and laid the cornerstone of sectarian tensions ripe for exploitation.

The Iraq insurgency that developed in the chaos of post-Saddam Iraq was a complex patchwork of groups.[45] The mix of pro-Saddam Baathist loyalists, Iraqi nationalists, Shi'ite radicals, local and foreign Salafi-jihadists lacked a common program other than agreement to defeat Coalition forces. While forming an alliance against the Americans, their ideological and sectarian divisions frequently hampered coordinated action and set the stage for future divisions.

Zarqawi's group stretched over a hundred square miles connecting Tikrit, Baghdad, and Ramadi. Known as the *Sunni Triangle* the region was the epicenter of Iraqi resistance movement. Zarqawi's network of foreign fighters, IED explosive factories, resistance fighters, media operations, and criminal activities involved over a thousand militants.[46] Their weight in the resistance while small was magnified by its nihilistic violence and sophisticated media campaign. Zarqawi's smuggling of foreign suicide bombers via established routes in Syria unleashed a contagion of violence in Iraq. During his leadership of AQI he, not bin Laden, was the focus of American counterterror operations.

Zarqawi's 2004 operations targeted US forces, foreign workers, Iraqi security services, and large scale reconstruction projects.[47] The group's first major attack was its car bombing against the UN Complex in August 2003 that killed dozens including United Nation's special envoy Sergio Vieiria de Mello. The Jordanian terrorist also struck at the Iraqi political establishment in an August 29, 2003 bombing in Najaf that killed 80 people including Shi'ite cleric Ayatollah Muhammad Baqir-al-Hakim.[48] Zarqawi followed up this attack with a sustained assault against foreign workers (including videos of ritualistic beheadings), and waves of suicide bombings and IED explosions against Coalition and Iraqi forces.

Zarqawi's role in the Iraqi insurgency was magnified by his propaganda campaign glorifying his network's jihadist exploits. Capitalizing on new communications technology (mobile telephones, social network sites, and internet) Zarqawi posted videos of suicide bombings, grotesque beheadings, attack coalition forces, and he used the internet to recruit funds and foreign fighters. As a consequence, Zarqawi contributed to the emergence of a virtual *jihadesphere* linking internet videos, chat rooms, Facebook, and You Tube activity.[49] His e-magazine *The Camels Hump* trumpeted his networks exploits, published information on car bomb making, IED fabrications, and insurgent guerilla tactics.⁵⁰ His organization, not al-Qaeda Central, was the forefront in the jihadist struggle to *vex* and *exhaust* Crusader-Zionist forces.

Zarqawi's internet video beheading of American Nicholas Berg was designed to inspire fear and revulsion from his enemies and admiration from his supporters. Emulating Khalid Sheik Muhammad's execution of American journalist Daniel Pearl and narcissistically upstaging al-Qaeda Central, Zarqawi beheaded Berg showing his head to a captive internet audience.⁵¹ Zarqawi's Iraqi network would be officially proclaimed Tawid wal Jihad (Unity and Holy War) in May of 2004 and was seen by authorities as the most dangerous group within the resistance.

By October 2004 Unity and Holy War had killed 675 Iraqis, executed 40 foreigners, and was responsible for 140 kidnappings.⁵² Zarqawi's daring exploits and media campaign had succeeded in creating a virtual cult of personality. Recognizing the destabilizing impact of Zarqawi's network the United States in June put a $25 million reward for his capture equaling OBL's bounty.⁵³

Zarqawi's desire to unleash a sectarian civil war

Despite his successful terror campaign, Zarqawi became convinced that his network needed a new strategy. Zarqawi reckoned that at most AQI could harass American and Iraqi government forces, but not decisively defeat them. Intercepted by US forces, Zarqawi's February 2004 to al-Qaeda outlines a sectarian strategy aimed at Shia civil population and its religious centers.⁵⁴ Zarqawi reasoned that a sustained campaign against the Shia could trigger a sectarian civil war and force US forces to withdraw. Once Iraq had devolved into separate sectarian enclaves, Zarqawi believed he would become emir of the Sunni Triangle and the region would become a fertile training ground for a new generation of Islamic terrorists making Abu Bakr Naji's vision of an Islamic enclave contained in *The Management of Savagery* a reality.

His February letter is full of rage and invective against the Shia for they are "the insurmountable obstacle, the prowling serpent, the crafty, evil scorpion, the enemy lying in wait, and biting poison." Zarqawi describes them as "the enemy" and that they conspired with the Americans in an anti-Sunni crusader assault.⁵⁵ His letter outlines a strategy against the Shia to unite the Sunni world against the Shia-American alliance to create a "Greater Israel" in the Arab heartland.

From February to October 2004, Zarqawi conducted negotiations with al-Qaeda Central about an alliance with his organization.⁵⁶ These talks were very tense bringing forth latent disagreements over the propriety of targeting Shi'ite civilians and the efficacy of Zarqawi's Iraq Strategy. The Jordanian's hatred of the Shia and his cavalier attitude toward sacrificing innocent Muslims horrified al-Qaeda Central. Bin Laden and Ayman Zawahiri urged Zarqawi to renew the fight against the American infidel and avoid sectarian attacks.[57]

By winter 2004, al-Qaeda Central had been eclipsed by Zarqawi's network in the "war in terror" and Iraq had become a new vital jihadist battlefield. Zarqawi became the focal point of internet jihadist chatter and Iraq a fertile recruiting ground for suicide bombers. Fearing they would be left behind in the jihadist struggle if they rejected his entreaties, al-Qaeda acceded to Zarqawi's request for support and alignment. It was a decision that they would later regret.

AQI was officially formed on October 17, 2004 with Zarqawi declaring fidelity to bin Laden.[58] By accepting Zarqawi's oath of allegiance, the central leadership endorsed AQI's sectarian strategy. In the span of a year, Zarqawi had rocketed to fame inspiring a mix of loathing, hatred and admiration. Al-Qaeda's alignment with Zarqawi's Iraqi operation proved to be a fatal decision. The high school dropout, moreover, had aspirations beyond Iraq that equally damaged al-Qaeda's reputation in the Arab world.

Zarqawi's renewed fight against the Jordanian apostate regime

Zarqawi's exploits in Iraq did not prevent him from targeting Jordanian interests. His network bombed the Jordanian embassy in Baghdad killing dozens. With operatives in Jordan, Syria, Iraq, and Europe, Zarqawi had substantial financial resources and fighters at his disposal. Foiled in April 2004 by the GID, Zarqawi's most ambitious plot involved suicide bombers crashing a truck into GID headquarters igniting 20 tons of chemicals.[59] The planned chemical fallout over Amman could have killed an estimated 80,000 people.

AQI's targeting of civilians and his nihilistic brutality invited many reproaches. Many clerics saw the unleashing of suicide bombers as un-Islamic. Zarqawi's spiritual mentor Abdul Mohammad al-Maqdisi renounced his former pupil's exploits, sectarian killings, and barbarism.[60] Whether Maqdisi had been pressured by the government in 2004 to denounce Zarqawi as a precondition for his prison release is a matter of dispute. The cleric's later refutation of his critique has only added further controversy.[61]

Frustrated in his bid to strike at the Hashemite monarchy Zarqawi redoubled his efforts. His lone "success" was a November 2005 attack on Amman hotels one of which hosted a wedding party killing some 60 people.[62] Zarqawi became an enemy in his own homeland and the symbolism of the wedding party bombing inspired mass protests. The Amman bombings greatly hurt his reputation that suffered further with his attacks against Shi'ites and anti-al-Qaeda Sunnis.

The war against the Shia

The Jordanian had targeted the Shia as early as August 2003 when two bombs exploded outside the Imam Ali Mosque in Najaf killing 83 people including a revered cleric and spiritual leaders associated with the Supreme Council of the Islamic Revolution in Iraq. This assassination and its death toll created mass grief in the Shia community. It was one of the first attacks in post-Saddam Iraq and was widely believed to be the work of Saddam loyalists. Subsequent investigation in 2005, however, revealed that Zarqawi's network was responsible.[63]

Zarqawi's pathological hatred of the Shia led him to target their mosques, pilgrims, clerics, and religious celebrations. His February 2004 letter to al-Qaeda describes the Shia in these graphic terms:

> These confirmed polytheists, who stand and pray at gravesides, who organized funeral possessions, who treat the Companions [of the Prophet] as infidels and insult the mothers of the faithful and the elite of this [Islamic] nation, do all they can to distort the Koran, presenting it as an offshoot of logical thought in order to disparage those who have a correct knowledge of it, in addition, they speak of infallibility of the [Islamic] nation . . . and in many other forms they give clear proof of atheism that abounds in their published works and original sources.[64]

Zarqawi anti-Shia strategy targeted the group's religious rituals like the commemoration of the death of Mohammad's grandson Husayn and he attacked shrines dedicated to his memory. The Shi'ite reverence for Ali (the prophet's son-in-law) similarly suggests to Zarqawi a multideity religion that is anathema to the Sunni tradition and its emphasis on the unity of Allah. Despite its irrational excesses, Zarqawi's 2004 letter to al-Qaeda contains the seeds of a strategy that almost succeeded in ripping Iraq asunder. He not bin Laden came closest to defeating America and becoming a regional emir in the heart of the Arab world.

Zarqawi hoped his attacks against Shia religious centers and political parties would lure the government and Shia cleric Muqtada al Sadr militia into retaliation. The prospect of sectarian war would have consequences beyond Iraq inviting a possible regional war as Sunni countries align against Baghdad and their American patrons. Relying on his impressive network of car bomb factories, IED manufacturing sites, and seemingly inexhaustible supply of suicide bombers, Zarqawi ruthlessly went about his strategy. The following were the most notable attacks:[65]

- The Karbala Ashoura massacre in March 2, 2004 where suicide bombers, car bombs, and insurgent sniper fire killed 178 people commemorating the death of Husayn.
- A series of car bomb explosions in the southern Shi'ite town of Basra killing 74 people.
- The November 18, 2005 attack against Shia Mosques in Khanaqin near the Iranian border killing over 70 people.
- The use of suicide bombers on September 14, 2005 to kill 160 people in a Shi'ite district in Baghdad.
- A triple suicide bombing of Baghdad's Shia Buratha mosque killing 85 worshipers.

During his 2004–6 campaign, Zarqawi also targeted Kurds, Sufis, and Christians. All of whom are described in disparaging terms in this February letter.[66] The utilization of car bombs, suicide bombers, IEDs, and insurgent gunfire had devastating sectarian consequences.

Communities that comingled for generations became hostile. Populations migrated to "safe" sectarian enclaves and formed militias. Christians left in a mass exodus as their Churches were bombed and their leaders executed. As Zarqawi anticipated the Shi'ite government death squads retaliated against the Sunnis and Muqtada al Sadr Mahdi army unleashed its fury. The Americans, above all, were hapless and ineffective to stem the religious warfare unleashed by al-Qaeda.

The sectarian conflict had reached levels that many believed unsustainable. Experts doubted that Iraq could avoid civil war. US Marine intelligence report in 2005 reported that Anbar Province had been lost to al-Qaeda and a dangerous and impenetrable terror sanctuary created. The weight of scholarly opinion, similarly, urged American withdraw and a containment policy to limit the regional impact of the disastrous Iraq war. Had this advice been heeded Zarqawi may have achieved his dream of defeating crusader forces and their Shi'ite apostate allies.

Zarqawi's strategy seemed to be working perfectly. What then happened to derail it? The answer is complicated but can be reduced to a number of factors that coalesced ironically at the point that Zarqawi achieved his greatest success.

Zarqawi's fall and al-Qaeda's collapse in Anbar Province

Fearing tragic consequences al-Qaeda's second in command Ayman al-Zawahiri warned Zarqawi in a 2005 letter that his strategy risked alienating Muslim support.[67] Intercepted by US forces his message suggests to Zarqawi that his sectarian strategy was unsustainable. Zawahiri writes that "in the absence of this popular support, the Islamic mujahidin would be crushed in the shadows" and "among the things which the feelings of the Muslim populace who love and support you will never find palatable—also are the scenes of slaughtering the hostages."[68] Zawahiri describes the sectarian factor secondary to the fight against the Americans and the creation of Baghdad based Islamic Emirate that would be a focal point for regional jihad.

Zawahiri prescience was lost on Zarqawi who never wavered in his sectarian approach. Yet there were other AQI missteps that proved more lethal than the dysfunctional effort to force religious civil war. Among the most important of these was Zarqawi's war against the Sunni Anbar sheiks.

By late 2005, the Iraqi Sunni insurgency once united against the Americans began to fragment.[69] Al-Qaeda's use of Anbar and the Sunni Triangle as a base of operations brought it into conflict with Sunni tribal sheiks who chaffed at AQI's efforts to cut into their smuggling operations and impose Sharia law.[70] While claiming to represent an authentic Iraqi resistance, al-Qaeda's core leadership and suicidal jihadists were predominately foreign born. Their priorities in Iraq began to diverge from Iraqi nationalists that were the core of the insurgency.

Zarqawi's alienation of the Shia, Kurds, Christians, and Iraqi Sunnis contributed to his death. Hunted by US forces with a $25 million bounty on his head, his time was limited. Based on an informant's tip Zarqawi was connected to a cleric whose movements were monitored by US task force.[71] Tracked to a rural safe house where Zarqawi met his spiritual advisor, US Special Forces took no risks bombing the edifice with two 500-pound bombs. Zarqawi's June 7, 2006 death was greeted with much jubilation in Shia dominated parts of Iraq.

The safe house provided information that led investigators to a great deal of Zarqawi's network. Al-Qaeda had been meticulous in storing computer based information of its commanders, operational cells, smuggling routes, financial sources, and local contacts. Subsequent US and Iraqi raids exacted a significant toll in Zarqawi's network.[72]

The transnational nature of al-Qaeda's agenda, its fixation on sectarian war, and its imposition of Sharia in towns it controlled created conflict with local leaders. Zarqawi's policy of supplanting tribal authority, his forced marriages of foreign fighters with local women, and his assassination of recalcitrant Sunni sheiks began to divide the insurgency. By late 2006, al-Qaeda was involved in a war with Sunni tribal leaders whose communitarian prestige could be exploited by coalition authorities and the Iraqi government.

During this period US forces in Anbar sought to "flip" the insurgency by uniting with the Sheiks in their battle against al-Qaeda. These negotiations bore fruit and becoming the basis of the *Sahwa* or *Awakening Movement* of tribal sheiks united to resist al-Qaeda in Anbar. Studies of the al Anbar *Awakening Movement* suggest that the Sunni insurgency against the government turned in late 2006.[73] Threatened by al-Qaeda's murderous suicidal bombing campaigns, its indiscriminate killing of civilians and its efforts to usurp tribal authority, Sunni Sheiks entered into an alliance with US forces. American arming of over a hundred thousand Sunni tribesmen tied to local sheiks is widely credited with weakening al-Qaeda and within a year driving its remnants to Kirkuk and Mosul.[74]

America's ability to consolidate tribal authority was facilitated by Anbar's sectarian homogeneity and intratribal loyalty. The US military used financial patronage and contracts funneled through tribal leaders to reinforce the sheiks economic power and popularity.[75] With the backing of US forces and weapons, tribal militias could withstand the al-Qaeda assault.

The deployment of tens of thousands of additional US forces in 2007 provided greater stability in Baghdad. Deaths of US troops and Iraqi civilians began to decline throughout 2007–8 with considerable reduction in the Sunni Triangle. Anbar would move from the most dangerous to one of the safes in early 2009. The consolidation of Prime Minister Nuri al Maliki cross-sectarian government and his successful military operation against Basra's Badar Shi'ite militias in

2008 forcing the Islamists into a ceasefire and subsequent truce also produced stability gains.

Without a charismatic presence to replace Zarqawi, US Special Force's attacks and armed Sunni tribesman exerted a considerable toll on AQI. By the year 2008, 2,400 al-Qaeda militants and allied groups had been killed by US and Iraqi security forces and some 9,000 AQI operatives arrested.[76] Foreign fighters entering Iraq have declined dramatically since 2007. Al-Qaeda's post-Zarqawi's reorganization has been plagued by internal factionalism, frequent leadership changes, and diminished operational capability. It continues to cling to Zarqawi's sectarian divide and rule strategy.

Al-Qaeda in post-Zarqawi Iraq and the US withdraw

Zarqawi's death and the unpopularity of his policies forced al-Qaeda to reorganize as a more authentic Iraqi insurgent group. Egyptian Abu Hamza al-Muhajir became al-Qaeda's new leader and he began his rule by courting Iraqi support and native leaders.[77] Hoping to put an Iraqi face on the organizations Abu Hamza joined ranks with local Islamist insurgent groups forming the ISI. Led by Iraqi Abu Omar al-Baghdadi who was widely considered Abu Hamza's figurehead, ISI seeks to rejuvenate the jihadist struggle.

Al-Qaeda's ISI reconfiguration has done little to blunt its loss of popular support. US and Iraqi counterterror operations killed Abu Hamza and Abu Omar in October of 2010.[78] Since its failed 2006-7 campaign, the groups has receded to cities like Mosul and Tikrit where religious and ethnic passions give it a supportive infrastructure.

ISI has a more bureaucratic command structure with a hierarchical direction over local cells that leaves it vulnerable to counterterror operations. Despite the dysfunctional nature of Zarqawi's sectarian strategy the new ISI continues to operate as though it were its only strategy. Iraqi Christians have been particularly vulnerable to the group's attacks as witnessed by al-Qaeda's 2010 siege and bombing of a Baghdad Catholic Church killing dozens.[79]

Al-Qaeda has exploited the exit of US troops and the failure of the Iraqi government to resolve contentious issues like provincial autonomy and the distribution of oil wealth between Kurdish, Shi'ite, and Sunni communities. Unable to secure a long-term security agreement with Baghdad, the Obama Administration withdraw at the end of 2011 all US combat troops and supporting personnel. Since the US departure there has been a sharp rise in sectarian conflicts and terror attacks against government forces and Shia civil and religious society. Fernando Reinares reports that terror incidents doubled after the US withdraw making hollow the claim that American occupation was the principal source of jihadist violence.[80] The Shia community continues to be targeted by the ISI with significant attacks against religious pilgrims and mass ceremonies. Such attacks will invariably result in Shi'ite militia retaliation against the Sunni minority. While the level of violence in Iraq has not reached the 2006-7 fatality rates, current trends are alarming. This is exactly what ISI desires.

While ethno-religious warfare could result in national dissolution allowing al-Qaeda to dominate some Sunni areas, this outcome is unlikely. Zarqawi's legacy of nihilistic violence and his terror campaign against Anbar Province's Sheiks limits ISI's potential power base in Sunni communities. This same cannot be said about the jihadist forces in the two-year-old Syrian revolt against the Assad regime. The prominence of Syrian jihadist groups and foreign fighters in the revolutionary movement offers al-Qaeda some opportunity for a terror sanctuary and recruitment base.

The Syrian Jihad against the Assad regime 2011-13

Jihadist revolts against the Syrian regime have strong historical antecedents. The Muslim Brotherhood insurgency between 1978 and 1982 challenged Hafez al-Assad Baathist regime's right to rule. The Baathists were secular Arab nationalists who borrowed ideological and organizational principles from European fascistic, anti-Semitic, and communist ideas.[81] They promoted a sectarian policy of support for Muslim and Christian minorities within the context of a secular-socialist state. They, however, were careful not to alienate the Sunni majority and under successive regimes forged alliances with Sunni economic elites.

The Syrian Baathists were not a unified movement. The party had diverse ideological currents which resulted in successive intraparty rivalries. Most of the movement's founders such as Michel Aflaq were expelled in 1965 power struggles that strengthened the military's position in the party. As a prominent commander in the Syrian Air Force, Hafez al Assad built a considerable following in the military and Baathist party structure.

His ambitions for complete control were realized with his 1970 seizure of power in a military coup against a party rival. Assad worked strenuously to reinforce the position of Christian, Druze, and Alawite minorities in Syria building upon France's colonial legacy of support of minority sects. Geographically concentrated in impoverished coastal northern mountains, Druze and Alawite minorities had been exploited for generations by the dominant Sunni landed gentry. They saw the Baathists state and party as a catalyst for progressive upward social mobility.

Baathist control over state apparatus promoted the economic interests of Druze, Christian, and Alawite minorities alienating many impoverished Sunnis. The Alawites were particularly prominent in the army, security, and intelligence circles with Assad's relatives in dominant key leadership positions. The regimes security services and militias ruthlessly repressed political opposition groups with dissident organizations banned after the party came to power in the early 1960s.

The Islamist opposition to Baathist rule grew dramatically in the 1970s with the Muslim Brotherhood mounting a serious challenge to Assad's regime. The Brotherhood's antipathy toward Assad's government was driven by many factors. The regime's secular Pan-Arabist socialist ideals offended the Brothers Islamist worldview that was exacerbated by the presence of Alawite Muslims in top political and security positions. The Alawites are the followers of a tenth-century religious movement that evolved from the Shia branch of Islam that believe that twelfth imam will liberate the world from injustice during the final days of humanity. Given the Christian parallel in Jesus' return to destroy Satan's rule, the Sunni Brothers considered the Alawites to be polytheistic heretics. The Islamists, moreover, wanted to reassert the Sunni postcolonial hegemony over Syrian politics.

Baathist rule exacerbated sectarian, economic, and ideological tensions finally sparking the Islamist 1979–82 rebellion. Revolts were especially strong in cities like Homs and Hama that became a center of Sunni resistance to Assad's regime. The regime was merciless unleashing the army and its *shabiya* militias to destroy the insurgency. Ten to twenty thousand Muslim Brothers and their civilian supporters were killed by government forces in Hama in the early 1980s. As Fouad Ajami notes in his book *The Syrian Rebellion* the 1982 Hama massacre casts a significant shadow over the current rebellion in which Islamist and jihadist elements are becoming more pronounced.[82]

Long thought impregnable by many observers the 2011 rebellion against Bashar Assad regime came as a surprise.[83] Bashar assumed the presidency after the death of his father in 2000 and Western analysts had hoped that the London trained optometrist would unshackle the regime's authoritarian system. Western governments engaged Bashar expecting that he would renew peace negotiations with the Israelis to resolve the Golan Heights territorial dispute. Despite such hopes, Bashar continued to use the Israeli threat to justify his Baathist dictatorship.

Bashar did, however, change the state's economic direction. He unshackled state controls and liberalized key service industries and agriculture. Privatization benefited party insiders and Assad loyalists. Some analysts believe that the economic inequality and crony capitalism of Bashar's regime contributed to popular resentment that surfaced in Deraa in March 2011 after security forces tortured and killed teenagers who sprayed antiregime graffiti on some of the town's walls. Hundreds turned out in civil disobedience to condemn the killings. Despite their peaceful character, protests in the town were brutally repressed by the regime. Bashar sought to emulate his late father's reputation for ruthlessness and brutality.

Throughout 2012, protests became larger and more numerous as hundreds of thousands streamed out into the squares and plazas of Syria's towns, cities, and villages. The demonstrations were matched by the severity of the regime repressive actions with *shabiya* militias and secret police brutalizing protesters. Government forces have destroyed mosques that are a key meeting place and symbolic center for the resistance movement.

Assad' regime has alternated between repression and conciliation. The Baathist state's abolition of an emergency law that allowed security forces unprecedented power to detain "terrorists" was an effort to placate the opposition. Assad's continued detention of protesters and opponents makes a mockery of this cynical and hollow gesture. Assad has detained hundreds of thousands since the uprising began.

The 2011 protests had a pronounced sectarian caste with Sunni towns and cities marked by violent demonstrations. As they had in the early 1980s cities like Homs and Hama were centers of antiregime resistance and fervor. Homs in particular was devastated by the fighting that victimized many civilians. Much of the city is destroyed, but it continues to be a defiant symbol of resistance. Fouad Ajami compares Syria's Homs to Bosnia's *Sarajevo* a Muslim city which was repeatedly savaged by Serbian militias some two decades ago. Ironically the international community's inaction in resolving Sarajevo's plight is a sad precedent that governs the West's indecision, fear, and "realist" caution characteristic of its current policy of nonintervention in the Syrian civil war.

With Assad's savage repression that killed thousands and imprisoned multitudes, peaceful protests catalyzed into armed rebellion. Unlike Egypt and Tunisia, the Syrian army did not stand aside. The Alawite character of the officer corps, Special Forces brigades, and militias facilitated Bashar's repressive tactics. The military and security apparatus are tied to the regime's survival. Widespread fear of a Sunni fundamentalist revolution additionally has forced Syrian Christian and Muslim minorities to support the regime. If Assad regime falls these minorities could fall victim to severe Sunni retaliation.

Dominated by exile groups like the Syrian National Council and military deserters who formed the Free Syrian Army (FSA), the resistance movement is badly fractured. Hundreds of local militias have also arisen to wage a military campaign to dislodge the regime. Like Libya, the rebels are a loose amalgamation of militias and vigilante groups. These groups often quarrel and clash. Kurdish and Syrian nationalists have fought each other close to the Turkish border to control territory and smuggling roots.

Despite these obstacles the rebels had conquered much of rural Syria by March of 2013 and the regime struggles to control key cities like Damascus and Aleppo. Continuous fighting in these both cities' suburbs illustrates the regime's precarious position. This pattern is reinforced by the fall of government airstrips and military bases to rebels in the countryside.

Syrian jihadists and foreign fighters from Iraq, Lebanon, Libya, and Jordan have joined opposition forces. What began as largely a secular uprising now has an increasingly Islamist character punctuated with AQI like suicide operations and massive car bombings. While comprising thousands of fighters, jihadists are a critical part of the resistance movement. The al-Nusra Front has emerged as the strongest jihadist movement that has mounted spectacular suicide operations against the regime's security, party, and intelligence apparatus.

Formed in January 2012 the al-Nusra is mainly Syrian but it does utilize foreign fighters from Libya, Iraq, Saudi Arabia, and Jordan for suicide operations.[84] The group's coordinated car bomb explosions and suicidal jihadists have killed thousands and many of the al-Nusra's operations are filmed and posted on Islamist websites. It has also been responsible for summary executions of Baathist loyalists and soldiers.

Within a year the al-Nusra Front has emerged as a key player in the Syrian resistance. It may be able to field up to 10,000 combatants. ISI provides fighters, money and logistical support for the group. Along with the foreign dominated Abdullah Azzam Brigade and Fatah al-Islam group, al-Nusra and ISI hope to overthrow the regime and replace it with a Sunni fundamentalist state.

Based on a study of martyrdom notices for foreign fighters on jihadi websites between 2011–13 some 130 suicide bombers have died in Syria with the bulk of the fighters coming from foreign countries like Saudi Arabia, Libya, Egypt, and Tunisia. Of the dozens of jihadist groups in Syria, al-Nusra Front is increasingly dominating in its recruitment of foreign suicide bombers. Not surprisingly some young men from Europe's Muslim Diaspora population have answered the call to jihad in Syria. British authorities are increasingly worried that extremist segments from the United Kingdom's 13,000 strong Syrian community are providing funds and fighters for jihadist networks. Based on some press reports hundreds of British, French, and Belgian fighters have augmented the ranks of the Syrian rebels.

In April 2013, ISI leader Abu Bakr al-Baghdadi announced that al-Nusra was a territorial extension of his network and that he has provided the group with half of its resources. Baghdadi's announcement is fraught with controversy. Al-Nusra websites initially confirmed the merger between the two organizations, but would later recant the attempted union. Ayman al-Zawahiri has publically reproached Baghdadi's efforts and says he supports al-Nusra's independent status. Baghdadi has openly criticized Zawahiri's interference. Accordingly, a new jihadist formation has arisen in Syria called al-Qaeda in Iraq and the Levant in Syria that swears fidelity to Baghdadi's vision. The group now openly competes with al-Nusra. The incident and its attendant consequences are emblematic of the divisions and confusion that are rampant in al-Qaeda's diffuse network of affiliates and associates.

The ascendance of jihadi organizations in the Syrian rebel movement is not surprising. Syria was a logistical network for the Iraqi resistance movement after the 2003 US invasion. The Assad regime actively supported the smuggling of foreign fighters and assisted AQI's development of a Syrian logistical and financial infrastructure. The regime is now of the receiving end of a network that it helped develop and Bashar now presents his regime as being in the front line in the war against al-Qaeda. As the war's virulence and death toll intensify, the rebel movement is likely to become more extremist and sectarian. Al-Nusra's popularity is growing and it is considered to be a vanguard jihadist group capable of attracting considerable numbers of Syrian and foreign fighters. The group is beginning to coordinate military action with the Free Syrian Army that has formed its own Islamist brigades.

The flow of Qatari, Kuwaiti, and Saudi money and weapons to extremist jihadi organizations amplifies this radicalization. The reluctance of Western nations to militarily intercede in Syria has exacerbated the violence and reinforced the growing role of jihadist organizations. The Obama Administration's reticence to fully arm the rebels is predicated upon fears that it could empower jihadists ISI recent merger with al-Nusra and their joint declaration of an Islamic state intensifies these concerns. Al-Qaeda has gained yet another affiliate that departs from its original *far enemy* design.

American caution has ceded ground to Gulf State patrons who have armed extremist groups. Until very recently the Obama Administration's inaction has assisted jihadi presence in the Syrian rebel movement. Recognizing the growing jihadist threat if a protracted struggle endures, the French and British have belatedly agreed to arm the rebels. The United States would later follow suit though the arms transfers are subject to congressional approval. It may be too late to counter the Islamization of the revolutionary movement.

Two years of civil war have resulted in over a 100,000 deaths and more than 2 million externally displaced people.[85] Syria's neighbors and international relief agencies are straining to meet the refugee needs. The sectarian fighting threatens to unleash a contagion of violence across the region. Lebanon has seen Sunni and pro-Hezbollah forces clash in Tripoli and other places in the restive South. The Sunni minority in Iraq experiencing the loss of US military protection and a repressive Shia dominated government have begun an incipient Sunni insurgency supported by al-Qaeda elements that hope to exploit the resulting chaos.

The tenth anniversary of Iraq's *liberation* was greeted by al-Qaeda and Sunni extremists by a series of car bombs and terror attacks aimed at government installations and Shia religious institutions and ceremonies. These attacks have the imprimatur of AQI and ISI operations that hope to exploit sectarian violence. Kurdish rebels in northern Syria, furthermore, could stoke secessionist pressures in neighboring Turkey reigniting irredentist pressures in Syria and Iran. Many years after Zawahiri's letter admonishing Zarqawi for his sectarian strategy, the Jordanian jihadist sectarian legacy continues unabated.

With 50,000 well-armed troops and militias led by relatives and coreligionists the Assad's regime may be able to stand for a number of years. This is especially true if the West wary of any intervention continues to be divided, fearful, and uncertain if it should act. Assad appears paranoid and may spare no measure to ensure his regime's survival. Some analysts believe the Baathist dictatorship may fall with its surviving elements retreating to Alawi dominated coastal areas, mountain villages, and a Latakia refuge to mount one last stand against Sunni opponents.[86] The resulting sectarian bloodbath could have profound regional ramifications as fighting spreads to neighboring Lebanon and exacerbates tensions across the region.

American and Europe's geopolitical interests in resolving the Syrian conflict are considerable. The overthrow of Assad's regime could blunt Iran's projection of power in the region and be a major blow to Hezbollah that has benefited from Syrian armed, logistical, and financial support. Both Iranian and Hezbollah forces have fought and died to save their Syrian ally and continue to struggle to preserve their presence in the region. The Assad regime has vast stockpiles of mustard, anthrax, and saran gas that could be transferred to Hezbollah or may fall into the hands of Sunni extremists.

Israeli Prime Minister Benjamin Netanyau recently told a group of American congressional representatives his options in Syria go from bad to worse. The Obama Administration has warned Assad's government that the use of chemical weapons is a *red line* that would trigger American military intervention.

In late April 2013 British and Israeli intelligence agencies reported that the regime had used chemical weapons against insurgents south of Damascus in a government counteroffensive that crossed the threshold to trigger an American military response. US government sources would later confirm these findings and the Obama Administration has decided to forward arms to Free Syrian Army brigades that have been vetted by the CIA to ensure that advanced weaponry is not acquired by jihadists.

The collapse of the Syrian Baathist regime could fuel a sectarian bloodbath. While jihadi organizations may join in violence against Christian and Alawite minorities, such a development is counter to bin Laden and Zawahiri's admonitions of sectarian war. The cycle of violence and revenge in a post-Assad Syria offers the real possibility that Shi'ite and Sunni extremists will kill each other. As Adam Garfinkle has cynically noted this is likely to strengthen, not harm Western and Israeli security interests.[87]

Al-Nusra efforts to create a Syrian base of operations will intensify efforts to dislodge whatever power base they may establish. A possible al-Nusra *sanctuary* will invariably be targeted by Alawite, Shi'ite, Christian, and Druse enemies. The jihadist war in Syria and Zarqawi's fall in Iraq are vivid testimony that foreign jihadists need to craft a strategy congruent with local interests but also one that adheres to al-Qaeda's war against the United States. So far such a balanced approach striking at both *near* and *far enemies* has not been easy to achieve.

Al-Qaeda' actions to create a transnational jihadist state in Iraq floundered against the needs and priorities of indigenous insurgents and local forces. Foreign jihadi attacks against Sunni tribal leaders in Anbar Province forced them to align with the Americans reversing al-Qaeda's spectacular initial gains. Jihadist penetration of the Syrian rebel movement, moreover, has exacerbated sectarian fissures that work against the implementation of al-Qaeda's *far enemy* strategy.

The Syrian jihad may result in more sectarian conflict and internal wars across the region. Fighting has broken out in neighboring Lebanon between Shi'ite Hezbollah and Sunni militants. Hezbollah's sending of thousands of its fighters to support Assad's beleaguered regime has catalyzed the Sunni jihadists to redouble their efforts to overthrow the Syrian regime. Jihadist groups across the Sunni Muslim world including Chechen and Pakistani extremist organizations have established combat units in Syria. Damascus not Washington is now the number one enemy of Sunni jihadists.

Success or failure of al-Qaeda affiliates and insurgents operating in Somalia, Yemen, and the Maghreb will also be dependent on whether they have learned from the failure of its Iraqi jihad. Judging from ISI and al-Nusra's stubborn commitment to a sectarian strategy their future prospects are anything but encouraging.

6

Al-Qaeda's Affiliates and Insurgent Groups in Somalia, Yemen, and the Maghreb

> *On the other hand, after the war expanded and the Mujahidin spread out to many regions, some of the brothers became totally absorbed in fighting our local enemies, and more mistakes have been made due to miscalculations by the brothers planning operations.*
>
> Osama bin Laden[1]

The rise of al-Qaeda affiliates and insurgent groups across the world demonstrates how Jihadism has morphed into a multifront decentralized and fractured struggle. AQIM, AQAP, and al-Shabaab represent diverse jihadist efforts to attack *near* and *far enemies*.[2] Often hailed as an al-Qaeda success making the *war on terror* more difficult, this is anything but true. These alliances represent mutual failure and frustration as local and international jihadists have repeatedly failed to achieve their objectives.

The collapse of al-Qaeda's terror sanctuary in Afghanistan led to its post-9/11 strategy to open multiple fronts in a policy of *vexation* and *exhaustion*.[3] This policy entailed many tactics including sponsoring lone wolf terrorist attacks in Western countries and assisting Islamic insurgents fighting foreign occupation forces. Frustrated in their inability to dislodge native regimes regional Islamists leapt at the opportunity to revive their struggle by aligning with al-Qaeda. These alliances hoped to convert singular failure into a joint success.

Al-Qaeda affiliates and insurgents have arisen in failed states where they have waged a jihadist war against numerous enemies. Al-Qaeda's relationship with these groups was built upon indigenous traditions of radical Jihadism.[4] Previous al-Qaeda presence in these areas and past joint ventures with local groups facilitated this alignment. These networks have risen in countries ravaged by civil wars, guerilla insurgencies, and states rocked by internal conflict. "Arab Afghans" have played roles in al-Shabaab, AQIM, and AQAP and they have contributed to an internationalization of the jihadist war.[5]

Somalia, Algeria, and Yemen have experienced years of chronic warfare that in the Somali case led to state implosion. Lawless since 1991 Somalia is a dire case with al-Shabaab at the height of its power controlling some two-thirds of the war-torn country.[6] Yemen also has been plagued by numerous insurgencies and is bordering on state collapse. This could allow AQAP opportunities to exploit a potential power vacuum. Algeria, similarly, was convulsed by a decade civil war that became the impetus for a variety of radical Islamist movements from which AQIM is the most recent manifestation. AQIM in turn has sponsored groups in Mali and Nigeria hoping to make West Africa a future jihadist front.

Al-Qaeda franchises developed in these countries because of chronic state failure, autocratic government, and tribal conflicts. Al-Qaeda's affiliates and insurgent groups are strongest in remote areas where central authority is weak and heavily resented. AQIM and AQAP have also benefited from tribal alliances and criminal activity that give them a secure base of operations.[7]

Formerly autonomous movements committed to native insurgencies, affiliates, and insurgent branches hope to diversify the scope of their operations by attacking the Western *far enemy*.

Al-Qaeda's incorporation of these branches envisions simultaneous wars against multiple enemies. The groups seek to target Western interests. This has invited concern form American and European security agencies. Of the three al-Qaeda affiliate/insurgent formations only AQAP has consistently targeted the Western homeland. AQIM and al-Shabaab, alternatively, have targeted manly regional and local enemies. Bin Laden's Abbottabad correspondence makes clear his disappointment with AQAP, AQIM, and al-Shabaab and their lack of commitment to his *far enemy* approach.

Al-Qaeda's franchise operations aspire to an equitable division of labor: with native groups receiving from al-Qaeda advanced training and skilled fighters, while the central organization enlarges its field of global operations to strike at Western enemies. Al-Shabaab, AQIM, and AQAP actions now have the trademarks (IED and suicide bombings) of al-Qaeda Central.[8] Significantly, none of these groups have been able to launch a major successful attack against al-Qaeda's American nemesis. AQAP's greatest "victory" was its encouragement of Major Nidal Hassan to kill 13 fellow servicemen at his Fort Hood Texas base. The bulk of AQAP operations are directed against Yemeni security services.

This cross-fertilization of activities, furthermore, has failed to stem the decline of regional jihadist networks. Al-Qaeda's affiliates are confined to the margin of failed states. One way to envision these groups is by conceptualizing them along a number of dimensions. Table 6.1 categorizes al-Qaeda inspired affiliates based on a number of factors. The variations between affiliates reflect their different

Table 6.1 Overview of al-Qaeda in Somalia, Yemen, and Algeria

Affiliate or Insurgent Groups	Failed State	Tribal Integration of Affiliate	Financial Support for Terrorist Activities	Enemies
Al-Shabaab	Somalia has been in a state of civil war since the fall of the Barre dictatorship in 1991 with repeated intervention by Ethiopian and AU troops to prevent an outright Islamist domination.	Efforts to supplant tribal authority to create trans-Islamic identity have floundered in light of clan and tribal resistance.	Protection for smuggling routes, Zakat, protection, and piracy. Initial support by Somali Diaspora.	Muslim apostates (Transitional Federal Government), and Ethiopian and AU troops oppose US interests and African states that have ethnic Somali minorities.
AQAP	Yemen has been the site of numerous civil wars, guerrilla insurgencies, and secessionist struggles that have plagued the country for two decades.	Yes, tribal connections to central government opponents and northern Sunni Tribes fighting Shi'ite insurgents.	Arms smuggling and external Saudi finance.	Muslim apostates, central government in Sana, and US interests and homeland are targeted.
AQIM	Remote areas of Algerian, Malian, Mauritanian, and Sahel are poorly governed and controlled by central authority.	Yes, AQIM has a relationship; Tuareg tribal leaders connection and cross-marriage ties.	Yes, hostage taking, arms, drugs, and cigarettes.	Muslim apostate governments; threats to conquer al Andaluz and attacks against colonial France and French citizens in the Sahel.

ethnic, tribal, geographic, and political contexts. What follows is an effort to look at these differences and similarities.

Al-Shabaab

The Somali jihadi organization is rooted in the Islamist Salafist groups of the 1970s whose clerics were trained in Saudi Arabia. Formed to oppose the Barre dictatorship, al-Shabaab's ideological ancestor Al-Ittihad al-Islamiyya (AIAI) mobilized in the 1980s to transplant Saudi Wahhabism in a country steeped in moderate Sufi traditions. This evolution reflects a general pattern of Saudi finance facilitating Islamic radicalism across the world. The effect has been especially pronounced in Africa as witnessed by the growth of Muslim fundamentalist movements like Nigeria's BH and the Malian AD.

The group's agenda was altered by the collapse of Barre Regime in 1991 and the disintegration of state authority as warring clans established their own fiefdoms. The country's descent into warlordism combined with draught led to massive starvation and death among the populace. By the early 1990s, Somalia exemplified the African failed state.

UN famine relief efforts were complicated when warlords seized grain supplies tragically contributing to the severity of the civil war. UN peace keepers expanded their mission in a failed effort to disarm the militias and restore order. Participating US forces in 1993 were caught in a deadly maelstrom dramatized by the downing of two Blackhawk helicopters and death of 19 US Special Forces soldiers in an effort in Mogadishu to capture a Somali warlord.

Operating in the region, bin Laden's network used Sudan as a base of operations to support radical Islamist groups fighting UN peacekeepers. Al-Qaeda in Sudan supported numerous East African Islamists radicals.[9] In its biggest act of terrorism al-Qaeda attacked American embassies in Kenya and Tanzania killing hundreds. This was bin Laden's first significant attack against US interests indicating global range of his network. Washington's subsequent retaliation (including striking al-Qaeda training camps in Taliban controlled Afghanistan and destroying a Sudanese plant suspected of manufacturing chemical weapons) failed to deter bin Laden's organization. Its ineffective response only enhanced OBL allure in the jihadist community.

The rise of Islamic Court Union (ICU) contributed to al-Shabaab's development as a major jihadist group. The ICU fought against the Western supported Transitional Federal Government that hoped to wrestle power away from the Islamist forces. The ICU's aim was to centralize authority, impose Sharia law, and eliminate warlordism. Al-Shabaab emerged as an ICU militia and due to Ethiopian military involvement in Somalia the group became more extreme in its jihadist ambitions.[10] The Transitional Federal Government's patchwork alliance of moderate warlords supported by Ethiopian Troops became involved in pitch battles against the radical Islamists.

Support for al-Shabaab by Somali Diaspora communities in the West resulted in the sending of money and jihadists to fight Ethiopian troops and the Transitional Federal Government.[11] The Somali community in Minneapolis was especially active and the local Diaspora population became an active recruiting base for young Somali-Americans to fight Ethiopian forces. They would be succeeded by Gulf Arab jihadists aligned with al-Qaeda. Al-Shabaab's insurgency and martyrdom operations inflicted considerable casualties on the Ethiopian army with over a thousand of its personnel killed between 2007 and 2009.

Many al-Shabaab leaders and foot soldiers were veterans of the Afghan campaign and Taliban training camps. Foreign fighters play a key role in the organization's Shura (Leadership Council) and have redirected the group's strategy toward greater Islamic militancy and the use of suicide bombers.[12] Some observers see increased patterns of cooperation between al-Shabaab and AQAP.[13] Many of these fighters, however, are widely resented by the local population with forced marriages involving native Somali women in common.[14]

The prominence of African jihadists in Bin Laden's movement and the notoriety of the Kenyan and Tanzanian embassy attacks were not ignored by US intelligence and security services. The CIA and the American military launched a number of strikes against Somali operatives including a 2002 Predator drone strike and Special Force's operations and air strikes that have killed key leaders.[15] Remaining leaders continue to be hunted by US intelligence and AU troops.

The internationalist agenda of al-Shabaab includes support for Somali irredentist movements in Ethiopia and Kenya and the group envisions a regional Islamic caliphate. Guerilla operations continue against the FTC and AU troops who replaced the Ethiopian forces in 2009.

Since Ethiopia's withdraw, external support has declined as many Somali supporters have become repulsed by al-Shabaab's tactics. The Somali radicals have failed to learn from Zarqawi's AQI's failures and their policies have alienated many local clans. The group's implementation of Shariah law (amputations are common), its brutalization of the Sufi populace, and its interference with food aid relief efforts have reduced al-Shabaab's popular appeal.[16] Bin Laden in his Abbottabad letters sharply criticized the group's tactics and he urged them to carry out social programs to assist the impoverished population.

Nonplused by the erosion in local and international support, al-Shabaab declared fidelity to al-Qaeda in 2010 and shortly after bin Laden's death Ayman al-Zawahiri gave his blessing to the group's incorporation into al-Qaeda's organizational umbrella. The group's Shura Council is dominated by Arabs and Somali exiles exacerbating its dependence on Salafist doctrine and inviting greater resistance from Sufi Muslim militias who have resisted al-Shabaab.[17] The Somali radicals continue to impose zakat or a tax on the local population and earned until quite recently revenue by protecting Somali pirates.

The range of al-Shabaab offensive capability has expanded beyond Somalia's borders with attacks in Uganda during the 2010 World Cup and in Fall 2013 in Kenya when a small group of terrorists killed over sixty people and wounded hundreds in a Nairobi shopping mall.[18] The bombings were al-Shabaab retaliation for AU support of the FTC government's campaign against Islamic militancy. The group's wider sphere of operations led to fears of an escalation of the conflict and the potential radicalization of Muslim minorities in Kenya, Ethiopia, and Uganda. Local militants no doubt played a key role in the World Cup bombings.

Despite these anxieties reinforced by al-Shabaab's control over South-Central Somalia, the group has suffered many reversals. Al-Shabaab's forces have been driven out of Mogadishu by AU and FTC forces. Recent US strikes have also devastated the movement targeting and killing key leaders. Last year al-Shabaab ceded control over the port city of Kismayo to advancing AU troops losing a major source of revenue that could reduce its offensive capacity. The group had used the port to levy taxes on lucrative charcoal exports to the Middle East and without this revenue the drain of resources may intensify al-Shabaab's taxation of the populace under its control. This is likely to exacerbate local resistance inviting more popular resentment of the group who refused international food aid during the 2011 draught. Because of al-Shabaab's rejection of Western famine relief efforts thousands perished in areas under its control.

The West Point's Combating Terrorism Center's (CTC) 2013 analysis of al-Shabaab recently listed three factors critical in the group declining fortunes. Among these are the effectiveness of Pan-African troops fighting the Islamists, clan disputes within al-Shabaab, and popular revulsion of the terror organizations efforts to impair the delivery of food aid.[19] According to the CTC study there are sharp intragroup divisions over al-Shabaab's *far enemy* strategy and its incorporation into al-Qaeda's global network. The group's dire condition mirrors the experiences of other al-Qaeda branches in Yemen and Algeria.

AQAP

Yemen is the ancestral home of bin Laden and a territorial base for Islamic radicalism. Salafism is firmly imbedded in the country's tribes and radical Islamic discourse resonates among much of the population.[20] Yemenis fought in the international jihadist killing fields of Afghanistan, Bosnia, Chechnya, and Iraq. The country was also the site of previous attacks against American interests including the aborted al-Qaeda operation against the USS Sullivan in 1999 and the networks successful 2000 bombing of the USS Cole.

AQAP's growth in Yemen can be traced to the Saudi government's 2003 crackdown on al-Qaeda operatives.[21] Saudi security services' repression of the al-Qaeda network was in retaliation for al-Qaeda's attacks against foreign workers' complexes and oil facilities. Al-Qaeda attacks during this period killed many Saudis reducing the network's popular standing in the Kingdom. Al-Qaeda had hoped to attack foreign workers and petroleum complexes to cripple the Kingdom's economy. Using established cross-border smuggling networks, many al-Qaeda agents escaped to Yemen.

Saudi fighters in Yemen have deep roots in the country's troubled past. Bin laden set up camps there to train jihadists to fight South Yemen's Marxist government during the 1994 civil war.[22] Al-Qaeda has been a presence in the country for decades and the network has established alliances with tribes opposed to the central government. These connections played a pivotal role in the recruitment of fighters for the Iraqi jihad and their incorporation into AQI ranks.[23]

Convulsed by southern and northern secessionist movements, Yemen has witnessed many civil wars. Despite the country's 1994 unification, Yemen remains the quintessential failed state with multiple insurrections that include a Shi'ite northern insurgency, revolts by antigovernment tribes, and southerners clamoring for independence. Al-Qaeda's has alternated in its support for these insurrections hoping to maximize its strategic position.[24] Given the upsurge in sectarian passions in the region animated by the legacy of the 2003 Iraq war and current Syrian civil war AQAP is assisting local tribes fighting Shi'ite secessionist in the northern areas.

Lawlessness pervades Yemen and the central government's recent amnesty of Islamist fighters only exacerbates the country's dire security situation. AQAP ranks were dramatically increased by a 2006 jailbreak in which many al-Qaeda agents escaped.[25] Some tribes support al-Qaeda in remote parts of Yemen. AQAP has successfully imbedded some of its leaders in Yemen's tribal structure supporting northern Sunni tribes against Shia rebels and assisting groups fighting the central government. AQAP has not repeated the failures of AQI and al-Shabaab and they have firmly imbedded foreign fighters into the country's native insurgent movement.[26]

AQAP's internationalist agenda includes targeting foreign workers and tourists and it has attacked the Saudi and Yemeni governments for their alliance with Washington's war on terror. The organization's 2009 failed assassination attempt against Saudi crown prince deputy interior minister underscores its dangerous capabilities. The network has made a major effort to recruit foreign jihadists to carry forth its war against the US *far enemy*. Chapter 8 of the book will analyze AQAP's *far enemy* strategy within the terror network's ineffectual efforts to strike the US homeland.

Born in New Mexico the late jihadist cleric Anwar al-Awlaki reportedly met a number of 9/11 attackers at California mosque when they attended some of his sermons. Trained in theological studies he initially condemned the 9/11 attacks but became radicalized by the wars in Afghanistan and Iraq.[27] Awlaki traveled to Yemen in 2005 preaching the cause of radical jihad.

Awlaki's fame in jihadist circles was abetted by his creation of an English language e-magazine *Inspire* and his encouragement of plots and attacks against America. His cyber jihadist exploits include internet communiques with American Palestinian Major Nidal Malek Hassan who Awlaki encouraged to kill 13 fellow American soldiers at Fort Hood in 2009. Despite knowledge of his radical views and support for jihad, the Army consistently promoted Major Hassan and his commanding officers ignored warnings about his jihadist sympathies. Radicalized by his deepening AQAP contacts and facing deployment to Afghanistan, Major Hassan carried out his personal form of jihad. Crippled by police bullets after his shooting, he has been found guilty by a military tribunal and been sentenced to death.

The Yemeni preacher was also involved in the aborted 2009 Christmas Day airplane bombing by Nigerian believer Farouk Abdulmutallab who met Awlaki in Yemen during his religious studies. He eventually became an AQAP agent. Boarding a plane in Amsterdam that was bound for Detroit, the Nigerian attempted to ignite underwear clad explosives over American airspace but was stopped by a fellow passenger and by members of the flight crew. The Nigerian has pled guilty to terrorism charges and is currently serving a life sentence in federal maximum security facility. Awlaki and AQAP were also involved in a 2010 US bound cargo jet bombing effort foiled by British and Saudi intelligence. The group's bomb-making expert Ibrahim al-Asiri continues to experiment with explosive designs capable of evading airport security.

By 2010 Awlaki's AQAP activities were considered the network's most dangerous threat to the American homeland. After a number of failed CIA assassination attempts, his 2011 killing in a Predator drone strike was a blow to AQAP's international operations. In the air strike Awlaki, his son, and his e-magazine editor Yemeni-American Samir Khan were killed. Given their status as US citizens there assassinations remain controversial among legal experts and critics of the drone program. Whether AQAP can recover its international capability after his death is actively debated. Recently American and Saudi intelligence operatives were able to penetrate AQAP with a double agent who was able to disclose key figures in the organization laying the basis for drone strikes that have killed key operatives.

AQAP additionally has many internal enemies. Its warfare against the Shia rebels and progovernment tribes leave it in a vulnerable position inviting inevitable retaliation. Even its alliances with existing tribes can be undone by state bribes and coercion. Despite its efforts to attack the US homeland bin Laden was disappointed with al-Qaeda's Yemeni external operations and its media outreach programs.

The 2010 insurrection against President Saleh's 33-year rule has, however, given AQAP a strategic opening.[28] The power vacuum created by Saleh's abdication allows an AQAP a sanctuary in towns governed by supporting tribal warlords. The Obama Administration has supported Saleh's successor government dominated by former regime officials who remain committed to fight Islamic extremism. Political divisions and rivalries within the post-Saleh government have complicated antiterror efforts and effective cooperation.

Denying AQAP a sanctuary is an Obama Administration priority. Failure to achieve this objective could give the network a larger sphere of operations to attack Western interests. Destroying the AQAP network is especially critical given al-Zawahiri's August 2013 elevation of AQAP emir Nasir al-Wuhayshi as general manager of al-Qaeda whose duties involve coordination of policy between al-Qaeda Central and its diverse affiliates. Some reports indicate that

AQAP has terror training camps in the coastal Abiyan Province and in remote mountainous places in the country.[29] Anxiety over state collapse in the Maghreb and the Sahel has also invited concerns that these regions may be ripe for the development of terror sanctuaries.

AQIM

Arabs veterans of the Afghan campaign against Soviet forces were pivotal in the rise of al-Shabaab and AQAP as they have contributed to jihadist development in the Maghreb.[30] This is especially true of the Algerians who had been in the forefront in the Bosnian, Chechen, and Kashmir campaigns as well being active in native insurgencies. The Arab-Afghan supporters of the GIA (Islamic Combat Groups) were prominently featured in the bloody Algerian civil war in the 1990s.[31]

In the Maghreb a number of Islamist organizations had gained political ascendance in the 1980s, most notably the Algerian Islamic National Front (FIS) that won municipal elections and swept the country's parliamentary elections in 1990. Fearing that the FIS would impose an Iranian type state, the military seized power.

The Islamists in retaliation mounted a brutal guerrilla and terror campaign against Algiers. Due to their training and combat experience the Arab Afghans who formed the GIA emerged as the most dominant insurgent group. Driven by brutal nihilistic rage and takfir doctrine they considered all opponents *apostates*; the GIA beheaded their enemies and destroyed entire villages.[32] Hundreds of thousands of Algerians died during the Islamist rebellion and the government's equally brutal counterinsurgency campaign.

Supported by radical Islamist elements in Algerian Diaspora communities in Europe, the networks attacked France for its support of the Algerian governments.[33] The war spread to France with a 1994 Air France hijacking in Algiers and a 1995 Paris Metro attack that killed six people. French intelligence officials believed that the Air France hijackers hoped to crash the plane into the Eiffel Tower. The flight, however, was diverted to Marseilles for refueling where French security forces successful stormed the plane killing the hijackers. The Paris Metro bombing would be ominous presentment of the Madrid train attacks and the London subway bombings many years later.

The GIA's barbaric tactics soon backfired. Their popular support evaporated and this contributed to the fragmentation of the movement with some factions entering into a dialogue with the regime, while others continued the fight against Algiers.[34] The GSPC formed from reformist wing of the GIA redefined the insurgency by targeting only government personnel. The group's ties to al-Qaeda would strengthen its international agenda playing a role in the ongoing war against the Western nemesis.

Algerians fighters were also pivotal in the Iraqi Jihad with the GSPC recruiting many fighters. GSPC emir Abdelmalek Droukdel and AQI leader Abu Musab Zarqawi's close partnership culminated in the sending of hundreds of jihadists to fight US forces in Iraq. Swelling the ranks of suicide bombers Algerians made a substantial contribution to AQI's foreign fighter operations.

The drain of rank and file jihadists to Iraq, however, weakened GSPC operations against the Algerian state. The government's counterterror operations and amnesty agreements weakened the Islamist insurgency.[35] GSPC consequently moved many of its operations to the Sahel where it has greater freedom of action. Aided by tribal alliances GSPC began to target Westerners working in the Sahel through kidnapping operations.

Recognizing the utility of an Algerian terror network capable of operating in the Sahel, the Maghreb, and Europe, al-Qaeda formed a 2006 alliance with GSPC. This association culminated in AQIM's creation in 2006 which resulted in rapid increase in attacks against government and Western targets.[36] AQIM 2007 attacks against the Constitutional Court and UN complex in Algiers resulted in a government renewed crackdown accelerating its redeployment to the Sahel.

After these high-profile attacks Western policy makers reacted with France taking the lead in security operations against AQIM's network in retaliation for the group's kidnapping of French nationals visiting or working in the region. In addition, the US inspired Trans Sahara Counter Terrorism Partnership is designed to coordinate antiterror measures among states in the Maghreb and the Sahel.[37]

Despite AQIM's early promise and its ample revenue due to kidnapping and smuggling operations the groups has failed to seriously compromise the security situation in the Maghreb. Confined to remote areas of the North Eastern Mountains of Algeria with the bulk of its operatives in the impoverished Sahel the group is highly factionalized and its criminal operations have degraded its jihadist credentials.[38]

The contrast between AQIM's aspirations and its attack record is striking. Numerous threats of war against colonial France have resulted only in kidnappings and killing of hostages. AQIM calls for the reconquest of Al Andaluz have failed to culminate in attacks on the Spanish mainland or in assaults against Spain's North African territories, Melilla and Ceuta.

AQIM has been given a boost by the Qaddafi regime's 2011 overthrow. The postwar chaos, the presence of Islamist militias, and an uncontrolled arms market offer some succor for the movement's revitalization.[39] Among the unintended consequences of NATO 2011 air campaign that assisted the rebel's successful revolt against Qaddafi is the empowering of AQIM affiliates operating in Libya and Mali.

NATO's 2011 war against Qaddafi's regime must be placed into a historic context. Libya has seen past-Islamist revolts. Libyan jihadists mounted a challenge to Qaddafi's regime in the 1990s and they were brutally defeated. Thousands of militants of the Libyan Islamic Fighting Group (LIFG) were killed or imprisoned by Qaddafi's regime during the revolt. Qaddafi's opening to the West following the 2003 Iraq war led to a latter amnesty of LIFG prisoners. Libyans, additionally, have played important roles in jihads in Afghanistan, Bosnia, Chechnya, and Iraq.

Not surprisingly Eastern Libya has seen a rise in Islamic militancy with the emergence of groups like Ansar al Sharia who stormed the US consulate on September 11, 2012 in Benghazi killing four Americans including the US Ambassador Christopher Stevens. Ansar al Sharia is rumored to be an AQIM affiliate and has established to substantial power base in the Eastern Libya. Like many of the hundreds of heavily armed militias that freely roam the country, Ansar al Sharia's activities complicate the central government's efforts to centralize power in post-Qaddafi democratic Libya. So far the government has failed to disarm these groups and its plans to incorporate militias into the national army are in disarray.

While the Benghazi attack is still under investigation, it created a political firestorm in Washington given the consulate's many communiques requesting additional security and the failure of the Administration to heed them. The State Department's failure to bolster the consulate's defenses left it vulnerable to militant attacks. The Department's Advisory Review Board in a December 2012 report indicates that there was a systemic failure to protect the consulate that was heavily dependent on lightly armed local police and militias.[40] At the time of the attack, the consulate had only five embassy security personnel that were forced to battle dozens of heavily armed militants. Significantly none of the attackers have been arrested by Libyan officials. The US government promises to bring them to justice. So far it has failed to do so.

The political situation in Libya is volatile. Democratic elections in 2012 brought a non-Islamist government to power that has failed to reign in the militias. Islamic militants in the East demand the imposition of Sharia and armed conflict with the new government in Tripoli is likely. Fighting between militias has intensified and groups like Ansar al Sharia and the Sheik Abdul Rachman Brigade have expressed solidarity with al-Qaeda.

AQIM's prospects for revitalization in Libya are complicated by the hundreds of militias that compete for power in the turbulent post-Qaddafi transition period. Given the fragmentation of Islamist forces, power struggles between contending factions are inevitable. Past-Islamist insurgencies in Egypt and Algeria have been damaged by group divisions and conflicts. This pattern is likely to resurface in Libya and limit al-Qaeda's potential scope for action.

AQIM's development of a Libyan terror infrastructure is also compromised by Tripoli's pro-Western government and the absence of an existing state patron. America's recent agreement with Niger to install a Predator drone base creates the potential for attacks against Libyan Islamists. The network's future may lie in neighboring Mali where the implosion of central authority in the northern part of the country and a Tuareg insurgency offer enhanced opportunities for regeneration. AQIM's Sahel network and its alliance with Tuareg national liberation and Islamist groups are explored in the next chapter.

Conclusion

AQIM, al-Shabaab, and AQAP have progressed from association with to formal integration into al-Qaeda. More organizationally symbolic than substantive, al-Qaeda franchises in Yemen, Somalia, and the Maghreb loosely coordinate their activities with al-Qaeda Central and these groups are largely autonomous.[41] The most advanced relationship has occurred between al-Shabaab and AQAP where the Yemenis and Saudis have played an important role in the East African terror networks' organizational growth and tactics.[42] AQIM moreover hopes to reinforce ties with West African jihadists in Mali and Nigeria.

Before his 2011 death, bin Laden lamented the performance of insurgents and affiliates tied to his organization. OBL believed that they were not pursuing his *far enemy* strategy and that they were preoccupied near enemy apostates. AQAP, al-Shabaab, and AQIM leaders were chastised by bin Laden for their human rights violations and sectarian agendas. The Saudi leader wanted to centralize their media operations and oversee the development of his franchises terror strategy. He urged al-Shabaab to create social welfare programs to win back the population.

These networks continue to be hunted by internal and external enemies that impair their operational capability. Al-Shabaab, AQAP, and AQIM operate in failing states whose criminal activity, instability, and supporting tribes offers some hope of survival. The dependence on crime, however, is highly problematic and it has contributed to their delegitimization.

Harassed by security services and threatened by US Predator drone strikes, these organizations do not have the luxury that historic al-Qaeda enjoyed in the 1990s Afghanistan and the Sudan. The reverses these networks have experienced have been exacerbated by their tendency toward factionalism and intragroup competition.

Al-Shabaab and AQIM face declining popularity due to their extremist excesses and the inability of their Salafi ideas to gain support among the populations they rule. Yemen offers AQAP some reprieve as security forces become more fragmented and weaker. There may be some short-term strategic opening created by regime change and instability in Libya. Groups like Ansar al Sharia may partner with al-Qaeda to attack local Western interests. AQIM has recently made significant advances in West Africa where tribalism, poverty, and Islamist radicalism offer a fertile recruitment base for jihad.

7

West Africa: The Latest Jihadist War

One of the wrong policies we think you carried out is the extreme speed with which you applied Sharia, not taking into consideration the gradual evolution that should be applied in a area ignorant of religion, and a people which hasn't applied Sharia in centuries. And our previous experience proved that applying Sharia in this way, without taking the environment into consideration will lead people rejecting the religion, and engender hatred toward the Mujahidin, and will consequently lead to failure of our experiment.

Emir Abdelmalek Droukdel[1]

Introduction

The post-9/11 dispersion of the jihadist movement continues to branch out into new territories. Harassed by Western and local security services, Al-Qaeda seeks affiliation with other jihadist movements to reinvigorate its offensive capability. West Africa, in particular, has seen a substantial rise in local Islamic militancy that has attracted al-Qaeda's attention. Such a development facilitates al-Qaeda's goal of deeper penetration into Africa to combat *Christian crusaders* and mount offensive operations against Western interests.

AQIM is moving many of its operations into West Africa and has supported many native jihadist groups.[2] Displaced from most of Algeria by government forces, AQIM Sahelian *katibas* have provided training and arms to the Nigerian BH and the Malian-Tuareg AD. Formerly part of AQIM, the transethnic Group Movement for Unity of Jihad in West Africa (MUJWA) is also part of this jihadist confederation. Some experts predict West Africa will be a major front in the "war on terror" for years to come.[3]

Such a development is surprising. While West Africa has experienced severe Muslim-Christian violence, it has never historically had a strong jihadist movement. West Africa is dominated by Sufi Islam noted for its ideological moderation and religious tolerance.

Recent political, religious, and economic forces, however, have changed the region's religious complexion. While ridding the world of Qaddafi, the Libyan war has had unintended and dangerous consequences. Among these are the expatriation to Mali of ex-Qaddafi African mercenaries and an intensification of the flow of surplus arms to Tuareg rebels and their Islamist allies. Both have conjoined to foster a rebellion in Mali.

Assisted by radical Islamist forces, the January 2012 Tuareg rebellion resulted in northern Mali falling under the control of al-Qaeda affiliates for close to a year. Islamist forces in April 2012 declared an independent Tuareg Islamic state of *Azawad* and by late summer they consolidated their power base.

Since 2009 Nigeria has experienced a determined Islamist terror campaign to break the North's ties with the central government.[4] BH, AD (Defenders of the Faith), and MUJWA have combined jihad with ethnic-tribal secessionism. The Salafi-jihadist movement has adopted West African separatist causes exploiting tribal grievances as a means to achieve a trans-Islamic state.[5] This potent combination threatens to explode across a region seething with sectarian and ethnic tensions.

BH and AD desire independent Islamic states that rigidly apply Sharia law. The Malian Islamists briefly achieved their goal by forming the Tuareg Islamic state of Azawad. AD, MUJWA, and other Salafi-jihadist groups retained control of the area from March 2012 to January 2013. Their ill-fated January invasion of the South triggered a French and West African military intervention ending their sanctuary and freeing populations that had been brutally suppressed by Islamist rule.

Despite its rapid growth, the West African jihadist movement currently does not threaten vital Western interests.[6] Its attacks against the West have been aimed at kidnapping of Europeans for ransom money and assaults on UN complexes. The Islamists have attacked mainly against local enemies and they seem driven by desires to achieve pure Islamic state. This fixation on fighting the *near enemy* some argue may change.[7]

BH and AD have good relations with AQIM.[8] Some of their members have received al-Qaeda training in IED fabrication and terror operations. BH's terror campaign has al-Qaeda trademarks complete with suicide and IED attacks.

Like AQI, BH and AD combine a viscous sectarian agenda with a penchant for ideological fanaticism.

Other West African groups are even better connected to al-Qaeda. MUJWA was part of the AQIM umbrella breaking away in 2011 to chart a struggle exclusively in the Sahel. The movement's goal is a West African caliphate with Mali being the foundation for a series of revolution across the region. AQIM, AD, and MUJWA were dominant in the northern Mali and had consolidated their grip on power by displacing moderate Tuareg rebels.

AD and MUJWA adopted the Tuareg independence movement hoping to transform what began as a local ethnic rebellion into a Taliban-like state. Their seizure of northern Mali, their subsequent displacement of the moderate Movement for the National Liberation of Azawad (MNLA), and their draconian imposition of Sharia law add credence to this theory.[9] What started as a Tuareg independence struggle became an opportunity for an al-Qaeda sanctuary that was ended by France's 2013 military intervention.

Events in Nigeria are almost as ominous. BH has killed over a thousand people in the past two years. The group has attacked police stations, beer halls, government buildings, and churches. The Islamists have mounted a fierce campaign against the government, killed many Muslim leaders, and attacked the Christian minority without mercy. The group has called for all Christians to leave northern Nigeria and their militants have targeted non-Salafi Muslims and BH critics.

With its endemic ethno-religious conflicts, weak states, and dilapidated economic base, West Africa is ideal recruitment area for al-Qaeda.[10] This is especially true with the rise of regional Salafist movements some of whom are committed to jihad. Fundamentalism in the region has resulted in the persecution of Christian and Sufi groups. BH and AD have endorsed a brutal agenda of ethnic cleansing. The French military intervention in February has succeeded in recovering much of northern Mali from Islamist forces and has spared the local population from further depredation. AQIM and its allies will undoubtedly wage a determined guerrilla campaign and Malian security will continue to be jeopardized by their operations.

AQIM and its allies' desecration of Sufi shrines in Timbuktu, the amputations of criminal's limbs, and the stoning of unmarried couples were eerily reminiscent of the Afghan Taliban. BH's fanatical violence, its exploitation of sectarian grievances, and its exaltation of Salafist Islam threaten to unhinge the integrity of the Nigerian state. This chapter discusses BH, AD, and MUJWA whom have aligned with al-Qaeda's Maghreb branch. It concludes with an evaluation of the regions importance in the *war on terror* and assesses al-Qaeda's jihadist capability in West Africa.

Boko Haram

Nigeria is plagued by ethno-religious violence that is a legacy of the British colonial experience. With its borders drawn for administrative convenience, imperial authorities had little concern for tribal homogeneity. Nigeria is home to hundreds of ethnic groups with long-standing political and religious animosities. Postcolonial internecine violence between Christians and Muslims has been a problem killing tens of thousands. So too has tribalism. Efforts to break away from the central government in Lagos have been brutally suppressed. The murder of 1 million Ibos in 1971 is but one of the more terrifying episodes in the country's modern era.

BH's extreme violence must be understood within this context.[11] Divided by an impoverished Muslim North and a relatively prosperous Christian South, Nigeria is a land of stark contrasts and disparities. These differences are aggravated by an autonomous northern culture where Islamic education poorly prepares students for the imperatives of modern society.[12]

The progression toward Islamic militancy and separatism has been abetted by Saudi Arabia's patronage of Nigerian clerics steeped in Wahhabi fundamentalism. Many of the Islamic rebellion movements that have convulsed Nigeria from the Maitatsine of the 1980s to today's BH have featured leaders trained in Saudi fundamentalism. Many northern Nigerians have positive attitudes on al-Qaeda with as much a third of the population expressing support for bin Laden's organization.[13]

Islamic school graduates trained in theological studies and Koranic recitation are resistant to Western culture and many lack skills to acquire employment. These *almejeri* form the cadres of BH and represent a lost generation committed to Islamist radicalism and violence.[14] The education system is but one example of a northern religious culture impervious to assimilation.

Nigeria's federal structure, furthermore, has empowered local elites to resist central state direction. Since 1999, 12 northern states have adopted Sharia law reinforcing the fundamentalist drift in the past decade. Dependent upon central government largesse and corrupt ion, the North's political elite has failed to address long-standing economic problems.

The economic laggardness of northern states which average 70 percent youth unemployment rates has exacerbated religious tensions.[15] Much of the population lives on less than a dollar a day. The litany of problems hardly ends there and includes endemic corruption, bad governance, brutal security services, extrajudicial killing, rampant crime, and an unbalanced national economy where oil wealth is concentrated in the Niger Delta and the South.

BH's origins have often been traced to the Maitatsine movement.[16] Started by Charismatic preacher Muhammad Marwa, the group initially adopted a Kanuri tribal agenda and made moderate demands on the government. As the movement grew, its agenda became more radical and trans-Islamic. In the 1970s, Marwa created a mass populist movement that extolled Salafi fundamentalism and Islamic millenarianism. Trained in Saudi Arabian Wahhabi fundamentalism, Marwa railed against Western values and advocated northern Muslim separatism. His impassioned and at times scatological speeches attracted many followers.

Marwa's demands for pure Islamic state, his provocations against the northern Muslim political elite and his attacks against federal institutions were often ignored by local authorities. His followers (mostly unemployed young men) numbered tens of thousands and Marwa was able to establish a power base in Maiduguri and other northern cities.

By December 1980, Marwa created a populist insurgency committed to attacks against police stations and state institutions. Ordered by the federal government to disband, Marwa and his followers revolted. The Nigerian army intervened and in 11 days of fighting some 4,000 people perished and hundreds of villages were destroyed.

The Maitatsine revolt was crushed by the army and its leader was killed. While many of the movement's followers disbanded they never gave up his call for Islamic rebellion and many were driven to avenge their fallen leader. Continued Christian-Muslim violence throughout the 1990s and the festering economic problems of the North created a conducive environment for the resurgence of an Islamic separatist movement.[17]

Formed in 2002 by preacher Muhammad Yusuf, BH is a virulent extension of the Maitatsine. Yusuf's populist rants, his Salafi ideology, and his attacks against traditional elites initially failed to elicit a firm response from authorities. Only late in the movements maturation did the state respond.

An admirer of the Taliban, Yusuf created a small fundamentalist rural outpost known for its drastic imposition of Islamic law. Billed "little Afghanistan" this area aroused considerable controversy.[18] Starting in rural Kanamma, Yusuf created a mass movement composed of unemployed graduates of Islamic schools and his movement spread to many northern states and cities. By 2008–9 Maiduguri and Kano were major areas of BH support and traditional Muslim elites and Christian minorities began to feel the brunt of the movement's violent wrath.

Roughly translated, BH combines Hausa and Arabic words meaning "Western education is forbidden." Central to the group's ideology is its rejection of Western civilization of which public schools are a very potent symbol. BH militants also chafe at traditional Muslim elites whose imposition of Sharia law in 12 northern states fails to meet their standard of Islamic purity.

The movement's solution to northern Nigeria's problems entail a return to traditional Islam and a separate state cleansed of Christian influence and minorities. BH's fanatical ideological imperatives drove into violent confrontation with the regional authorities. BH's assaults against police stations and federal buildings and the group's assassination of Muslim politicians opposed to its agenda inspired government repression.[19]

The state's brutal response resulted in a deadly spiral of violence that lead to a police raid against a suspected BH bomb-making facility. BH responded to the arrest of members of its explosives fabrication unit in late July 2009 by mounting a general insurrection. The revolt lasted for 4 days spreading to 6 Nigerian states and resulted in the death of over 1,400 people.

Arrested by police in a chicken coup farm owned by his father-in-law, Yusuf died under police custody. The government's subsequent judicial inquiry called Yusuf's death an extrajudicial killing.[20] With its historic leader dead and its members scattered, BH's secondary leadership fled to Chad and Niger.

BH's remaining leaders made contact with AQIM in exile and received bomb making and terrorist training.[21] AQIM leader Droukdel in a June 2010 message pledged arms and training to BH in its war against *Christian crusaders* making good on al-Qaeda's intent to achieve greater strategic depth in Africa.[22]

Reorganized by BH's current leader Abubakar bin Muhammad Shekau, the group has come raging back.[23] Thought killed in the 2009 violence, Shekau gave the group a greater international focus, sectarian edge, and jihadist orientation. His stewardship of the BH fortified by AQIM's black African militants has unleashed an ultraviolent terror campaign that departs considerably from past assaults.

The group's violence has resulted in over a thousand deaths. Police stations, army barracks, government buildings, shopping complexes, churches, beer halls, and political officials have been targeted. Among BH's most notable attacks have been the following:

- a prison assault in September 2010 freeing over a hundred BH members
- seven IED attacks in Jos during Christmas Eve 2010 celebrations killing seventy Christian worshipers
- bombings of polling places to protest the April 2011 elections resulting in reelection of Christian President Goodluck Jonathan
- the use of suicide bomber destroying a UN building in August 2011 in Abuja killing 23 people
- coordinated attacks on police barracks in November 2011 in Damaturu and Potiskum killing hundreds
- Christmas Day bombings in 2011 in Abuja killing 42 worshippers
- attacks in Kano in January 2012 against police stations and federal buildings killing 185 people.[24]

BH attacks have included IEDs, vehicle born bombs driven by suicidal jihadists, and a more sophisticated arsenal capable of multiple, simultaneous attacks that are the hallmark of al-Qaeda affiliates. The attack against the UN complex in Abuja is considered by some experts as a turning point in the organization's strategy suggesting a more internationalist posture.[25] BH websites promise to take the jihadist war to the Western *far enemy* that so far has been limited to taking Westerners hostage.

BH's call for Christians to vacate the North, its brutal sectarian attacks, and fixation on Taliban rule is sadly reminiscent of Zarqawi's al-Qaeda legacy in Iraq. Similarly, BH has targeted Muslim critics killing moderate clerics, civic leaders, and politicians.

Federal and local officials have responded to the BH assaults by vigorously arresting and killing large numbers of BH militants. The Jonathan Administration has declared a state of emergency in 15 states affected by the group's violent campaign. The army has assisted police in the fight against the group. Recently the government has offered an amnesty program for repentant members who put down their arms. It is unlikely that most of BH's militancy will be swayed by such pacifying measures.

The year 2012 in northern Nigeria was especially bloody with a reported 2,600 people killed in violence between BH and security forces.[26] Islamist fanaticism has resulted in both severe government repression and the fracturing of the jihadist movement repeating patterns found in Algeria and Mali. The emergence of Ansaru a BH jihadist splinter group in January 2012 committed to a regional caliphate and a *far enemy* strategy complicates Nigeria's security environment. Ansaru broke from BH's ranks because of the group's indiscriminate killing of Muslims. The group has kidnapped dozens of Westerners working in Nigeria and has killed a number of them when Nigerian or French forces have attempted to rescue the hostages.

Ansaru reportedly has a strong relationship with AQIM leader Mohktar Belmokhtar whose Sahelian brigade has earned millions in ransom money.[27] The group's website promised to take its jihad to the West. BH rejects hostage taking as a legitimate form of struggle and has a competitive tense relationship. This fracturing of the Nigerian jihadist movement repeats patterns seen elsewhere in Algeria, Egypt, and Mali where internecine leadership and strategy conflicts splinter organizational unity. Lagos may be able to exploit these divisions in its counterterror policy.

At present it is unclear if the central government's repressive policies will have a demonstrative effect in the near future. There is, however, some recent evidence that BH's terror campaign is less popular among Muslims and the organization is financially strained employing fewer suicide bombers, more machete attacks, and primitive explosive devices.[28] This may reflect government efforts to deplete the BH's financial support base by investigating and prosecuting charities and mosques affiliated with the terror network.

Despite these hopeful signs, terror driven insurgencies typically endure for over a decade before counterinsurgency measures succeed.[29] Algeria went through a bloody civil war before the Islamists were driven to the Sahel where they continue to battle against Algerian security forces. What is clear, however, is that the Nigerian state is strong enough to deny BH, Ansaru, and its AQIM supporters a terror safe haven in the North. This may not be true elsewhere in West Africa.

West Africa's Afghanistan: Northern Mali, AD, and the MUJWA

Al-Qaeda's drive for strategic depth in West Africa has been assisted by calamitous events in Libya and Mali. The Maghreb branch of al-Qaeda has established good relations with Tuareg tribes in the Sahel assisting their smuggling operations and encouraging the Berber peoples resistance against West African governments.[30] Some AQIM leaders have furthered this relationship by marrying Tuareg woman connected to important tribal families.

Spread over Algeria, Mali, Niger, and Libya, the Tuaregs have rebelled on many occasions desiring to create an "Azawad" national homeland. Their last rebellion occurred in the mid-1990s in Mali and was quelled by a Qaddafi brokered peace agreement.[31] The self-proclaimed Libyan "King of African Kings" reinforced his military capability by forming Tuareg militias, providing employment for thousands of impoverished young men.

These mercenaries were used by Qaddafi to combat the Libyan Spring 2011 revolt that eventually received armed Western support. Faced with NATO airstrikes and hostile Libyan rebels, thousands of heavily armed pro-Qaddafi Tuareg mercenaries streamed across the Libya's border into Mali.

The flow of arms and tribal fighters into northern Mali altered the balance of power igniting a Tuareg revolt. The Movement for the National Liberation of Azawad (MNLA) rebel force joined with Islamist AD and its allies and made substantial progress against government forces.

A March 2012 military coup in Bamako by rogue Malian army officers overthrew the civilian government and created a northern power vacuum.[32] With the dissolution of army units in the North, the Tuareg rebels and their Islamist partners marched into Kindal, Goa, and Timbuktu. By April, the rebels had announced an independent Islamic Tuareg state.

Fighting quickly erupted between MNLA and its Islamist allies. AD and MUJWA dislodged moderate Tuareg rebels consolidating Islamist control over the northern part of the country. Described as a "jihadist condominium" by Spanish terror expert Fernando Reinares, AQIM, AD, and MUJWA consummated a power sharing arrangement aimed at creating a jihadist training sanctuary and a pure Sharia state.[33]

Such a jihadist confederation is extraordinary. AQIM and MUJWA have had conflicts over past policy. Formed in 2011, MUJWA was part of AQIM breaking from the organization to chart a purely West African path of jihad.[34] The group's leadership is predominately Mauritanian brandishing an ideology that combines West African nationalism with jihadist fanaticism.[35] Some observers have argued that racial tensions between the black African MUJWA and the Algerian dominated AQIM forced the separation, while some others claim the division was over leadership and strategy issues.

AD is a Tuareg dominated Islamist militia led by Iyad Ag Ghali who had played an important role in past ethnic revolts. Known as Defenders of the Faith, AD forged a relationship with MNLA in January 2012 and brokered the AQIM-MUJWA reconciliation. By most accounts, AD was the dominant faction in the jihadist grouping.[36]

Al-Qaeda, moreover, has historically played a role in the region. AQIM's relationship with Tuareg tribes is based on partitioning lucrative smuggling routes. With its Tuareg roots AD's role within the rebel movement, furthermore, catalyzed revolutionary unity. The AD and MNLA alliance, however, did not last. By late April 2012 the Islamists violently displaced the MNLA transforming a separatist revolt into a quest for new West African Afghanistan. AD and MUJWA rapidly secured major northern cities and their forces marched southward relatively unopposed. Salafi-jihadist forces wasted little time erecting a Taliban-like state with a religious police and draconian policies. Dispensing with the mirage of Tuareg independence, AD and its allies desire a trans-Islamic state where Sufi shrines were desecrated, alcohol users were whipped, and unmarried couples were stoned. Thieves had their limbs amputated without medical supervision, instruction in biology was forbidden, and the population was brutally subjugated.

Clearly in a supporting role, AQIM had only few hundred men in northern Mali.[37] Under AD protection, it established terror camps and intensified recruitment efforts. AQIM's websites promise a new jihadist war against *Christian crusaders*. The al-Qaeda affiliate's criminal activities result in millions of dollars obtained in Western hostage money to give it considerable financial means. The flow of heavy arms (including thousands of shoulder fired missiles) into North Mali congeals nicely with Islamist efforts to fend off competitors.

During its brief sanctuary jihadist rule in the region was widely unpopular. The Islamists destruction of Sufi burial sites and mosques additionally engendered the international community's opprobrium. The jihadist's brutal application of Sharia ignited local protests as many chafed under Talibanesque rule. Many others fled to more secure regions in the South.

The AD-AQIM and MUJWA dominance over North Mali created countervailing international, national, and regional efforts. The March 2012 military junta in Bamako was short lived. Faced with the threat of international sanctions by the United Nations, rebellious army officers agreed to step down from power in April, allowing for a new civilian transitional government in Bamako and democratic elections.

Civilian rule in Bamako was fortified by regional and European efforts. The ECOWAS was readying a 3,000 man Pan-African army to mount an invasion of the North. Given its status a former colonial overseer the French spearheaded efforts to train this military force and provide it logistical support.

Not content with their northern sanctuary, jihadist forces in early 2003 moved toward the South. Al-Qaeda militant's southern offensive, however, changed the international community's strategy and the timetable for intervention. Fear that a Salafi-jihadist dominated state could spread jihad southward were vindicated by Islamist incursions into central Malian territory. By early January 2013 Islamist forces were marching against the capital. Panicked Mali's interim president called for immediate French assistance. Faced with the logistical problems of preparing a Pan-African force that would not be ready until fall 2013, France militarily intervened to insure the safety of the Malian state and protect its expatriate population.

France's Operation Serval involved major air strikes against main rebel positions in the North followed by a ground campaign aimed at securing towns around major highways in North Central Mali. By late January 2013 Islamist bastions of Gao, Kindal, and Timbuktu fell before the Franco-African troops who encountered scarce resistance. Fears that the Islamists would use shoulder fired rockets against French aircraft have not been vindicated. Troops were greeted enthusiastically by the local population that had been brutally suppressed by Islamist rule. Many of al-Qaeda supporters in the liberated North were killed by angry mobs.

The French army forged a path for an assault against AQIM and AD's northern desert and mountainous fiefdoms. By early March 2013, one of AQIM's historic leaders (Abdel Mehid Abou Ziad) had died in the fighting and his brigade were shattered by combined French airstrikes and Chadian ground forces. The Islamists are likely to mount a protracted guerilla war with IED attacks and suicide bombings against the internationally trained Pan-African force. This strategy seeks to emulate al-Shabaab's tactics against AU soldiers.

What is clear is that Islamists overreached and miscalculated. By moving southward they lost their northern sanctuary. Like the Algerian case, Islamists forces fragmented in response to battlefield reverses. Some factions of AD appear willing to negotiate with Bamako; others have promised to continue the quest for a Sharia state. Currently Islamist forces are in complete disarray. They no doubt will launch retaliatory attacks. Some of these may involve children trained as suicide bombers.

Surprised by the scale of France's military intervention, Islamist forces have been temporarily routed. They hope to regroup in the mountains near the Algerian border. They are unlikely to take back what had been for ten months a genuine terror sanctuary and experiment in extremist Islam. The United States agreement with Niger to host a Predator drone base to assist French and African forces additionally weighs against Islamist resurgence.

The Malian civil war, draconian Islamist rule, and its attendant humanitarian catastrophe require urgent and immediate attention. Close to a million people have been displaced and Mali's neighbors can ill afford the expense of a refugee epidemic. Some fear that withdrawing jihadist forces could spread terror to other African states and possibly threaten the Western homeland.[38]

Assessing West Africa's jihadist capabilities

The rise of BH and AD is a concern for Western governments. AQIM's support for these networks suggests a coalescence of regional jihadist forces. Israeli terror expert Michael Tanchum argues that al-Qaeda wants to unite BH, AD, and East Africa's al-Shabaab in a continental war against Western interests.[39]

While this may be their aspiration, it is unlikely. BH and AD's plans against *Christian crusaders* and the *far Western enemy* have resulted in a struggle waged against local enemies. These formations are largely autonomous movements driven by ideological imperatives to cleanse their societies.[40] Al-Qaeda has limited influence over their future direction.

Created in 2006. AQIM has never attacked the Western homeland. Given the presence of large Algerian Diaspora communities in Europe, the failure to attack "Crusader France" or recover Al Andaluz may reflect AQIM priorities not to disrupt its lucrative European drug routes. The Maghreb network has the most successful and financially profitable criminal operations within the al-Qaeda organization.

The group's taking of Western hostages is an effort to accrue financial resources to combat regional governments. In early January 2013, AQIM aligned groups attacked an Algerian gas complex in Amenas operated by Norwegian and British companies taking hostage of 41 foreign workers and hundreds of Algerians. Orchestrated by an ex-AQIM leader, the hostage takers demanded an end to French military intervention in Mali and the release of hundreds of Islamic militants from Algerian jails. The dozen or so terrorists were distinctly international with some Libyan, Egyptian, Algerian, Canadian, Tunisian, and Malian nationals participating. The Amenas operation was facilitated by Libya's porous borders where Islamic militants easily cross into Algeria.

Algerian security forces assaulted the complex hoping to free the hostages. After 4 days of fighting and 3 military assaults, hundreds escaped, and dozens of terrorists and 38 hostages were killed. Given that hundreds of hostages had been held, the outcome cannot be interpreted as an Islamist victory. BH has followed this tactic by kidnapping a French family vacationing in a park in Chad and in March 2013 killed a number of foreign workers including one Britain that they were holding for ransom.

AQIM's financial avarice and its interests in smuggling and narco-trafficking belie its jihadist credentials.[41] Its main war is against Algeria and Sahelian states. BH and AD hope to transform ethno-tribal conflicts into a trans-Islamic jihadist war against local Christian crusaders and Muslim apostates. Like AQIM they have taken Western hostages to earn money for their movement. Their aim of achieving a pure Islamic state and desire to cleanse society of Western influence harkens back to the origins of Islamist doctrine that fixated on local enemies and grievances.

The Nigerian and Malian Islamists want to legitimize their struggle and gain recruits though their al-Qaeda affiliations. Both AQIM and al-Shabaab are *linked* to al-Qaeda Central but neither has attacked the West. BH and AD have little incentive to attack the United States. Such efforts could result in American retaliation that could jeopardize their rule and utopian plans for Islamic purity. So far they have been content to take Western hostages or attack UN missions and complexes. While the French military intervention in Mali may change this situation their retaliatory capacity seems limited to local operations against Western interests.

This does not mean that these groups are not dangerous. BH and AD pose difficult strategic challenges. Both groups have entered an early ultraviolent stage that may endure for a considerable amount of time. They show little inclination to renounce their jihadist struggle.

Reminiscent of the Algerian Islamic Combat Group (GIA) who contributed to a 1990's civil war that killed hundreds of thousands, BH's bombing of churches and AD's sacking of Sufi shrines reflect an ideological fanaticism that will take years to reverse. As in previous Islamist insurgencies in Algeria and Iraq, their ranks are rising with zealous recruits ready for jihad.

The fight against the jihadists will be difficult. Studies of counterterror/counterinsurgency campaigns estimate such measures take ten or more years to exert a considerable impact.[42] The Algerian government was able to defeat the insurgency through a protracted policy of targeted killing, amnesties, and divide and conquer policies that forced the Islamic militants to the Sahel.[43] Similarly, American counterinsurgency policy in Iraq by 2009 had blunted the Islamist terror campaign by Special Force's strikes and financing Anbar Sunni militias to fight al-Qaeda militants.[44] French and African forces in Mali are likely to face a prolonged guerilla war mostly in AQIM northern mountain safe havens.

Nigeria and Mali will need a comparable strategy where victory is never total. What ultimately will defeat such groups is their own totalitarian impulses and blind adherence to religious purity. Their ideological trajectory forces them to brutalize the local population and indiscriminately kill real and imaginary enemies.

Before French and African troops recovered much of North Mali in March 2013, the Islamists encountered local resistance. Bamako is readying northern non-Tuareg militias to combat AD and its al-Qaeda allies and regional actors like the ECOWAS are with European assistance creating a Pan-African force to stabilize North Mali.

Having evolved from the failed GIA terror campaign in Algeria, AQIM has not learned from past lessons. It continues to adhere to a dysfunctional totalitarian worldview that also impels BH into counterproductive actions. Such mistakes are inevitable for fanatics are oblivious to the ramifications of their actions. The cycle of violence and revenge started by BH and AD should come back to defeat them.

Ironically, AQIM leader Abdelmalek Droukdel presciently advised his forces in Mali to relax their repressive rule in a July 2012 letter found by the Associated Press in Timbuktu. In his missive he admonishes his militants and writes:[45]

> Some of the examples where we feel you were hasty in applying Sharia ... include ... the destruction of the shrines ... and the application of the had (religious punishment) in the case of adultery, in the lashing of people and the use of force to stop things are haram, and the fact that you have prevented women from going out, and prevented children from playing and searched the houses of the population ... so your officials need to control themselves and commit themselves to the guide that we will elaborate here.

Droukdel feared that AQIM's excesses would invariably invite Western military intervention ending the group's safe haven. His militants failed to heed his advice.

Seized by US forces in their raid against his Pakistani compound, bin Laden's Abbottabad letters similarly express dissatisfaction with the errors of his affiliates in Somalia, Yemen, Iraq, and the Maghreb. His correspondence speaks of a diffuse, unwieldy, and dysfunctional al-Qaeda oblivious to the *correct* path to jihad. BH and AD would be well advised to read his letters.

Until his 2011 death bin Laden remained committed to attacking America. He was convinced that American moral rot, weakness, and decay would crumble under al-Qaeda's *vexation* and *exhaustion* strategy. The inability of his organization and its diverse *branches* to repeat its Holy Tuesday success angered and frustrated him. There have been over fifty al-Qaeda inspired or planned attempts to strike at the terror network's incarnate enemy since 9/11, only three of these efforts succeeded in killing Americans on their native soil. Excluding the 2013 Boston bombing that is under investigation, total American fatalities due to al-Qaeda inspired activity and its fanatical quest to strike the US homeland stands at fourteen individuals.

8

Al-Qaeda Plots and Attacks against the United States after 9/11

Al-Qaida concentrates on its external enemy before its internal enemy. Even though the internal enemy is considered to be a greater non-believer, the external enemy is more clearly defined as a non-believer and is more dangerous at this stage of our life. America is the head of the nonbelievers. If God cut it off, the wings [Muslim apostate states] will be weakened.

Osama bin Laden[1]

Bin Laden's far enemy strategy and the doctrine's "durability" within the al-Qaeda's network

Bin Laden's Abbottabad correspondence makes clear his frustration with the inability of his affiliates to attack the United States. Equally deplorable for bin Laden were al-Qaeda branches emphasis on combating fellow Muslims and their wanton sectarian bloodletting. Al-Qaeda's historic leader repeatedly urged them to refocus on attacking American interests across the globe and especially on its national territory.

Bin Laden may have been driven by fear and anxiety about his personal legacy and the viability of his *far enemy* policy. His doctrine of attacking the United States was unique among jihadist groups that had warred unsuccessfully for a generation against Muslim apostate states. It is clear that he was very worried that affiliates were damaging al-Qaeda's reputation in the Muslim world with their use of indiscriminate violence. So anxious was bin Laden that he wanted to centralize media operations within his fragmented organization and make final approval of affiliate operations in the province of al-Qaeda's central hierarchy.

This chapter reviews al-Qaeda's record in sustaining its *far enemy* strategy and the role of affiliates and homegrown terrorists in attacking the US homeland. It begins by examining Bin Laden's emphasis on hitting the United States and then analyzes the role of AQAP, TTP, and homegrown terrorists in the planning and executing the most important attacks and plots against the US homeland. These conspiracies and attacks have failed to hit the United States in a decisive way and most of the attempts on American soil have involved amateurs whose efforts did not even an operational stage.

The majority of these plots were foiled by FBI and police sting operations. "Homegrown" terrorists inspired by radical Islamic ideology were able to attack unarmed civilians in April 2013 during the final leg of the Boston Marathon killing three Americans and wounding hundreds. This is a far cry from 9/11 or Madrid and London attacks. Al-Qaeda's inability to hit the US homeland in a devastating manner represents its greatest singular failure.

Bin Laden's *far enemy* strategy was Sunni Jihadism's last desperate chance for victory. His approach was built upon the mythical foundations of the role of Arab fighters in the Afghan war and their defeat of Soviet forces as well as the purported weakness and decay of the United States. Driven by past failure against the *near enemy*, Bin Laden's doctrine sought to attack the United States and force its military disengagement from the region. It hoped to arouse Muslim passions against America in a campaign of *vexation* and *exhaustion* that al-Qaeda failed to sustain. Within the larger context of jihadist movement, this result is probably not surprising. Al-Qaeda was an outlier among jihadist groups that for a brief period was able to align with associated movements to attack the West.

Bin Laden sought to capitalize on the 9/11 attacks, the Afghan war, and Zarqawi's early successful campaign in Iraq in the successful implementation of its *vexation* and *exhaustion* strategy. Some groups bought into Bin Laden's *far enemy* strategy and the organization was able to use the Indonesian JI and the MICG to attack Western interests in Bali and Madrid. Many groups, moreover, hoped to gain from al-Qaeda's expertise in explosives and training that could be used to attack Muslim apostate regimes. Their adoption of bin Laden's *far enemy* strategy was short lived with most groups reverting to combat against *near enemy* adversaries and the brutalization of sectarian minorities.

Al-Qaeda's approach had notable early victories including attacks in Bali, Istanbul, Madrid, London, and AQI's initial insurgency and terror campaign.

Much al-Qaeda's success was built on Zarqawi's high stakes gamble of stoking a sectarian war in Iraq that almost succeeded. By 2005–6 Iraq was on the brink of collapsing and al-Qaeda seemed poised to establish a terror sanctuary in the Sunni Triangle. Despite its reservations about his networks attacks on the Shia, al-Qaeda's central leadership endorsed the Jordanian's leadership. It would be a decision that they would later regret.

Zarqawi's death and the excesses of his sectarian campaign eventually produced revulsion among the Iraq populace and the Jordanian's efforts to establish an AQI base in Anbar Province by warring against Sunni Tribal Sheiks boomeranged, dividing, and weakening the insurgency. Attacks by Anbar Province's Sons of Iraq militia and US Special Forces greatly hollowed the ranks of AQI. Today AQI's successor ISI has transplanted operations to religiously mixed areas like Kirkuk and Mosul where they hope to capitalize on growing sectarian conflicts in the region. ISI's current leader Abu Bakr al-Baghdadi attempted merger of his group with the Syrian al-Nusra Front. Despite their leadership quarrels, both organizations continue AQI's sectarian strategy that runs counter to bin Laden's *far enemy* policy.

Zarqawi's bloody Iraq campaign did not enhance al-Qaeda's image in the jihadist community. Despite this disastrous legacy, al-Qaeda Central was able to incorporate AQAP in 2009 and al-Shabaab in 2012 due largely to Zawahiri's endorsement. Both integrations may be due to bin Laden's mythic image and leadership that will likely recede in the future. Al-Qaeda Central in Pakistan continues to emphasize its *far enemy* strategy with greatly diminished results and has found that sectarian and *near enemy* concerns more paramount for the network's affiliated branches.

The transcendental utility of attacking the United States

Bin Laden's visceral hatred and contempt for the United States leads him to view an Islamic world that is assaulted by a nefarious Crusader-Zionist conspiracy and betrayed by corrupt Muslim apostate rulers. The psychological value of attacking America he reckoned could shake the Muslim masses from their lethargy. The presence of American troops in Afghanistan and later in Iraq would impel large numbers of jihadists to travel to Dar al Harb to combat, *vex*, and *exhaust* crusader forces. Like the Soviet defeat in Afghanistan, mujahidin victory against the United States he believed was inevitable.

Al-Qaeda accordingly hoped to awake a slumbering ummah and break the strictures of jahiliyya ignorance by tapping into prejudice and mythology. Fortified by their theological rebirth caused by 9/11's aftermath, bin Laden hoped Muslim militants would defeat a morally rotting super power. This anti-American tactic is not new for isolation and hatred of the foreign other as a catalyst for group cohesion is a staple of most totalitarian movements. As Walid Phares notes in *The Coming Revolution*, Pan-Arabist rulers employed the same technique against Jews, Berbers, and other minorities.[2]

Tapping into anti-Americanism has always a refuge for demagogues of various ideological persuasions.[3] Globalization, social inequalities, and resentment have served as convenient canvasses for elite mobilization of enraged masses. Bin Laden's Crusader-Zionist Conspiracy employs much neo-Marxist and fascist rhetoric about capitalist exploitation and Jewish financial control. This strategy combined with selective Koranic interpretations to defend Islamic interests in the post-9/11 war bin Laden hoped would act as a catalytic device to rally a beleaguered, dormant ummah.

The final cornerstone of al-Qaeda's utopian fantasy is its reliance on divine intervention to compensate for missing logical connections. The mystical belief that Islam will be victorious over Satanic forces drives al-Qaeda to attack the United States in the hope of inducing its inevitable capitulation, a goal made difficult after the loss of its operational command and control after the American counterstrike.

Al-Qaeda's diminished offensive capability to compel America's regional disengagement has forced it to cede most offensive capability to affiliates, associates. and homegrown terrorists not completely under central headquarter direction. Frequently this has led to embarrassing failures, missteps, and disappointing results.

Al-Qaeda's difficulties in implementing its post-9/11 far enemy strategy

The loss of al-Qaeda's Taliban protected sanctuary and erosion of direct control over operations has been quite challenging. Given heightened American security after 9/11 hitting the US homeland was an especially vexing. Much of al-Qaeda's cellular network was broken up after the WTC and Pentagon attacks. Other impediments exacerbated this challenge.

The American Muslim community is far more moderate and assimilated than its European counterpart.[4] The population has a unique and distinct profile. Muslim Diaspora communities are dispersed across the United States and the lack of densely clustered populations impedes strong community identities and radicalization. Most American Muslims are fairly prosperous and well educated.

The United States, moreover, has not historically been a base for al-Qaeda aligned terror networks. Unlike France or Spain, the GIA, GSPC, MICG, LIFG have no real network in the country. The dismantling of al-Qaeda's cells in the United States after 9/11 and tighter controls on visa requirements require the selection of candidates that do not fit the typical terrorist profile. Under such circumstances, the recruitment of second generation Muslim Americans, naturalized citizens, and converts is necessary to realize a successful *far enemy* strategy to attack American interests. While the absence of organized networks and extensive community radicalization impair mobilization they do not make homegrown terrorist attacks impossible.

Lorenzo Vidino study of US Jihadism notes that a small subsection of American Muslims are radicalized and al-Qaeda can through internet communication and external support influence them to attack the United States.[5] Radicalized groups and alienated individuals in America include new immigrants, second generation Muslims, and converts. Al-Shabaab's operations, for example, have featured Somali-American suicide bombers who joined the network after abandoning a reasonably comfortable life in Minnesota.[6] Joseph Jay Carafano reports that most of the 50 terrorist conspiracies to hit America since the 9/11 attacks are without substantial al-Qaeda links.[7] Forty-two of these failed conspiracies have involved homegrown Muslim terrorists acting autonomously.

In a 2010, New American Foundation-Syracuse University Maxwell School statistical study of post-9/11 plots and attacks finds most were planned by recent immigrants, ex-prisoners, and converts.[8] A majority of these conspiracies were broken up by police and intelligence efforts that involved amateurs vulnerable to police and FBI sting operations. This underscores some of the dangers of al-Qaeda's reliance on homegrown novices and the critical importance of external training, financial and logistical support.

The most serious attacks and plots against the United States have been commissioned with the help of al-Qaeda affiliates or inspired directly by al-Qaeda Central. Al-Qaeda, AQAP, and TTP networks are committed to attacking the American *far enemy* and have forged relationships with radicalized American citizens and immigrants. Both Fort Hood and the 2009 failed Christmas Day bombing had links to AQAP which has emerged as al-Qaeda's most dependable affiliate. It, however, failed to live up to Bin Laden's expectations with most of its offensive operations waged against Yemeni security forces.

Bin Laden's most "loyal" but "imperfect" branch AQAP and its *far enemy* strategy

The Saudi-Yemeni al-Qaeda branch shares bin Laden's antipathy toward the United States and its strong alliance with the Kingdom's royal family. The *far enemy* strategy has been a persistent theme of AQAP's operations but even here it is a minority current. Some factions within AQAP like Ansar al Shariah, for example, are exclusively devoted to attacking the *near enemy*.[9] While most of AQAP's operations are conducted against the central government and Sana's supporting tribal militias, the network has mounted sustained operations against the American homeland. It is arguably the most dangerous of al-Qaeda's post-9/11 branches and an anomaly within al-Qaeda's organizational umbrella. What accounts for AQAP's distinctiveness among the networks other branches?

Among some salient explanations are its unique profile and its loyalty to bin Laden. Many in AQAP are veterans of the Afghan campaign who served with late leader and continue to revere him. They remain committed to his personality cult and his vision of attacking the heart of the Crusader-Zionist alliance. Driven from Saudi Arabia after the Kingdom's post-2003 crackdown, many militants blame America for strengthening the hated Saudi royal family and exploitation of the country's oil. They desperately want revenge.

The Wahhabi chauvinism and jihadist pretentions of AQAP militants who seek to protect Mecca and Medina from the crusader *onslaught* and are eager to secure the Kingdom from globalization's *cultural pollution* may also account for their visceral hatred for the United States and their preoccupation with the *far enemy* approach. Like many jihadists, AQAP militants and leaders long to luxuriate in the divine radiance of Allah by resurrecting a version of Muhammad's early caliphate. They believe that this can only be done by crippling strikes against America forcing it to jettison its Saudi ally. Denied American military and economic support, the Kingdom they believe would fall to *heroic* mujahidin revolutionaries. Jihadist dreams of genuine Islamic state in the *land of the two sanctuaries* could they reckon be realized.

Saudi extremist juxtaposition of Islamic cultural superiority with Western decadence also accounts for the appeal of attacking the United States. It remains a fundamental motif of al-Qaeda propaganda and one of the foundations of Abu Bakr Naji's *The Management of Savagery*.[10]

The inevitable mujahidin triumph against America and the regional disengagement of US forces via a policy of *vexation* and *exhaustion* is a key theme of AQAP media operations and its English language e-magazine *Inspire*.

Despite its *far enemy* policy, Bin Laden was an AQAP critic who felt the organization had misplaced goals, amateurish propaganda, and a failed strategy at attacking the central government. The historic leader urged them not to declare a Yemeni Islamic state and divert resources away from attacking security forces toward assaulting US interests.[11] His critique of AQAP operations also suggests that he was resentful of the emergence of Yemeni-American cleric Anwar al-Awlaki and the prominence of his English language media operations. Bin Laden refused to recognize the American citizen as AQAP emir believing him too young and untested.

Al-Qaeda's Abbottabad correspondence paints a fractured and divided organization plagued by personality conflicts and rivalries. Bin Laden's reluctance to embrace the American cleric and his criticism of its media operations suggest an element of resentment. Fearing another Zarqawi like public relations disaster, bin Laden kept his distance from his affiliates, their leaders, and refused to recognize any of al-Qaeda's branches in Yemen, Somalia, and the Maghreb. When recognition was forthcoming, it was Ayman al-Zawahiri that gave his blessing to the incorporation of AQIM, AQAP, and al-Shabaab.

Bin Laden's reticence to endorse Awlaki is perplexing given the Yemeni-American's personal fidelity to the *far enemy* strategy. Under Awlaki's leadership AQAP was able to orchestrate two 2009 attacks: one at a Fort Hood Texas military base in November killing over a dozen Americans and one on Christmas Day nearly bringing down a Northwest passenger plane bound for Detroit that could have killed hundreds.[12] Given his emphasis on the *far enemy* approach, bin Laden's reluctance to endorse Awlaki may be attributable to the Yemeni's notoriety and AQAP's designation as its most dangerous branch. By 2010 Awlaki's prominence in the jihadi community frequently eclipsed bin Laden's mythic but diminished status.

AQAP external operations against America have furthermore remained intact after America's killing of bin Laden and Awlaki. The Saudi-Yemeni network's *far enemy* strategy, moreover, has been emulated by al-Qaeda's Pakistani associate

TTP that has attempted to launch attacks in America and Europe.[13] Al-Qaeda's affiliates and associates have had to rely on alienated homegrown terrorists not fully under their operational control; this has frustrated effective implementation of bin Laden's doctrine. Of the more than 50 attempts to strike America a total of 14 Americans have been killed in al-Qaeda's post-9/11 *far enemy* strategy. The most lethal attacks and failed plots, moreover, were under partial al-Qaeda sponsorship. Given al-Qaeda's titanic ambitions, the results of its post-9/11 campaign have been meager.

Externally assisted post-9/11 attacks and conspiracies involving American citizens, immigrants, and foreign agents

The Fort Hood shooting

Major Nidal Malek Hassan shooting rampage killing 13 American servicemen on November 5, 2009 remains al-Qaeda's greatest seminal *achievement* since the 9/11 attacks. As documented in numerous US Army reports Hassan was a deeply conflicted and troubled man with a mediocre performance record.[14] Despite his erratic behavior and overtly jihadist sympathies he was given a medical fellowship and promotions that he did not deserve. Army superiors failed to discipline or demote him despite the many complaints of his psychosis and anti-American views. His tenure as an Army psychiatrist at Walter Reed Medical Center was fraught with controversy with presentations extolling the virtues of jihad and intimations that he could kill fellow servicemen in the performance of religious duties.

Born in Virginia and raised by a Palestinian family Hassan entered the Army in the late 1990s getting a medical degree and serving as Army psychiatrist at Walter Reed Medical Center often counseling veterans who served in Afghanistan and Iraq. His radicalization evolved over time and may have been exacerbated by his work at Walter Reed and troubled personal life. Those who knew him say he was plagued by his inability to find a suitable spouse and that he had difficulty adjusting to the 2001 death of his mother.

During his six-year residency at Walter Reed Medical Center Hassan's extremism increased dramatically as a consequence of the Iraq war. The hospital required doctors to give periodic presentations on medical issues. In some of his power point presentations Hassan openly declared his jihadist sympathies and stated his opposition to the deployment of American troops on Muslim lands.[15] He even intimated that Muslims serving in the US military had a right to kill fellow servicemen in the defense of their Muslim brothers.

When some of colleagues complained of Hassan's behavior, Army commanders either ignored the complaints or defended Hassan's right to articulate unpopular views. Clint Watts notes that Hassan's officer evaluation reports were frequently sanitized and he was promoted despite a mediocre performance record. Fearing cries of anti-Muslim discrimination, Hassan's commanding officers often acted out of political correctness in their dealings with him.[16] It is highly unlikely a white supremacist or black African nationalist would have received such favorable treatment.

Hassan's radicalism was intensified by his contact with AQAP leader Anwar al-Awlaki whose communications with him on jihadi internet forums may have been a final factor in his decision to kill his fellow servicemen. The two men share a long history. Major Hassan had met Awlaki before 9/11 when the Yemeni-American cleric preached at a Virginia mosque. During the final year of his postdoctoral fellowship Hassan had numerous e-mail exchanges with Awlaki who urged him to kill US military personnel. Most of their conversations centered on Muslim obligations to commit jihad and focused on the propriety of killing innocents in defense of the ummah. Hassan's reservations about killing his colleagues were gradually erased by his e-mail chats with the AQAP leader. Awlaki urged Hassan to follow the example of Sergeant Mohammad Hassan Akbar who had killed two of his fellow servicemen in the early stages of the 2003 Iraq war.

These conversations caught the attention of FBI intelligence agents who failed to alert Hassan's superiors and who mistakenly concluded that Hassan's exchanges were a form of scholarly investigation. Major Hassan's "research" would have tragic consequences. Having fulfilled his postdoctoral fellowship Hassan was sent to Fort Hood Texas military base to facilitate his scheduled deployment to Afghanistan. Hassan's erratic behavior and conflicted loyalties were repeatedly discounted by his superiors.

When he arrived at the Texas base Hassan continued to intimate his displeasure at the prospect of being deployed to Afghanistan. Prior to his November 4, 2009 shooting rampage, Major Hassan sold his belongings and when he was outside the base he wore a white robe symbolizing his impending martyrdom. In the early November afternoon Hassan entered a medical facility organized to ready troops for deployment; he sat for a while and steadying his nerves arose screaming *Allah Akbar* and opened fire at every soldier he saw in the facility. Using a subautomatic pistol and several revolvers Hassan fired over 200 rounds, killed 13 comrades, and wounded 30 others.[17] Fort Hood civilian police responded quickly to the incident wounding Hassan and paralyzed him from the waist down. Major Hassan was found guilty by a military tribunal and has been sentenced to death for the Fort Hood shooting.

The Army's failure to expedite Hassan's trial exacerbates past mistakes. The Senate Select Committee on Intelligence Report on the Fort Hood shootings found systematic errors in the way the military dealt with Hassan's case.[18] Given his ample warnings to his superiors, the failure to discipline Hassan was inexcusable. The report also finds that the FBI failed to take appropriate action and underestimated the gravity of the colonel's communications with AQAP leader Anwar al-Awlaki. It was yet another lamentable mistake made by an intelligence community that in the post-9/11 era that continues to make reference to "complex environments" and "unforeseeable consequences" to justify its inaction. It is an apologia that will be repeated after the Fort Hood shooting.

Hassan's "workplace violence" was quickly endorsed and praised by AQAP's media operations. The Fort Hood attack began a concerted but failed campaign by the Saudi-Yemeni branch of al-Qaeda to attack the United States homeland. Two months after the Fort Hood attack, AQAP embarked on an ambitious project to blow up a US passenger jet over America's heartland.

The failed 2009 Christmas Day passenger jet attack

Umar Farouk Abdulmutallab was the highly educated son of a former President of the First Bank of Nigeria. Born to a wealthy family and educated in England, Umar was a devout Muslim who was very much a loner. Like Hassan he was sexually repressed and had no girlfriends. Umar traveled to England to attend London's prestigious University College eventually receiving a degree in mechanical engineering. Abdulmutallab was involved in radical Islamist student organizations during his university years in London. As President of the School's Islamic Society he organized rallies and protests against the United Kingdom's involvement in Afghanistan and Iraq. Despite the July 2005 London subway bombings, Londinstan remains an important hub for radical Islamist organizations and exiles. After graduation Umar traveled to Dubai to study for an MBA.

Abdulmutallab's jihadist views were no secret. His e-mail conversations with his father suggested violent jihadist orientations and a desire to abandon his business studies. Worried by his son's radicalization and erratic mood swings his father warned the American consulate in Abuja of Umar's desire to attack American interests. Consulate officials informed the regional CIA office of the possible terror threat. Intelligence officials in the United States reviewed the case and entered his name in a government terror data base. His name, however, was not placed on the FBI's terror watch and airline no-fly lists.[19] As a consequence, he was able to get a valid US student visa to travel to America.

By August 2009 Umar abandoned his MBA degree studies in Dubai and went to Yemen to study Arabic and pursue religious studies. He came into contact with AQAP agents and met Anwar al-Awlaki who sought to provide him training to bring down an American passenger jet. Umar received instructions by AQAP's master bomb-maker Ibrahim al-Asiri who was experimenting with different combinations of explosive materials capable of evading airport security. Asiri developed a powder based explosive materials that could be mixed with liquid acid once on the airplane. Awlaki prepared Abdulmutallab for his *martyrdom* operation by providing religious and ideological instruction.

Asiri's explosives concoction had been used in previous terror attacks including a failed August 2009 effort to assassinate Saudi Crown Prince and Intelligence Minister Mohammad bin Nayef who narrowly missed being killed when Asiri's brother Abdullah ignited explosives that had been hidden in his rectum.

The mixture was sewed into Umar underwear and Asiri hoped Umar would be able to ignite the explosive with a syringe to bring down the plane. After three months of training Umar left Yemen, traveled to Ghana, and then boarded a series of planes that led him to Amsterdam's Skipol airport where he evaded airport security and boarded on December 25th Northwest Flight 253 bound for Detroit. As the plane crossed over American airspace and headed toward its final destination, Abdulmutallab spent some 20 minutes in the plane's restroom mixing the chemicals. He emerged from the bathroom covered in a blanket with his trousers ablaze where he was wrestled to the ground by an alarmed passenger. The fire was extinguished by the flight crew and Abdulmutallab was restrained with badly burnt legs for the duration of the flight. He offered little resistance.

Once in custody Umar confessed and relayed to police and FBI officials details on his meetings with Awlaki and Asiri. The Christmas Day Plot was the most serious attempt to attack the United States since shoe bomber Richard Reed's failed 2001 effort to ignite a similar mixture on an American bound passenger jet that was foiled by passengers and flight attendants. The failed attack underscores enduring problems with airport security and intelligence in the post-9/11 era. Freely admitting his guilt, Abdulmutallab was found guilty on seven counts of terrorism related charges and is serving a life sentence in federal maximum security prison.

AQAP praised Abdulmutallab's effort to bring down a US passenger jet. Undaunted the network continued to target the American homeland. Its explosives export Asiri in October 2010 constructed timed bombs hidden inside printer cartridges to be sent to a Chicago based Jewish Center. Foiled by Saudi and British intelligence the bombs were intercepted in the United Kingdom and Dubai before the cargo jets flew to their American destination. US and Saudi intelligence operators in 2012 were successful in recruiting a double agent who during his training to be a martyr on board a American bound passenger jet was able to provide details of AQAP key operators many of whom later be killed in a CIA Predator drone attack.

The recent disclosure of a drone base in Saudi Arabia underscores the serious nature of AQAP threat to Saudi and American security. American targeting of the group's leaders abetted by Saudi intelligence has been able to weaken AQAP's offensive capability. The *Long War Journal* reports that the CIA and US military launched 31 drone strikes in 2012 killing an estimated 193 al-Qaeda in the Arabian Peninsula leaders and militants.[20]

Recent al-Qaeda plots against NYC public transport systems

Not content to delegate offensive operations exclusively to its affiliates, al-Qaeda Central in Waziristan has directly assisted disgruntled American Muslims to attack the United States. In 2009 Bryant Neals Vinas pled guilty to terrorism charges for his involvement in an al-Qaeda effort to bomb a NYC's Long Island Railroad commuter train. Arrested in Peshawar, Pakistan by local intelligence he confessed to the FBI that he had traveled to Pakistan in the hope of fighting US forces in Afghanistan. Vinas a Hispanic convert to Islam received al-Qaeda bomb-making training in Waziristan for close to a year.

Al-Qaeda hoped to follow up Vinas' planned attack by assisting Afghan-American Najibullah Zazi and three of his high school friends in bomb-making capability. These four radicalized American Muslims had traveled to Pakistan in 2008 to receive training by al-Qaeda Waziristan operations. Zazi hoped to emulate al-Qaeda's attacks in Madrid and London subway systems by blowing up NYC metro trains. Their main goal was to protest America's military intervention in Afghanistan and express solidarity with the Taliban.

Zazi returned to the United States where he worked as a Colorado airport shuttle driver. He prepared hydrogen peroxide based bombs stored in backpacks with detonators. The Afghan-American communicated with senior al-Qaeda leaders via e-mail that was picked up by US intelligence who also received information about the plot from an informant. Zazi prepared the bombs in Colorado and drove to NYC to meet his classmates to mount martyrdom operations. They planned to enter four different subway trains at Grand Central and Time Square Stations and to ignite their backpack explosives during morning rush hour to inflict maximum damage. Had the plan been implemented the attacks could have killed more than the 3/11 Madrid bombings.

Once he arrived in New York, Zazi and his friends were informed by family and friends that police and the FBI were inquiring about their activities. The Madrid style operation was aborted with Zazi flying back to Colorado where he was subsequently arrested under terrorism conspiracy charges. He like Abdulmutallab pled guilty to these charges and faces the prospect of life imprisonment without parole.

AQAP is not the only aligned or associated group to remain faithful to bin Laden's *far enemy* strategy. Pakistan's TTP has been involved in numerous efforts to strike the American homeland. Prior to the Times Square attack, TTP's most ambitious operation involved a failed 2008 effort to bomb the Barcelona subway. TTP leader Hakimullah Mehsud is an important al-Qaeda ally whose organization has mounted a fierce insurgency and terror campaign against Islamabad and has actively assisted the Afghan Taliban.

The 2010 Times Square attack

On May 1, 2010 a car bomb failed to detonate next to a theatre in New York Times Square District. Conceived by Pakistani born American citizen Faisal Shahzad the bomb's cell phone triggered ignition device malfunctioned. Trained in 2009 by the Pakistani Taliban in their Waziristan camps, Shahzad hoped to avenge the CIA's killing of TTP leader Baitullah Mehsud.

The TTP provided bomb-making training to Shahzad during his five months in Pakistan. Born to wealthy parents, Faisal came to America in 2006 under a student visa. Living in Connecticut he married a US citizen which facilitated his naturalizations. Despite being well educated his business ventures failed and by 2009 he was bankrupt.

Radicalized by the *war on terror* and drone strikes in Pakistan he became a TTP agent. With his Taliban training and internet bomb-making notes he erected a complex gasoline-fertilizer based bomb that he put into the trunk of a rental car later parked outside the Time Square theatre. Shahzad hoped to trigger the explosives by cell phone. Faisal bomb design, however, was poor and it failed to explode as planned. Police were alerted to the car bomb when two street vendors noticed smoke streaming from the rental car. Police cordoned off the area and robots deactivated the bomb.

NYC investigators were able to link Faisal to the failed bombing by cell phone and rental car records. Shazhad was detained by police aboard an Emirates flight to Dubai. He later confessed to terrorism conspiracy charges and is serving life sentence without the possibility of parole. TTP involvement in the plot is incontrovertible for Shahzad is featured in one of the network's video sitting next to leader Hakimullah Mehsud praising his impending martyrdom.

Despite their relative ineffectiveness externally supported attacks and conspiracies represent a clear danger to the American homeland. The security threat posed by organized networks greatly eclipses the danger of homegrown and lone wolf terrorists. Of the 50 foiled plots against the American homeland only a handful reached operational phase. In his Heritage Foundation Study, James Jay Carafano designated 42 of these aborted efforts as homegrown conspiracies.[21] Most were conceived by a mix of immigrants, black Muslims, converts, disgruntled immigrants, and ex-convicts enraged by America's war on terror. Most of these amateur jihadists had fallen prey to FBI and police sting operations and informants.

Many had hoped to target US military bases, synagogues, Jewish cultural centers, transport infrastructure, and corporate-financial institutions. The groups were small often comprising a network of friends and family members energized by the prospect of martyrdom. Some of the jihadists sought to travel to Pakistan and receive training from al-Qaeda or its affiliated branches. A few claim that they had contact with late AQAP leader Anwar al-Awlaki.

Among the most notable recent efforts by al-Qaeda's inspired homegrown terrorists to attack the American homeland are as follows:[22]

- May 2007 Plot conspired by a group of six immigrants to attack US soldiers stationed at Fort Dix New Jersey with assault rifles and grenades. They were convicted on terrorism and weapons charges and sentenced to over 30 years in prison.
- A June 2007 conspiracy by four Caribbean immigrants to blow up aviation fuel tanks at JFK Airport. All were tried and convicted and are currently serving life sentences.
- Plan by four men in May of 2009 to use stinger missiles against synagogues and Jewish cultural centers in NYC. The four were convicted and were sentenced to 25 years in prison.
- Effort by a Raleigh North Carolina Jihad Group in July 2009 to attack the US Marines stationed at Quantico. Their trial is pending.

The "homegrown" terrorist Boston Marathon attacks (April 2013)

Not every effort by "homegrown" jihadist operating in America has failed.

On Monday April 15, 2013 two Chechen immigrant brothers (Tamerlan and Dzhokhar Tsarnaev) implanted improvised bombs timed to explode at the finishing line of the Boston Marathon. Two "pressure cooker" bombs packed with nails detonated killing three people and wounding over two hundred people. Widespread video footage of the attack scene shows severed limbs, billowing smoke, substantial debris, and widespread panic. Not since 9/11 had Americans been subjected to such a widely publicized and filmed terror attack.

In the ensuing days an extensive manhunt finally encountered the perpetrators of the attack but only after the brothers killed a police officer on the campus of Massachusetts Institute of Technology (MIT). After they assassinated the MIT patrol officer the brothers commandeered an SUV and held the owner hostage. The SUB's owner did manage to escape leaving his activated cell phone in the vehicle. When alerted of the stolen vehicle, the police used the cell phone to locate the Boston bombing suspects' geographic position.

When cornered by police in Watertown, Massachusetts neighborhood, Tamerlan and Dzhokhar responded with automatic weapons and explosive devices severely wounding a policeman. In the resulting firefight the elder brother Tamerlan jumped out of the vehicle firing wildly at police and in the confusion was killed when his younger brother accidently ran over him when he tried to evade the police dragnet. Dzhokhar was able to escape the police and later abandoned the vehicle. As a consequence of Dzhokhars' flight, Boston promptly closed its mass transit system fearing a potential subway or bus bombing.

Badly wounded in the shootout and near death the 19-year-old Dzhokhar was later found by police hiding in a parked boat in a neighborhood backyard. The neighbor reported to police that he saw a substantial amount of blood on the boat. The police surrounded the residence and negotiated with Dzhokhar who eventually surrendered to officials.

Police and FBI agents believe that the brothers acted alone and were not part of an organized conspiracy hatched by a foreign terror network. The Tsarnaevs had lived in America for ten years and based on accounts by friends and family the elder brother had become very religious in past few years. Though having radically divergent personalities, the Tsarnaev brothers were very close with the senior brother seemingly serving as a mentor leading quiet, carefree Dzhokhar down a violent jihadist path.

Complicating the investigation is the damage sustained by the younger brother's vocal cord caused in his firefight with police that press reports indicate his impaired speech capacity. Despite such obstacles Dzhokhar freely admitted to investigating officials his complicity in the attack, his jihadist sympathies, and he further disclosed that the pair acted alone. During his declarations, he said that the brothers had downloaded bomb-making instructions from an English language AQAP website. Based on an AQAP design manual they fabricated the pressure cooker bomb with circuit board timers used in the attack.

The specific motives for the attack still need to be clarified and further developed. Based on interviews of friends and family, Tamerlan had undergone a profound religious transformation five years ago. Encouraged by his mother's deepening Islamic faith and a troubled personal life characterized by alcohol and spousal abuse, Tamerlan became increasingly radicalized. His fundamentalist views sparked a number of controversies within his family in Dagestan and with parishioners at a Cambridge, Massachusetts mosque. The 26 year old had an accomplished amateur boxing career with aspirations to become a professional that he abandoned because of his deepening religious views.

He appeared frustrated and alienated with American society. Tamerlan's transformation to jihadist commitment in the West mirrors many of perpetrators behind the 9/11 attacks, Madrid and London bombings. Based on disclosures by family members to FBI investigators exploring possible links to regional terror organizations, Tamerlan's conversion to Jihadism was triggered by his association with an older Armenian convert to Islam only known as "Misha" who "brainwashed" the impressionable young man into becoming an Islamic fundamentalist. If verified by subsequent findings, the transformation mirrors the path of the members of the Hamburg cell who encountered an older man who served as a catalyst for jihadist commitment. Tamerlan's mother defends her son's association with "Misha" claiming it was a "positive" development pivotal in her son's commitment to Islamic values. She continues to believe that hers sons are being framed for the attacks.

Tamerlan's radical views were known to the FBI that was alerted by the American consulate in Dagestan. Embassy officials had received warnings in 2011 from Russian intelligence agencies who were alarmed by his radical views. Russian security services had monitored Tamerlan phone conversations with his mother during which he confessed his commitment to jihad and perhaps a willingness to travel to Palestine.

FBI officials investigated the case interviewing Tamerlan at one point in 2011 but they could not find any real evidence that he had dangerous jihadist proclivities. Having no criminal record with only one reported incident of violent behavior involving an unprosecuted domestic abuse allegation from a former girlfriend, the FBI failed to pursue the matter further. He was put on a number of terrorist data bases associated with various American security agencies that fell short of the famous "no-fly list."

The 26 year olds six-month visit to Dagestan at his family home before the Boston Marathon bombings is a source of concern for investigators who suspect he may have received explosives training from a foreign Islamist terror network. Given that the region has been the scene of nationalist insurgencies that are increasingly infused with jihadist elements such concerns are valid. Tamerlan's You Tube posting of a local jihadist killed by Russian security forces after his return from Dagestan reinforces these anxieties. The inquiry especially the FBI's handling of Russia's warnings of Tamerlan's jihadist sympathies and possible security threat remains under severe Congressional scrutiny and criticism.

Al-Qaeda, moreover, has adopted the Chechen cause and the role of Arab jihadists in the insurgent movement is not insubstantial. While the inquiry is far from complete, there are no proven links between the Tsarnaev brothers and a jihadi regional or global network. It is, however, uncommon for terrorists to successfully construct pressure cooker bombs without some formal training creating the possibility that Tamerlan in his six-month visit to Dagestan and Chechnya had some contract with an organized network with links to al-Qaeda. FBI officers are currently in Dagestan capital Makhachkala to determine if Tamerlan had met any Chechen or local jihadist network members during his visit to his father's home. Regional jihadist organizations in Dagestan have repudiated the attacks and claim their real war is with Russian Federation and deny any link with Tamerlan's activities.

So far al-Qaeda's role in the attack appears limited to Tamerlan's download of an AQAP bomb-making manual quaintly titled *Make a Bomb in the Kitchen of Your Mom*. The bombings depart from al-Qaeda's methodology in a number of important ways. First, there is no preattack warning or postattack endorsement. Both the Madrid and London bombings had al-Qaeda presentiments of attacks against European states assisting America in its wars in Afghanistan and Iraq as well as official recognition by al-Qaeda affiliated media organizations. Second, the global jihadi organization typically targets US military and corporate facilities and has never attacked a sporting event. Third, the amateurish nature of the attacks that featured the lack of a postattack escape plan militates against al-Qaeda's extensive involvement. Still one must be cautious in arriving at premature conclusions for investigators initially erred in labeling both the Madrid and London bombings as the work of *homegrown* terrorists.

The US Justice Department on April 22, 2013 charged Dzhokhar Tsarnaev with the using of weapons of mass destruction in his terror attack underscoring the Obama Administration's commitment to use the criminal justice system to prosecute terrorism cases within the United States involving American citizens. Weeks after the bombing the Justice Department charged Dzhokhar's two Chechen schoolmates with obstructing justice when they sought to eliminate evidence of his culpability by dumping his computer in a dumpster and charged a third student friend with making false statements to investigating authorities.

The Boston Marathon case is fraught with some legal controversy including police and FBI failure to read the surviving suspect of his Miranda Fifth Amendment rights upon his arrest. Using a national security emergency exception established by an Obama Justice Department to override this constitutional obligation, police and FBI justify their actions. He would later be apprised of his constitutional right to remain silent when formally charged by a magistrate as he convalesced from his wounds in a Boston medical facility.

Despite the criticisms of human rights and civil liberties groups of police SWAT team's departure from constitutional protocol, extensive video footage prior to the attack clearly identifies Tamerlan and Dzhokhar laying backpacks full of explosives near the finish line of the race with film of subsequent explosions taking the lives of three spectators and wounding over two hundred people. On July 10, 2013, Dzhokhar pled innocent to the Justice Department's 30 count indictment and he confronts of being convicted and sentenced to death. Given the extensive video coverage of the crime scene, evidence of his guilt appears overwhelming.

The international ramifications of the attacks have been substantial as security officials fear that aspiring jihadists may emulate the Tsarnaev brothers targeting high-profile sports events. Alarmed by two Maghrebi immigrants praising of the attacks on radical jihadi websites, Spanish police arrested Algerian Nou Mediouni and Moroccan Hassan El Jaauani for being part of a wider AQIM terror network to attack Spanish interests. Given the imminence of the Madrid Marathon just a week after the Boston bombings local officials decided to take no chances and decided to detain the pair.

Like the conspirators involved in many of the aborted plots in the United States, the two jihadists had been monitored for over a year by Spanish intelligence agents. Arraigned and charged within the Spanish justice system, the two had extensive contact with al-Qaeda in the Islamic Maghreb with at least one of the suspects hoping to travel to Mali for terrorist training during AQIM's brief sanctuary. The two suspects appear to be working in isolation and not part of a wider conspiracy. Like the brothers the two immigrants were radicalized in the West rejecting a society that permitted their entry and provided them safe refuge.

Plots to attack sporting events in Spain by al-Qaeda linked terrorists are not without precedent. In the summer of 2013 two Chechens and one Turk were arrested by Spanish antiterror police for a plot to use toy airplanes piloted by remote control to drop explosives on a sports stadium. Spain continues to be the target for al-Qaeda that seeks to recover the *lost lands* of al Andaluz.

The foiled 2013 al-Qaeda Canadian passenger train plot

Canadian officials ironically arrested two Muslim immigrants in Toronto and Montreal on the same day that Dzhokhar was charged by a federal judge for his role in the Boston Marathon bombings. The Royal Canadian Mounted Police

(RMCP) alleged that the two Arab immigrant suspects (Chiheb Esseghaier and Raed Jaser) are linked to an Iranian linked al-Qaeda supported plot to attack an Via line or Amtrak passenger train traveling between Toronto and NYC. Monitored by Canadian and American intelligence agents for over a year the plan never reached operational stage. Investigating officials have made underscored that the plot is unrelated to the Boston Marathon attack. The conspiracy's outcome mirrors many of the plots averted by the US government since 9/11 that failed to reach maturation and fell prey to government surveillance operations.

The alleged al-Qaeda plot is especially intriguing given the Iranian connection. Bin Laden's Abbottabad correspondence suggests a complex and conflicted relationship with Iran's revolutionary republic with repeated concern for the safety of relatives that escaped to Iran after the Taliban's overthrow. The historic leader apparently feared that some members of his family would be used as a bargaining chip by Iranian officials in their deliberations with US intelligence agencies. The RCMP have promised to be more forthcoming in providing details of the al-Qaeda "orchestrated" conspiracy when the suspects are formally charged in the court system. Early reports indicate that the police were informed of the plot by a Toronto based imam who knew the terror plot suspects.

Both terror suspects have denied the allegation with one of them challenging the legitimacy of proceedings not governed by Sharia law. The legal case against them may take year to reach fruition.

Al-Qaeda's failed *far enemy* approach

Post-9/11 homegrown and lone wolf terrorism linked to al-Qaeda has killed 14 Americans on their native soil. Colonel Hassan's execution of 13 fellow servicemen at Fort Hood and jihadist Carlos Bledsoe's drive by killing of Arkansas military recruiting office represent al-Qaeda's greatest success in getting Americans to kill in the name of jihad. Al-Qaeda's failure to strike the American homeland decisively is emblematic of the organization's decay. The network's reliance on amateurish homegrown terrorists and recalcitrant affiliates is dramatic proof of the erosion of its offensive capability.

Bin Laden's 2011 death is likely to intensify al-Qaeda's fragmentation and weaken its ability to direct the jihadist war against the *far enemy*. The turmoil of the Arab Spring, moreover, may channel Jihadism toward more localized enemies and a greater sectarian orientation. Despite the objections of bin Laden and American Adam Gadahn to the sectarian targeting of Muslims, ISI, and Zarqawi's successors have accelerated their attacks against the Shia, Christians, and Kurds. Al-Nusra partnership with ISI has targeted Alawites and Druse minorities. Ayman al-Zawahiri's endorsement of al-Nusra in Syria is a vivid indication that al-Qaeda's strategy has been transformed into a struggle against the Muslim apostate *near enemy*. With Osama gone, Jihadism is likely to morph into directions that al-Qaeda Central has historically rejected.

9

Is Al-Qaeda on the Brink of Defeat? Bin Laden's Death and the Impact of the Arab Spring

Regarding the Brothers in Waziristan in general, whoever can keep a low profile and take the necessary precautions, should stay in the area and those who cannot do so, their first option is to go to Nuristan in Kunar, Gazni or Zabil. I am leaning toward getting the brothers out of the area. We can leave the cars because they are targeting the cars now, but if we leave them, they will start focusing on houses that will increase casualties among women and children. It is possible that they have photographed targeted homes. The brothers who can keep a low profile should stay, but move to new houses on a cloudy day. . . . A warning to the brothers: they should not meet on the road and move into their cars because many of them get targeted while meeting on the road. They also should not enter the market in their cars.

Osama bin Laden[1]

Is al-Qaeda on the brink of defeat?

Eleven years have passed since 9/11 and al-Qaeda's greatest success. The *war on terror* has drastically reduced the terror organizations' capabilities. Al-Qaeda and its affiliates operate precariously in failed states. Its leaders and members are continuously threatened by internal and external enemies. Many senior and midlevel commanders have been killed in antiterror operations. Ironically al-Qaeda's key leadership seems fearful of impending death. Martyrdom has lost its allure for many of the networks leaders.

The organization has fractured along ethnic, regional, and ideological lines.[2] Bin Laden's death will likely exacerbate the organization's centrifugal pressures. Internal correspondence seized by US Special Forces in their May 2, 2011, raid on bin Laden compound vividly illustrate the organizations divisions and anxieties.[3] Al-Qaeda's senior leaders are internally divided, unable to control affiliates, short on cash, and convulsed by the effectiveness of the Predator drone campaign.

The death of bin Laden is a consequence of a targeted killing policy that has achieved devastating results.[4] More than 70 senior and midlevel al-Qaeda leaders have been killed in the past decade. The pace of Predator drone attacks has increased since 2008 and the attacks have neutralized al-Qaeda operations in Pakistan, Yemen, and Somalia. The success of the drone campaign is predicated upon local intelligence sources that over the years have improved.

Drone strikes have been accompanied by US Special Force's attacks that have reached the inner core of al-Qaeda. Killing bin Laden remains America's greatest strategic victory in the *war on terror* that has deprived the terror organizations of its spiritual and ideological center.[5] He is irreplaceable.

With the death of its historic leader, al-Qaeda is splintering even further. Its greatest challenge, however, may be the Arab popular protests that overthrew regimes in Egypt, Tunisia, and Libya. Prodemocracy activists have been the driving force for many of these changes. Arab protestors were able to do peacefully in Egypt and Tunisia what violent jihadists were unable to do for decades.

The Muslim Brotherhood's acceptance of democracy in Tunisia and Egypt complicates and contradicts al-Qaeda's narrative of an omnipotent *Crusader-Zionist* conspiracy to exploit and colonize Muslim lands. The electoral success of Islamist political parties in the Arab world creates a viable alternative to al-Qaeda's messianic violent ideology. Al-Qaeda appears to be losing the war of ideas in the Muslim world.[6]

This chapter examines bin Laden's death, the weakening of al-Qaeda's Pakistani tribal supporters, and gauges the Arab Spring's effect on al-Qaeda's future. It begins by analyzing the illusive hunt for bin Laden, explores the changes made in counterterror strategy during the Obama Administration, and assesses the impact of Osama's killing and the weakening of the al-Qaeda's TTP and Haqqani allies in its Waziristan *sanctuary*. The concluding section examines the Arab protest movement and analyzes the ambiguous impact of the Arab Spring on the terror organization's future.

Bin Laden: Wanted dead or alive!

Before 9/11, Bin Laden had been targeted by US and international intelligence agencies. Though the 1993 WTC bombing and the 1996 bomb attack against US air base in Saudi Arabia had little direct connection to bin Laden, the perpetrators were inspired by his networks message and its *far enemy* strategy. These assaults highlighted the national security dangers of a global jihadist campaign against the United States.

Al-Qaeda's 1998 bombings of the US embassies in Kenya and Tanzania killing hundreds and bin Laden and Zawahiri's proclamation of war against the United States prompted American military retaliation. The cruise missile strikes launched after the embassy bombings killed only a handful of al-Qaeda and did nothing to deter the organization that struck against the USS Cole in Yemen 2 years later killing 17 sailors.

The Cole bombing did not elicit a US military retaliation. Clinton's attack on al-Qaeda after the African bombings was very much of an anomalous action. The Administration was intent on pursuing a law and order model touting its successful criminal prosecution record of the 1993 WTC defendants. Controversy exists about the Clinton Administration's handling of al-Qaeda and whether more could have been done to derail the trajectory of 9/11 attacks. Some analysts have argued that the Administration had underestimated the jihadist threat and lacked the will to confront al-Qaeda.[7] In retrospect this seems to be an accurate assessment.

Neither the Clinton nor Bush Administrations took decisive action to disrupt and destroy al-Qaeda prior to WTC and Pentagon attacks. Despite a CIA plan to launch a military assault against al-Qaeda operations in Afghanistan, neither Clinton nor Bush took substantive action. 9/11 is their shared legacy.

When the attacks occurred the Administration was unprepared and in 9/11's aftermath it appeared in disarray. Only weeks after did the Administration recover rallying the nation and building a vast network of allies to isolate al-Qaeda and its Taliban patrons.

President Bush's visit to an NYC emergency response team of fireman with a promise that al-Qaeda would be on the receiving end of American retribution galvanized the nation. The President's declaration that he wanted bin Laden "dead" or "alive" personified America's struggle with the Saudi jihadist and put a premium on swift decisive action.

Despite the impassioned rhetoric, the Administration pursued a cautious strategy negotiating with the Taliban for a potential bin Laden's handover and relying on Pakistani intelligence services as intermediaries. While planning for an attack against al-Qaeda and the Taliban, the Administration lost precious time to trap bin Laden and his Egyptian deputy Ayman al-Zawahiri in Afghan territory. When the retaliatory attack did come bin Laden had ample time to escape to the Pakistani frontier where Taliban allies could shield him, his closest family, and associates.

Despite such errors the CIA-Special Forces attacks that included laser guided aerial bombing and NA proxy forces devastated the Taliban and their al-Qaeda allies. Thousands of radical Islamists were killed in a rapid campaign that toppled the Taliban and implanted a national unity government led by anti-Taliban Pashtun Hamid Karzai.[8]

America's best opportunity to kill bin Laden prior to the Abbottabad raid came in December 2001 at bin Laden Tora Bora mountainous redoubt. Limited US ground forces in the area necessitated reliance on mass air power and Afghan allies.[9] Despite the Administration's hope to kill bin Laden, the air campaign did not prevent him from slipping over the Pakistani border under the protection of the Taliban.

We will never know if the Administration had deployed the tenth Mountain Division to seal the border if bin Laden could have been killed or captured. The failure to deploy sufficient forces was the least of the Administration's errors which were magnified by its reliance on Pakistani intelligence.[10] This situation continues as American officials become increasingly skeptical of Pakistani intentions to curb the power of the Afghan and Pakistani Taliban.

Pakistan's patronage of the Afghan Taliban to achieve "strategic depth" against India and its close ethnic and ideological ties to Islamic militants has not been overcome by American financial largesse. While the border between Pakistan and Afghanistan makes Islamabad an invaluable conduit for logistical and military operations, Pakistani support for jihadist causes and movements makes it an inconsistent and often unreliable partner. Only when its security was compromised by the Pakistani Taliban rebellion in 2007 did Islamabad take forceful action against jihadist forces and begin to coordinate attacks with its US ally. Pakistan, however, has assisted in the hunt for al-Qaeda whose network seeks Islamabad's overthrow.

The President's bin Laden wanted "dead" or "alive" promise would hound the Bush Administration on two terms. Only at Tora Bora did the Administration have the slightest chance to kill the Saudi jihadist. It would not have a second real opportunity.

The mystery of Bin Laden and America's unfulfilled desire for justice

Once bin Laden had slipped over the border intelligence leads on his whereabouts were hard to find. Most informed opinion had thought that he was being protected by Pakistani Taliban in Waziristan. Historically the region had been largely autonomous and Islamabad's influence over the region was quite low. Given the dominance of pro-Taliban Pashtun tribal confederations in the region it was quite logical that bin Laden would seek refuge. Friendly warlords with whom bin Laden had personal contacts were more than willing to shield him. Especially critical will be the support of the Haqqani network for al-Qaeda in North Waziristan that allowed the jihadist group the geographic space to briefly resuscitate after 9/11. Given that the Haqqani have long been utilized by Pakistan as a proxy force to achieve strategic depth in Afghanistan and Kashmir the territory has been relatively free of military incursions.

Al-Qaeda agents elsewhere in Pakistan were not so fortunate. KSM, Abu Zubaydah, and Ramzi Bin al-Shibh were arrested by Pakistani officials in big cities where Islamabad had real authority. The FATA in contrast seemed a natural bin Laden hiding place. We now know that the Waziristan lead was inaccurate.

Far from residing in a remote cave, bin Laden for five years lived in a spacious villa in the medium sized town called Abbottabad.[11] How bin Laden was able to maintain a clandestine life in a town close to Pakistan's most prestigious military academy is a *mystery*. It has prompted considerable speculation of Pakistani complicity in shielding bin Laden from America's intense manhunt. Leaked to the Qatari news network Al Jazeera, a special Pakistani government report on the Abbottabad raid found systematic intelligence failures in the ISI's inability to locate bin Laden and even suggests that there could be some intelligence agency complicity with al-Qaeda top leadership.[12]

Materials taken by US special forces in the May 2011 raid may provide some clues. Unfortunately, only 17 letters drafted by bin Laden and his associates have been released and they do not indicate of any Pakistani state protection of the al-Qaeda leader.[13] What the letters demonstrate is that al-Qaeda had a conflicted relationship with the Pakistani based fundamentalist group TTP that no doubt was instrumental in assisting al-Qaeda fugitives.[14]

US authorities were able to track bin Laden to Abbottabad from the CIA's questioning of al-Qaeda suspects at Guantanamo. Much of this questioning apparently involved *enhanced interrogation* techniques like waterboarding. The name of a Kuwaiti courier was discovered as a possible link to bin Laden in one of these sessions.[15] The courier (Abu Ahmed al-Kuwaiti) connection to bin Laden was confirmed by multiple sources including KSM. Once the courier had been identified in 2010 his movements were tracked by the CIA to the Saudi jihadist Abbottabad refuge.

The CIA staked out the compound for half a year waiting to see any sign of bin Laden. Prior to the President's authorization of the raid, intelligence was badly divided on whether bin Laden was in the safe house.[16] Trying to ascertain the identity of the inhabitants in the villa, United States used a Pakistani doctor whose main task was to inoculate children in a disease eradication campaign. They hoped that this campaign would lead to bin Laden's children.

The inoculation campaign did not provide any real substantial evidence. Authorities knew that a family was hiding in the house and national security officials were divided on the propriety of an attack on the compound. The raid was quite risky for it violated Pakistani sovereignty, secretly moved dozens of commandos in helicopters across hundreds of miles and could potentially end in complete failure. Fortunately the raid succeeded resulting in the death of bin Laden, his son, Abu al-Kuwaiti, and al-Kuwaiti's wife and brother and a treasure trove of information.

Faced with a damaged helicopter whose rough landing made it inoperable, Special Forces left the compound without bin Laden's spouses and children. They were, however, able to secure thousands of documents stored in disks and computer thumb drives that would be of invaluable assistance in bringing down bin Laden's closest confidents. Some of whom like Abu Yahya al-Libi would later die in Predator drone strikes.[17]

Bin Laden's assassination is a culmination of a decade of intelligence work and represents a strategic victory in the *war on terror*.[18] Osama's death creates a leadership void in the terror organization. No other leader has his mythic presence or charisma. For Americans, OBL personified al-Qaeda and the 9/11 attacks.

Until bin Laden was dead Americans could not have closure in the *war on terror* and his killing ended the Saudi jihadist aura of invincibility. The late leader's secret burial at sea and the Administration's refusal to publish photos of his dead body denied him martyrdom status. Significantly, only the Pakistani Taliban mounted mass demonstrations to protest his death and al-Qaeda has not been able to successfully retaliate against America to avenge his death.

Bin Laden's mystique ended when Special Forces killed him in a gun battle. The visceral way he died is far more potent psychologically than any Predator drone strike or 1,000-pound bomb. Had he died in an air strike, identification would not be secure and his mythology may have endured.

Beyond the cathartic importance of his death, there are very practical consequences. Al-Qaeda will likely be engulfed in internecine power struggles as leaders jockey for a dominant position.[19] Despite his elevation as al-Qaeda leader, a month after bin Laden's death, Ayman al-Zawahiri does not command a huge following in the organization. Zawahiri is disliked by the al-Qaeda's Saudi-Yemeni leadership who had tense past relations with the Egyptian terrorist.[20]

Released by the West Point Combating Terrorism Center the Bin Laden's correspondence suggests Zawahiri had little influence in the organization and that bin Laden's closest associates were Abu Yahya al-Libi and Mahmud Atiyya.[21] West Point analysts, furthermore, believe that al-Qaeda correspondence hint at a rift between bin Laden and Zawahiri on incorporating affiliates into al-Qaeda.[22] It is quite telling that Zawahiri blesses al-Shabaab integration into al-Qaeda shortly after bin Laden's death. Osama was openly critical of the Somali jihadist network and its upstart leader the now deceased Anwar al-Awlaki.

The declassified letters, moreover, paints an al-Qaeda plagued by inner feuds, convulsed with constant fear of attacks and short on cash.[23] The correspondence further indicate bin Laden was reluctant to endorse affiliates operating under the al-Qaeda banner for fear of another Iraq like debacle. Al-Qaeda Central messages to AQAP, TTP, and al-Shabaab leaders implore them to end their indiscriminate slaughter of Muslims and refocus their efforts against the Western *far enemy*.[24] Bin Laden appears frustrated and perplexed by the behavior of affiliated groups and his inability to control their actions. Al-Qaeda media expert American Adam Gadahn argued that al-Qaeda should disassociate from its affiliates because of their wanton shedding of Muslim blood.[25]

The growing separation between al-Qaeda, its affiliates, and the wider jihadist community is increasingly apparent in *jihadesphere* activity. Daniel Kimmage reports that al-Qaeda's media operations confront a changing media landscape where its fixation on Afghanistan-Pakistan region has lost resonance with jihadists.[26] As-Sahab's share of the *jihadesphere* audience is in decline which is more interested in the Palestinian issue that traditionally has not been a focus of al-Qaeda attacks.[27] Al-Qaeda seems frustrated that its message to the wider community no longer registers strong support.

Bin Laden's killing furthers al-Qaeda's organizational and ideological weakness. His mythic presence ensured some unity and fidelity. Without his commanding presence, al-Qaeda lacks the capacity to prevent further organizational fissures. It is doubtful that Zawahiri will be able to maintain any semblance of organizational unity over the fractious movement.

Affiliates have not heeded Osama's advice and they continue to fight against Muslim *apostate* states and groups. Al-Shabaab and AQIM affiliate AD have brutalized Sufi Muslims and other minorities. Only AQAP has targeted the Western homeland with aborted efforts to bring down passenger and cargo jet planes. Yet AQAP's war is mainly waged against Sana and its security forces.

Obama's drone war against al-Qaeda and its Taliban allies

Al-Qaeda's organizational disarray is in part a consequence of more effective US counterterror policies. The CIA and Joint Operations Special Forces Command (JSPC) have become more effective in tracking down and killing al-Qaeda operatives across the globe. Wars in Iraq and Afghanistan have accelerated the use of drones and Special Forces operations that have devastated al-Qaeda operatives and their allies. *The Long War Journal's* 2013 statistical study of Predator drone strikes documents that large numbers of al-Qaeda and Taliban senior commanders have died in the CIA's 2004–13 assassination campaign.[28]

Based on the Journal's February 2013 tabulation 2,492 al-Qaeda, Taliban, and aligned extremist organizations operatives have died in unmanned aerial vehicle (UAV) strikes in Pakistan.[29] Since 2008 among the most notable "kills" in descending chronological order are as follows:

- Hakimullah Mehsud (TTP leader, 2013)
- Mullah Nazir (Taliban South Waziristan warlord, 2013)
- Abu Yahya al-Libi (al-Qaeda chief of staff, 2012)
- Abu Mqdad al-Masri (chief of al-Qaeda external operations, 2011)
- Abd al Rahman al-Yemeni (al-Qaeda official responsible for external operations, 2011)

- Abu Hafs al-Shahri (al-Qaeda official responsible for Pakistani operations, 2011)
- Abu Ziad al-Iraqi (al-Qaeda financial officer, 2011)
- Ibn Amin (senior al-Qaeda-Taliban commander, 2010)
- Saleh al-Somali (al-Qaeda commander responsible for external operations, 2009)
- Abu Musa al-Masri (al-Qaeda bomb maker, 2009)
- Mustafa al Jaziri (senior al-Qaeda military commander, 2009)
- Baitullah Mehsud (TTP leader, 2009)
- Tahir Yuldashev (leader of Islamic movement of Uzbekistan, 2009)
- Abu Hamza (al-Qaeda bomb maker and external operations chief, 2008)
- Abu Laith al-Libi (al-Qaeda senior commander of Brigade 055, 2008)
- Abu Khabab al-Masri (al-Qaeda weapons of mass destruction program, 2008)
- Abu Sulayman Jazairi (al-Qaeda chief of operations against the West, 2008).

The Predator drone program impact on midlevel commanders and foot soldiers has been even more devastating.[30] Starting in 2008 the Bush Administration began to accelerate the use of pilotless drones to kill al-Qaeda agents. Prior to this period, the Administration pursued a limited application of drones for fear of alienating Islamabad.

Drone arracks violate Pakistani sovereignty and given inevitable civilian casualties the strikes have aroused severe opposition. The drop in Pakistani cooperation in tracking down al-Qaeda in the last years of Bush's term, and the evidence that the Pakistani military and intelligence were supporting the Afghan insurgents fighting US troops, convinced the Bush Administration to accelerate attacks to disrupt al-Qaeda operational ability during its final year.

The Obama Administration has pursued an even more aggressive strategy targeting al-Qaeda militants.[31] The pace of Predator drone attacks was accelerated peaking in 2010 with over a hundred attacks. The Administration, moreover, has emphasized Special Forces operations against the network. The Obama Administration's concentrated strategy on "disrupting," "dismantling," and "destroying" al-Qaeda has paid dividends. Counterterror policy has become more lethal, targeted, and effective.

The Administration's decisive and focused policy is surprising. During the 2008 election Obama promised to pursue a law enforcement model by closing Guantanamo and using civilian tribunals to try al-Qaeda suspects.[32] Out of strategic necessity the Obama Administration has kept the Cuban camp open and has initiated military tribunal justice for al-Qaeda terrorists.

Obama's targeted killing policy is similarly pragmatic. Drone technology is uniquely situated for failed states where governments are nonexistent or too weak to assist in the capture of al-Qaeda suspects.[33] The precise nature of laser guided Hellfire missiles, furthermore, permits a more selective use of force that limits civilian causalities. Demarcations of noncombatants in unconventional wars are notoriously difficult for women and children have provided support for terror networks and they have been used to mount suicide missions. Accordingly, estimates of "civilian" casualties caused in drone attacks vary dramatically with the *Long War Journal* reporting 10 percent and Peter Bergin and Kathleen Tiedemann claiming close to a third of the drone program's deaths are civilians.[34]

Critics of the drone program have, however, few alternatives to advocate. Law enforcement cooperation is not available in these areas so capture and arrest are not viable. Mass bombing campaigns would kill too many civilians and a refusal to use drones would accelerate safe havens from which attacks could be launched at American interests. US military incursions into Waziristan to capture militants would be injurious to America's relations with Pakistan.

Quoting former Secretary of Defense Leon Panetta "drones are the only game in town."[35] A moral case can also be made for the use of drone technology. Insurgent groups frequently hide among civilian populations willingly exposing them to military retaliation.[36] As Amatai Etzioni persuasively argues, terrorists who subject civilian populations are ultimately responsible for any civilian casualties due to state retaliation.[37] UAV attacks have also hurt al-Qaeda Waziristan protectors.

The weakening of al-Qaeda's Pakistani Taliban, Uzbek, and Haqqani protectors

Given FATA's traditional autonomy and fierce tribes, Pakistan has been historically reluctant to initiate military action in Waziristan. Washington's *war on terror* and the presence of al-Qaeda along the Afghanistan-Pakistan frontier forced Islamabad to change its policy. The government's 2002 and 2004 military campaigns in the region were poorly executed resulting in many civilians deaths.

The Pakistani military absorbed many losses and halted its incursions into Waziristan after hastily arranging truces with Waziri tribal militants.

These peace treaties helped insulate al-Qaeda allowing the network to operate relatively securely. Under the protection of Pakistani and Uzbek militant networks al-Qaeda was able to rebuild some operational capability. By 2006 al-Qaeda rebuilt its ability to mount offensive operations against the West by working with affiliates, insurgents, associates, and homegrown terrorists. In addition, some analysts argued that the movement's diversification into Iraq, Somalia, Yemen, and the Maghreb made it an even more formidable and complex terror threat.[38] Indeed, the Iraqi jihad was so fierce that it appeared the country was headed for civil war and national dismemberment. One could persuasively argue during this time that al-Qaeda had successfully regrouped.

This temporary resurgence was illustrated by the dramatic growth of al-Qaeda and affiliated media operations. Starting modestly after 9/11 al-Shabaab has spawned a vast al-Qaeda *jihadesphere* network with websites for al-Qaeda's Maghreb, Iraqi, Somali, and Yemeni branches with many videos distributed by the central organizations main distribution outlet Global Islamic Media Front. Al-Qaeda's network offers its audience attack videos, leadership statements, training manuals, documentaries extolling the virtues of jihad against Crusader and apostate enemies. It is a communication link between al-Qaeda central and its affiliates, associates, and lone wolves in its overall *vexation* and *exhaustion* strategy. Al-Sahab, for example, produced 90 videos in 2007 quintupling the number of its productions two years earlier.[39]

Al-Qaeda's affiliates have been even more prolific. AQI's website (Al Fajr) has frequently been a catalyst in the production of high-tech videos and documentaries eclipsing al-Sahab in the number and quality of its offerings.[40] AQI's website served as an important recruitment tool for foreign fighters interested in martyrdom complete with travel information, ideological indoctrination, and explosives training. The restoration of Arab honor by exacting revenge upon Crusader forces is a preponderant theme of al-Qaeda's framing of its conflict with America.

Al-Qaeda in 2006–7 was poised to win the *war on terror*. Events in Waziristan, moreover, pointed to a consolidation of militant networks that cooperated with and protected al-Qaeda. Baitullah Mehsud's formation of TTP in 2007 seemed to secure al-Qaeda's Waziristan sanctuary. As a jihadist umbrella organization merging dozens of organizations operating along the frontier, the TTP's presence threatened Islamabad, Kabul, and Washington. Different from previous prior militant networks that enjoyed state support, TTP sought *defensive jihad* against the Pakistani state. Enraged by Islamabad's support for Washington's antiterror campaign and its erratic policy of military incursions and fragile truce agreements, TTP mounted a fierce terror war against Pakistani state and civil society. By 2009, tens of thousands of Pakistanis have died in TTP suicide martyrdom operations and bomb attacks. TTP victims include former Pakistani Prime Minister Benazir Bhutto who was killed in a TTP bombing during a campaign rally.

The TTP support for the Afghan insurgency and its sponsorship of plots to bomb the Barcelona and NYC subways resulted in a CIA drone campaign against the group that killed Baitullah Mehsud in 2009 and targeted its senior and midlevel commanders.

Al-Qaeda's Pakistani and Uzbek allies have also been targeted by the CIA drone program in South and North Waziristan. The majority of attacks have been directed against four networks connected to the Afghan insurgent movement. The Haqqani, Mehsud, Mullah Nazir, and Gul Bahadar organizations have been particularly damaged with leaders, senior and midlevel commanders killed.[41] After Baitullah Mehsud's assassination his successor Hakimullah Mehsud was repeatedly targeted by the CIA and killed in a 2013 drone attack. Al-Qaeda' Uzbek allies have similarly suffered severe losses with leaders and cadres killed. Starting in 2009, al-Qaeda's Waziristan sanctuary was becoming increasingly less secure.

Al-Qaeda's Waziristan allies are under severe pressure. The drone program has recently focused on disrupting the Haqqani network whose guerrilla force has played an important role in the Afghan insurgency. Since 2008, US military strikes in Pakistan have targeted areas in North Waziristan where the group uses the territory to resupply the Afghan Taliban. Since 2004, the *Long War Journal* reports that the US covert air campaign has struck the Haqqani network 82 times killing 13 senior commanders including Muhammad and Saifullah Haqqani and that 71 percent of attacks have been conducted against its North Waziristan tribal agency.[42]

The CIA program peaked in 2010 with over 117 strikes with 89 percent of them conducted in North Waziristan inflicting severe damage on the Haqqani and Baladar networks.[43] The intensity of the US air campaign in the tribal areas has put severe pressure on al-Qaeda and its key allies. Pakistan has also begun to renew military operations in South Waziristan that also feature CIA attacks against key TTP leaders. Al-Qaeda's paramilitary wing (Lashkar al-Zil) in Pakistan and Afghanistan that conducts joint operations with the Taliban and Haqqani organizations has seen many of its top military commanders killed in US air strikes.[44]

The Taliban in South Waziristan have also seen some reverses. Faced with a movement that threatened its security, Pakistan moved aggressively. The military battled TTP forces in Swat Valley and Waziristan. The TTP's terror campaign and its Talibanization policy in these areas have altered Pakistani perceptions of the war on terror. Public opinion polls after 2008 indicate great support for Islamabad's military campaign against the TTP.[45] Growing number of Pakistanis see the TTP as a threat to country's survival. CIA drone strikes have been coordinated with the Pakistani military's campaign. This indicates that Islamabad will cooperate with Washington when its strategic interests are threatened.

Brian Glyn William's analysis of the CIA covert drone war notes that polls in Waziristan show greater public support for the program. He argues that TTP's Talibanization of the region and assaults on tribal elites are heavily resented by the local populace.[46] The *Long War Journal*, furthermore, finds that the drone program has been timed with Pakistani military operations to maximize TTP and aligned group's losses.[47] The TTP-al-Qaeda relationship, furthermore, is strained.

The Abbottabad letters indicate that the al-Qaeda hierarchy has been critical of the group's targeting of Pakistani civil society.[48] In a December 3, 2010 letter addressed to TTP leader Hakimullah Mehsud, al-Qaeda leaders Abu Yahya al-Libi and Mahmud al-Hasan (both later killed by the drone program) write to him of the concern over his strategy:

> We have several important comments that cover the concept, approach, and behavior of the TTP in Pakistan, which we believe are passive behavior and clear legal and religious mistakes which result in a negative deviation from the set path of jihadist movement in Pakistan, which also are contrary to the objectives of jihad and to the effects exerted by us.

The CIA drone program and sustained Pakistani military operations after 2008 have made Waziristan less of a refuge for al-Qaeda. Persistent attacks against al-Qaeda and its aligned networks have hollowed and weakened jihadist groups. So convulsed was OBL about the CIA's drone war that he urged operatives to leave Waziristan and before his death the historic leader contemplated moving al-Qaeda central to Yemen believing it to be a more secure location.[49] It is now clear that al-Qaeda's resurgence in its Waziristan "sanctuary" stalled in 2009 and has been in progressive decline. This is dramatically illustrated by the TTP's recent offer of a truce with Islamabad for it seeks a respite from American-Pakistani joint operations that have badly degraded its capability.[50]

While counterterror operations have succeeded in degrading al-Qaeda's ranks, they are not capable of winning the "war of ideas." Here al-Qaeda confronts a deeper crisis that has emerged in the Middle East. The Arab street has risen up against autocratic regimes in Egypt, Tunisia, Yemen, Libya, and Syria with demands for democracy and personal liberty.

The protests by the Arab masses and the rise of Islamist parties accepting of democratic systems create an alternative narrative to al-Qaeda's brand of violent Jihadism. Having preached violent activism against autocratic regimes for decades al-Qaeda has seen nonviolent civil disobedience movements succeed where it has failed. This does not mean that al-Qaeda is destined to lose the war of ideas on the Arab street for the impact of the regions progression toward democracy is uncertain and still to be determined.

Al-Qaeda and the Arab Spring

Only a few years ago it was expert opinion that the Arab Middle East was impervious to democratic revolutions. Many analysts held that Arab civil society trampled by dictatorial and monarchial regimes had little capacity to break autocracy and repressive rule.[51] Tribalism, Islam, and autocratic culture were accordingly impediments to democratization not found elsewhere.

Historically monarchs and populist dictators had crushed liberal and Islamist opposition movements by relying on nearly omnipotent and ruthless security services. Seemingly Arabs were predestined to be ruled by strongmen like Qaddafi, Bin Ali, Assad, and Mubarak. Accordingly, there would be no Prague Spring equivalent in the Arab world.

These experts were clearly wrong. Social media networks, cell phones, and internet technologies undermined the foundations of Arab autocratic society.[52] By February 2011, Ben Ali and Mubarak were history and the Libyan revolt was underway with the help of NATO overthrowing Qaddafi's generational dictatorship. Visions of Qaddafi's corpse no doubt linger in the memory of

Bashar al-Assad whose regime appears to be teetering on the edge of collapse after two years of revolt.

Arab civil society and its demands for democratization are viewed by some analysts as a hopeful sign.[53] The use of nonviolence and civil disobedience campaigns in Tunisia and Egypt were a marked departure for a culture steeped in violence, blood honor, and revenge. Some commentators believe that this nascent liberalism can effectively counter al-Qaeda's radical jihadist message and make the network defunct.[54]

The Arab masses in Tahrir Square who brought down the Mubarak regime reinforce this view. Young people demanding liberal, secular democracy, and the scarce participation of Islamist groups suggested a powerful movement was emerging in the Middle East that could facilitate better Muslim-Western relations. Globalization and democratization seemed finally to have reached the region.

Al-Qaeda took months to respond to the sweeping changes in the Arab world. Like many regional experts they were perplexed and surprised by the fall of Bin Ali and Mubarak.[55] The collapse of the hated Egyptian and Tunisian *near enemy* must have produced ambivalent feelings in al-Qaeda's leaders.

Al-Qaeda is delighted that these regimes are history. Ayman Zawahiri spent much of his life fighting Mubarak's regime. The Egyptian blessed the revolutionaries in his early communiques and pledged al-Qaeda's solidarity with the protests. The organization's ideologues seek to project the fall of Mubarak, Qaddafi, and Bin Ali as a fulfillment of their aspirations and plans.[56] Bin Laden's Abbottabad correspondence, for example, sees the mass protests as a "significant event."[57]

Despite these pronouncements, the emergence of liberal and Islamist civil society must be disquieting to al-Qaeda's leadership. The challenges the jihadist organization faces in confronting the Arab Spring are huge and unprecedented. Al-Qaeda had no role in the Egyptian and Tunisian rebellions and the means the protesters used must worry al-Qaeda. Given its violent jihadist ideology, civil disobedience and nonviolence are anathema to al-Qaeda.

Even more disquieting for the movement must be the Arab street's demands for democracy and the emergence of an Islamist civil society accepting of elections and majority rule. Al-Qaeda condemns democracy as a Western perversion and a colonial trap to destroy Islam and deny Allah's will for a global Islamic state, al-Qaeda's rejection of democracy harkens back to Sayyid Qutb's argument that all systems divorced from Sharia law are illegitimate and that Muslims have a divine mandate to destroy such governments.⁵⁸ For the jihadists efforts to replace God's rule for man's rule is the epitome of evil that deny Allah's will.

Islamist parties in Tunisia and Egypt who formed coalitions with secular parties and authorities are equally vexing for the movement. Al-Qaeda could offer ideological instruction to these parties to change course and impose a Sharia dominated autocratic state. If Islamist parties continue to participate in elections and maintain democratic governance, this could lead to an al-Qaeda war against Muslim Brotherhood inspired parties. The prospects of an internal Islamist civil war does not provide much succor for al-Qaeda for it is likely to be on the losing side. AQI's war with the Anbar Sheiks was disastrous and greatly diminished the jihadist cause in the country.

Despite these challenges the Arab Spring does present opportunity for al-Qaeda growth. The terror networks regeneration may lie in failed democratic transitions that could degenerate into civil war and nation-state implosion.⁵⁹ Radical jihadists have benefitted from the overthrow of the regions governments. The dismantling of security services, the repeal of emergency laws, and general amnesties granted to Islamist political prisoners in the postrevolutionary era has enlarged al-Qaeda capabilities. Ansar al Shariah's assault on the US embassy compound in Benghazi killing Ambassador Christopher Stevens and three other Americans may be an ominous portent.

Recent events in Egypt may offer some succor for the jihadist movement. The July 2013 military coup deposing the Muslim Brotherhood dominated government paving the way for a new constitution and new parliamentary and presidential elections has been rejected by many Islamist forces. Al-Qaeda Central no doubt sees the putsch as a golden opportunity for popular rebellion. The Muslim Brotherhood, moreover, has called for an uprising against the military interim government.

Since Mubarak's fall jihadist forces in the Sinai have been particularly active with attacks against Egyptian security forces. Recently formed Ansar al Sharia has called for a consolidation of jihadist forces and open revolt against the Egyptian army and its interim regime.⁶⁰ Given his struggle in the Egyptian jihadist movement for over 40 years Ayman al-Zawahiri is likely to make renewed effort to destabilize the new regime.

Some believe that the "Arab Spring" leaves al-Qaeda the biggest winner.⁶¹ The collapse of regimes in Yemen and Syria could offer promise of safe havens and territories to mount jihad. AQI militants, for example, joined the Syrian rebellion against the Assad regime. Tied to al-Qaeda, the Syrian jihadist group al-Nusra has carried out suicide missions and bombings that have had a devastating impact on Assad's security forces and political supporters. The creation of a terror sanctuary in Syria offers numerous opportunities to attack Israel that in the past has largely eluded al-Qaeda's assaults.

AQIM's dramatic reversal in Mali, however, illustrates the tenuous nature of terror sanctuaries. Thought secure in its northern Mali *sanctuary*, the Islamists march on Bamako was a gross miscalculation. France's military intercession with the support of African troops recovered much of North Mali and forced katiba battalions into mountain where Chadian troops were able to kill AQIM's main Sahelian leadership.

The collapse of the Yemeni regime could increase AQAP's operations and ability to mount attacks against the *far enemy*. The conflict between Sunnis and Shi'ites in Syria, Iraq, and Lebanon may give an ideological impetus to al-Qaeda's branches committed to sectarian war. Polarization of the Shia-Sunni sectarian divide may strengthen jihadist movements. Such sectarianism, however, diverts the struggle away from the *far enemy* and is contrary to al-Qaeda's Central plans to *vex* and *exhaust* America.

Democratic transitions in Tunisia, Libya, and Egypt are not complete. Under the best of circumstances, civil war and regime collapse may give al-Qaeda short-term advantages. The record of Islamic radicals capitalizing on chaos, however, is not very good. AQIM's precursor the Algerian GIAs failed to gain traction despite having huge swaths of territory under its control in the heyday of the 1990's civil war.[62]

The GIA's totalitarian Islamic ideology and its savaging of the civilian population invariably invited popular revulsion. In Yemen, Mali, and Somalia, al-Qaeda is plagued by internal feuds, rival groups, and international counterterror policies. Having lost much of South-Central Somalia to AU troops, al-Shabaab is besieged by internal and external adversaries and has failed to launch one attack against the Western *far enemy*.

The role of illicit finance in al-Qaeda operations has a corrupting effect undermining its puritanical message. AQIM, for example, has evolved into a criminal enterprise and its jihadist message is secondary to reaping profits from drugs, arms, and tobacco. At best the movement will operate in the periphery of failed states, hunted by enemies and shielded by temporary and tenuous tribal alliances. It has few other places to go.

Whither al-Qaeda?

Whether al-Qaeda can respond to the ideological challenge of the Arab Spring and capitalize on its insecurity is difficult to forecast. The obstacles appear daunting. Al-Qaeda has failed to defeat its enemies since its 1988 formation. The movement is ideologically exhausted, financially depleted, and internally fractured. International and domestic counterterror policies have killed many of its leaders and degraded the network's capabilities.

Al-Qaeda has failed in its grand objective to force a Western disengagement from the Middle East. Its last great attack was eight years ago in London and the pace of subsequent serious attacks has slackened. The fracturing of the movement into uncontrollable affiliates has refocused Jihadism toward the *near enemy* and is contrary to bin Laden's wishes. Driven by Sunni-Shia tensions in the region with conflicts raging in Syria, Iraq, Lebanon, and Bahrain, jihadist groups have a pronounced sectarian caste contrary to al-Qaeda founder's wishes. Al-Qaeda's war with the West is today more aspirational than real. Its network appears *vexed* and *exhausted*.

Bin Laden's Abbottabad letters complain that affiliates lack a strategy against the West and they have a propensity to slaughter Muslims. Similarly, the Abbottabad letters indicate the sorry state of the movement's finances.[63] Al-Qaeda's financial drain is severe and by some accounts donations from Gulf supporters has drastically declined.[64] The movement's dependence on illicit trade diminishes its jihadist message and diverts resources to criminal enterprise. While these problems are significant, al-Qaeda's greatest failures have occurred in its struggle against apostate regimes.

Its assaults against its most hated foes have failed. After al-Qaeda's 2003–4 terror campaign, the Saudi Kingdom repressed its militants driving them into Yemen. The movement is harassed by Jordanian, Yemeni, and other Mideast security services that have imprisoned and killed hundreds of operatives. Al-Qaeda affiliates in Yemen, Mali, and Somalia have a precarious territorial base which they have failed to use effectively.

In Afghanistan and Pakistan, al-Qaeda Central's ranks have been depleted by air and Special Forces assaults. The Egyptian regime fell not because of al-Qaeda attacks but to a social movement that rejects al-Qaeda's core values and tactics. With the Muslim Brotherhood's embrace of democratic politics, al-Qaeda faces the prospect of waging an assault against an Islamist movement with whom it shares a common ideological lineage. A war it is unlikely to win.

Al-Qaeda's failures are also a consequence of its own totalitarian worldview. Its dreams of attacking the United States and provoking a confrontation with American forces in the Islamic world failed to ignite a mass Muslim conversion to its cause. Philosophical systems that negate individual freedom and pluralism irrationally attempt to impose order onto a chaotic and unpredictable world. Such movements can only succeed by using extreme coercion that invariably invites mass resistance.

Al-Qaeda's lack of a popular following is also due to its elitist ideology and character. Its violent takfiri ideology and its exaltation of elitist vanguards limit its mass appeal. Bin Laden's grand vision of breaking the strictures of jahilli ignorance by provoking and attacking the United States has not resulted in mass Muslim conversion to al-Qaeda's cause.

Where Islamists have sought to create genuine Sharia states, the zeal of their militants have inspired rebellion. Sufi militias have risen against al-Shabaab to defend their rights and Tuareg rebels have challenged AD and AQIM in northern Mali. AQI's nihilistic violence in Iraq continues to haunt the organization and AQIM's brief tyrannical rule in Mali created the seeds of failure inviting French and African intervention.

AD's destruction of Sufi burial sites and mosques in the historic city of Timbuktu is the latest incarnation of al-Qaeda's collective insanity that inexorably is self-defeating.

Like the Nazis of the past, al-Qaeda's embrace of irrational myths and their extremist vision will lead to their eventual destruction. The terror network's demise will most likely be secured by Muslim majorities that reject its extremist message.

Notes

Introduction

1 Osama bin Laden's letter to Sheik Mahmud designating him successor to Sheikh Sa'id after his death in a CIA predator drone assassination strike. Sheik Mahmud will also die in a Predator drone strike. Nelly Lahoud, Stuart Caudill, Liam Collins, Gabriel Koehler-Derrick, Don Rassler, and Muhammad al-`Ubaydi, *Letters from Abbottabad: Bin Laden Side Lined?* West Point Combating Terrorism Center Harmony Program (US Army: West Point, NY, 2012) accessed at www.ctc.usma.mil SOCOM-2012-0000019.
2 Peter Bergen, *Holy War Incorporated: Inside the Secret World of Osama bin Laden* (Simon and Schuster: New York, 2002).
3 Chris Dishman, "The Leaderless Nexus: When Crime and Terror Converge" in Johjn Horgan and Kurt Braddock (eds), *Terrorism: A Reader* (Routledge: New York, 2012) 20.
4 Ibid.
5 George Grayson, "Los Zetas: The Ruthless Army Spawned by a Mexican Drug Cartel" *FPRI E-Note* (May 2008) accessed at www.fpri.org/enotes/200805.grayson.loszetas.html
6 Dishman, "The Leaderless Nexus."
7 Daveed Gartenstein-Ross, *Bin Laden's Legacy: Why we are Still losing the War against Al Qaeda* (John Wiley & Sons: Hoboken, 2011); Michael Scheuer, *Imperial Hubris: Why the West Is Losing the War on Terror* (Potomac Books: Dulles, 2004).
8 Michael Radu, "News from Spain: Terror Work" *FPRI E-Note* (March 16, 2004) accessed at www.fpri.org/enotes/20040316.americawar.radu.terrorworks.html
9 James Dobson, "Who Lost Iraq?" *Foreign Affairs* 86 (2007) 61–75; James Fearon, "Iraq's Civil War" *Foreign Affairs* 85 (2006) 2–15; Stephen Biddle, "Seeing Baghdad, Thinking Saigon" *Foreign Affairs* (March/April 2006) 2–16.
10 Clint Watts, "Major Hassan Nidal and the Fort Hood Tragedy: Implications for the U.S. Armed Forces" *FPRI E-Note* (June 2011) accessed at www.fpri.org/articles/201106.watts.fort.hood.html
11 *Letters from Abbottabad.*
12 Pascale Siegel, "AQIM's Playbook in Mali" Combating Terrorism Center at West Point *CTC Sentinel* 6 (2013) 10–12.

13. Ibid.
14. M. W. Zackie, "An Analysis of Abu Musab Suri's Call to Global Islamic Resistance" *Journal of Strategic Security* 6 (2013) 1–18.
15. Abu Bakr Naji, *The Management of Savagery: The Most Critical Phase through Which the Ummah Will Pass* accessed at http://wcfia.harvard.edu/Management%20of%20-%2005-23-2006.pdf
16. Marc Sageman, *Leaderless Jihad* (University of Pennsylvania: Philadelphia, 2007).
17. James Jay Carafano, Steven Bucci, and Jessica Zuckerman, "Fifty Terror Plots Foiled since 9/11: The Homegrown Threat and the Long War on Terror" *Heritage Foundation Backgrounder* 2682 (April 26, 2012) accessed at www.heritage.org/research/reports/2012/04/fifty-terror-plots-foiled-since-9-11-the-homegrown-threat-and-the-long-war-on-terrorism

Chapter 1

1. Osama bin Laden's May 2011 letter to Sheikh Mahmud designating him successor to Sheik Sa'id; *Letters from Abbottabad*, SOCOM-2012-0000019.
2. Michael Radu, "Al Qaeda Confusion: How to Thinks about Jihad" *FPRI E-Note* (July 2007) accessed at www.fpri.org/enotes/200707.radu.alqaedajihad.html
3. John Esposito, *The Islamic Threat: Myth or Reality* (Oxford University Press: New York, 1999); Bernard Lewis, *What Went Wrong? The Clash between Islam and Modernity* (Harper Perennial: New York, 2003).
4. Thomas Hegghammer, "Jihadi-Salafis or Religious Revolutionaries? On Religion and Politics in the Study of Militant Islamism" accessed at http://hegghammer.com/_files/hegghammer_-_jihadi-salafis_orreligiousrevolutionaries.pdf; Andreas Ambrose, "Religious Fundamentalism and Terrorist Acts" *Defense against Terrorism* 2 (2009) 51–91.
5. Fawaz Gerges, *Rise and Fall of Al Qaeda* (Oxford University Press: New York, 2010); Walid Phares, *The War of Ideas: Jihadism versus Democracy* (Palgrave MacMillan: New York, 2008); Gilles Kepel, *The Trail of Political Islam* (I.B. Taurus: New York, 2006).
6. Tarek Fatah, *The Tragic Illusion of an Islamic State* (John Wiley & Sons: Toronto, 2008).
7. Paul Berman, *Terror and Liberalism* (W.W. Norton: New York, 2004); Johan Calvert, *Sayyid Qutb and the Origins of Radical Islam* (Columbia University Press: New York, 2010).
8. Mehdi Mozaffar, "What Is Islamism: History and Definition of a Concept" *Totalitarian Movements and Political Religions* 8 (2007) 17–33; Berman, *Terror and Liberalism*.

9   Ephraim Karsh, *Islamic Imperialism: A History* (Yale University Press: New Haven, 2007); Lewis, *What Went Wrong?*
10 Phares, *The War of Ideas*.
11 Ambrose, "Religious Fundamentalism and Terrorist Acts."
12 Karsh, *Islamic Imperialism*.
13 Vali Nasr, *The Shia Revival: How Conflicts Within Islam Will Shape the Future* (W.W. Norton: New York, 2007).
14 Karsh, *Islamic Imperialism*.
15 Daniel Benjamin and Steven Simon, *The Age of Sacred Terror: Radical Islam's War against America* (Random House: New York, 2002).
16 Nasr, *The Shia Revival*.
17 Bernard Lewis, *The Assassins* (Basic Books: New York, 2002).
18 Karsh, *Islamic Imperialism*.
19 Ahmed Ibrahim Abousouk, "The Ideology of the Mahdi in Muslim History: The Case of the Sudanese Mahdiyya" *Pakistan Journal of History and Culture* 30 (2009) 43–60.
20 Christopher Henzel, "The Origins of Al Qaeda's Ideology: Implications for U.S. Policy" accessed at www.carlisle.army.mil./USAWC/parameters/articles/05spring/henzel.pdf
21 Calvert, *Sayyid Qutb and the Origins of Radical Islam*.
22 Karsh, *Islamic Imperialism*, 40–2.
23 Phares, *The War of Ideas*; Berman, *Terror and Liberalism*.
24 Lewis, *The Assassins*. The Napoleonic period in Egypt appears to have been a pivotal event in forcing Muslim societies to adapt to Western traditions and invited a sharp conflict between traditionalists and modernizers that continues to this day.
25 Henzel, "The Origins of Al Qaeda's Ideology."
26 Dale Eikmeier, "Qutbism: An Ideology of Islamic Fascism" *Parameters: U.S. Army War College Journal* (Spring 2007) 85–97.
27 Aziz Ahmad, "Mawdudi and Orthodox Fundamentalism in Pakistan" *Middle East Journal* 21 (1967) 369–80.
28 Gerges, *Rise and Fall of Al Qaeda*.
29 Calvert, *Sayyid Qutb and the Origins of Radical Islam*, 69–70, 218–28.
30 Berman, *Terror and Liberalism*, 77–102.
31 Calvert, *Sayyid Qutb and the Origins of Radical Islam*, 232–4.
32 Ibid. The author does an excellent job in tracing the influence of Bolshevik theories on Qutb's philosophical development and his pivotal role in providing a connection between neo-Marxist and Koranic principles that al-Qaeda's theorists Abu Bakr Naji and Abu Musab Suri represent in their work.
33 Henzel, "The Origins of Al Qaeda's Ideology."

34. John Calvert, "The Mythic Foundations of Radical Islam," *Orbis* 48 (Winter 2004) 29–41. In this article Calvert emphasizes Qutb's quest for mystical explanations and a means to divine Allah's true intentions. It represents many of the utopian premises behind al-Qaeda unbridled and misguided optimism that has led to many strategic mistakes.
35. Berman, *Terror and Liberalism*, 42–3, 45–6.
36. Assar Moghadan, "Salafi Jihad as a Religious Ideology," Combating Terrorism Center at West Point *CTC Sentinel* 1 (2008) 14–16.
37. Calvert, *Sayyid Qutb and the Origins of Radical Islam*, 197–229. Calvert's sympathetic view nicely traces Sayyid Qutb's metamorphosis into totalitarian worldview. His brilliant book struggles mightily to humanize a man who at his base seems egomaniacal and irredeemably selfish.
38. Nasr, *The Shia Revival*, 129–30.
39. Eikmeier, "Qutbism: An Ideology of Islamic Fascism."
40. Robert Soloman, *Anti-Semitism: The Longest Hatred* (Schocken Press: New York, 1994).
41. Calvert, *Sayyid Qutb and the Origins of Radical Islam*, 250–73.
42. Ibid.
43. Oliver Roy, *The Failure of Political Islam* (I.B. Taurus: New York, 1994).
44. Gilles Kepel, "The Future of Political Islam and the War on Terrorism" accessed at http://www2./se.as.uk/IDEAS/publications/reports/pdf/su003/il
45. Peter Bergen, *The Longest War: The Enduring Struggle between the United States and Al Qaeda* (Simon and Schuster: New York, 2011).
46. Kepel, *The Trail of Political Islam*. Gilles Kepel repeatedly argues that Islamic radicalism was frustrated by its inability to defeat home governments and this frustration lead to an existential search for a new strategy to revitalize a moribund movement.
47. Gerges, *Rise and Fall of Al Qaeda*, 43–6.
48. Bergen, *Holy War Incorporated*.
49. Peter Pham, "Foreign Influence and Shifting Horizons: The Ongoing Evolution of Al Qaeda in the Islamic Maghreb," *Orbis* 55 (Spring 2011) 240–54.
50. Ray Takeyh and Nikolas Gvosdev, "Radical Islam: The Death of an Ideology," *Middle East Policy* 1 (2004) 86–95.
51. Michael Knapp. "The Concept and Practice of Jihad" accessed at www.carlisle.army.mil/USAWC/parameters/articles/03spring/knapp.pdf
52. Calvert, *Sayyid Qutb and the Origins of Radical Islam*, 230, 276.
53. Yousef H. Aboul-Enein, "Ayman al-Zawahiri: The Ideologue of Modern Islamic Militancy" accessed at http://cpc.au.af.mil/pdf/monograph/aymanzawahiri.pdf
54. Henzel, "The Origins of Al Qaeda's Ideology."

Chapter 2

1. Osama bin Laden's 1996 fatwa declaring war against the United States; PBS News Hour (August 23, 1996) full text of Bin Laden's fatwa accessed at www.pbs.org/newshour/terrrorism/international/fatwa_1996.html
2. Bergen, *Holy War Incorporated*.
3. Andrew McGregor, "Jihad and the Rifle Alone: Abdullah Azzam and the Islamist Revolution" *Journal of Conflict Studies* 23 (2003) 92–104.
4. Brian Glyn Williams, "On the Trail of the Lions of Islam: Foreign Fighters in Afghanistan and Pakistan, 1980–1990" *Orbis* 55 (2010) 216–39.
5. Thomas Kean and Lee Hamilton, *The 9-11 Commission Report: The Final Report of the National Commission on Terrorism Attacks upon the United States* (US Government Printing Office: Washington, DC, 2004) 73.
6. Abdullah Azzam, *Defense of Muslim Lands* accessed at www.kalamullah.com/Books/defence.pdf
7. Williams, "On the Trail of the Lions of Islam."
8. Lawrence Wright, *The Looming Tower* (Borzai Books: Toronto, 2006) 11–12.
9. Bergen, *The Longest War*; Gerges, *Rise and Fall of Al Qaeda*; Wright, *The Looming Tower*.
10. Wright, *The Looming Tower*, 139–40.
11. Ibid., 173–4.
12. Rohan Gunaratna, *Inside Al Qaeda: Global Network of Terror* (Berkley Book: New York, 2002) 30–1.
13. Bergen, *Holy War Incorporated*, 58.
14. Henzel, "The Origins of Al Qaeda's Ideology."
15. Ibid.
16. Kean and Hamilton, *The 9-11 Commission Report*, 59–61.
17. Henzel, "The Origins of Al Qaeda's Ideology."
18. Bergen, *The Longest War*, 18–19.
19. Soloman, *Anti-Semitism*.
20. Berman, *Terror and Liberalism*. Berman in his book establishes strong connections ideological and historical connections between the Islamist movement and the Nazis. Their rejection of bourgeois liberal capitalism and individualism seeks a mystical and irrational collective purpose to drive mankind. Berman's comparison between the Muslim Brotherhood and the Nazi movement has been pilloried by Islamic experts who cannot tolerate any connection between the two movements despite their strong historical linkage.
21. Karsh, *Islamic Imperialism*.
22. Wright, *The Looming Tower*, 224–6.

23 Ibid., 226–8.
24 Kean and Hamilton, *The 9-11 Commission Report*, 59–61.
25 Lorenzo Vidino, "The Arrival of Islamic Fundamentalism in the Sudan" *Al Nakalah: Fletcher School Journal of Southwest Asian and Islamic Civilization* (Fall 2006) accessed at www.fletcher.tufts.edu/alNakhahl/archives/_/media/fletcher/microsites/alnakhlah/archives/2006/vidino.asht
26 Wright, *The Looming Tower*, 165–6.
27 Vidino, "The Arrival of Islamic Fundamentalism."
28 Kean and Hamilton, *The 9-11 Commission Report*, 61–2.
29 Vidino, "The Arrival of Islamic Fundamentalism," 4–16.
30 Ibid., 6.
31 Ibid., 7.
32 Wright, *The Looming Tower*, 224–36.
33 Kean and Hamilton, *The 9-11 Commission Report*, 61.
34 Wright, *The Looming Tower*.
35 Kean and Hamilton, *The 9-11 Commission Report*, 60.
36 Bergen, *Holy War Incorporated*, 136–9.
37 Wright, *The Looming Tower*, 165–6.
38 Vidino, "The Arrival of Islamic Fundamentalism," 7.
39 Wright, *The Looming Tower*, 219.
40 Ibid., 166.
41 Ahmed Rashid, *Taliban* (Penguin Book: New York, 1999).
42 Ibid., 85–90.
43 Ibid., 89–97, 137–8.
44 Ahmed Rashid, *Descent into Chaos: The U.S. and the Disaster in Pakistan, Afghanistan and Central Asia* (Penguin Books: New York, 2007).
45 Bergen, *The Longest War*, 89–90.
46 Rashid, *Taliban*, 138–9.
47 Ibid., 131–40.
48 Bergen, *Holy War Incorporated*, 167–8.
49 Ibid., 160–4.
50 Gerges, *Rise and Fall of Al Qaeda*, 60–1.
51 Bergen, *The Longest War*, 90.
52 Kean and Hamilton, *The 9-11 Commission Report*, 63–70.
53 Gunaratna, *Inside Al Qaeda*, 208–19.
54 Ibid., 222–93.
55 Kean and Hamilton, *The 9-11 Commission Report*, 145–53.
56 Wright, *The Looming Tower*, 237–44.
57 Kean and Hamilton, *The 9-11 Commission Report*, 169–70.

58 Wright, *The Looming Tower*, 262–4.
59 Bergen, *Holy War Incorporated*, 114.
60 Vidino, "The Arrival of Islamic Fundamentalism."
61 Wright, *The Looming Tower*, 127.
62 Ibid., 270–7.
63 Bergen, *The Longest War*, 40–1.
64 Wright, *The Looming Tower*, 275–6.
65 Noam Chomsky, *9-11* (Seven Stories Press: New York, 2001). Chomsky's comparison between the Sudan chemical plant strike and 9/11 is yet another illustration of his effort to establish moral equivalence between established states and terrorists. He like many partisans of the post Marxist Left refer to Israel as a terrorist state and evoke South African Apartheid to explain Israeli settlement and occupation policies in the West Bank.
66 Wright, *The Looming Tower*, 310–20.
67 Ibid., 277.
68 Kean and Hamilton, *The 9-11 Commission Report*, 152–3.
69 Bergen, *The Longest War*, 40–1.
70 Kean and Hamilton, *The 9-11 Commission Report*, 153–60.
71 Wright, *The Looming Tower*, 178–9.
72 Ibid., 176–7.
73 Ibid.
74 Ibid., 176.
75 Ibid., 203–5.
76 Gunaratna, *Inside Al Qaeda*, 232–72.
77 Kean and Hamilton, *The 9-11 Commission Report*, 145–6.
78 Gunaratna, *Inside Al Qaeda*, 233–8.
79 Wright, *The Looming Tower*, 205.
80 Ibid., 301–4.
81 Kean and Hamilton, *The 9-11 Commission Report*, 153–60.
82 Ibid.
83 Ibid.
84 Wright, *The Looming Tower*, 301–10.
85 Michael Radu, *Europe's Ghosts: Tolerance, Jihadism and the Crisis in the West* (Encounter Books: New York, 2010); John Esposito, *The Future of Islam* (Oxford University Press: New York, 2010).
86 Kean and Hamilton, *The 9-11 Commission Report*, 163–5.
87 Marc Sageman, *Understanding Terror Networks* (University of Pennsylvania: Philadelphia, 2004).
88 Kean and Hamilton, *The 9-11 Commission Report*, 160–8.

89 Ibid., 165.
90 Wright, *The Looming Tower*, 311–12.
91 Kean and Hamilton, *The 9-11 Commission Report*, 254–67.
92 Ibid.

Chapter 3

1 Naji, *The Management of Savagery*.
2 Sageman, *Understanding Terror Networks*; Sageman, *Leaderless Jihad*; Bruce Hoffman, "The Myth of Grass Roots Terrorism" *Foreign Affairs* (May/June 2008).
3 Simon Franzen, "Unity in Terrorism the Relationship between Al Qaeda, the Taliban and Militants in Pakistan" Institute for Middle Eastern Democracy accessed at www.instmed.org/wp-contnet/uploads/2012/10/Al-Qaeda_and=Taliban.pdf; Barbara Suide, "Al Qaeda Central: An Assessment of the Threat Posed by the Group in the Afghanistan-Pakistan Border" *Counter Terrorism Strategy Initiative Policy Paper* (February 2010) accessed at www.counterterrorismnewamerica.net
4 *Letters from Abbottabad*.
5 Khurum Iqbal, "Tehrik-e-Taliban: A Global Threat" *Conflict and Peace Studies* 3 (October/December 2010) 125–38.
6 Shazad Qazi, "An Extended Profile of the Pakistani Taliban" *Policy Brief 44* Institute for Social Policy and Understanding (August 2011) accessed at www.ipsu.org/...?ISPU%20Policy%20Brief%20Profile%20Pakistani%20Taliban.pdf
7 Seth Jones, "Al Qaeda's Persistent Sanctuary" *ARI Real Instituto Elcano* 67 (April 13, 2011) accessed at www.realinstitutoelcano.org; Fernando Reinares, "Las amenazas terrorista en EEUU y el fallido atentado de Times Square" *ARI Real Instituto Elcano* 84 (May 14, 2010) accessed at www.realinstitutoelcano.org/wps/portalrealelcano/contenido?wcm_global_context.html
8 Fernando Reinares, "El terrorismo global:el fenomeno polimorfo" *ARI Real Instituto Elcano* 84 (July 23, 2008) accessed at www.realinstitutoelcano.rog/wps/portalrealelcano/contenido?_global_context.html
9 Phares, *The War of Ideas*; Gartenstein-Ross, *Bin Laden's Legacy*; Bergen, *The Longest War*; Gerges, *Rise and Fall of Al Qaeda*.
10 Bob Woodward, *Bush at War* (Simon and Schuster: New York, 2002).
11 Wright, *The Looming Tower*.
12 Ahmed Rashid, *Descent into Chaos: How the War against Islamic Extremism Is Being Lost in Pakistan, Afghanistan and Central Asia* (Penguin Books: London, 2008).

13 Wright, *The Looming Tower*.
14 Gerges, *Rise and Fall of Al Qaeda*.
15 Rashid, *Descent into Chaos: The U.S. and the Disaster*, 4.
16 Brynjar Lia, *Architect of Global Jihad: The Life of Al Qaeda Strategist Abu Musab al-Suri* (Columbia University Press: New York, 2008).
17 Rashid, *Descent into Chaos: How the War*, 75–85.
18 Bergen, *The Longest War*, 77–9.
19 Rashid, *Descent into Chaos: How the War*.
20 Williams, "On the Trail of the Lions of Islam."
21 Daanish Mustafa and Katherine E. Brown, "The Taliban Public Space and Terror in Pakistan" *Eurasian Geography and Economics* 51 (2010) 496–512.
22 Qazi, "An Extended Profile of the Pakistani Taliban."
23 Grant Holt and David Grey, "The Pakistani Fifth Column: The Pakistani Inter-services Directorate Sponsorship of Terrorism" *Global Security Studies* 2 (2011) 55–69.
24 Rashid, *Descent into Chaos: How the War*.
25 Bergen, *The Longest War*.
26 Brynjar Lia, "Does Al Qaeda Articulate a Consistent Strategy: A Study of Al Qaeda Leadership Statements 2001–2009" accessed at http://ffi\terra.jihadstudies.netbrynjarlia.com
27 Gerges, *Rise and Fall of Al Qaeda*; Bergen, *The Longest War*, 2010; Gartenstein-Ross, *Bin Laden's Legacy*.
28 Lia, *Architect of Global Jihad*; Paul Cruickshank and Mohammad Hage Ali, "Abu Musab al-Suri: Architect of the New Al Qaeda" *Studies in Conflict and Terrorism* 30 (2007) 1–14.
29 Sarah E. Zabel, "The Military Strategy of Global Jihad" (October 2007) accessed at www.strategicstudiesinstitute.army.mil
30 Sageman, *Leaderless Jihad*.
31 Lia, *Architect of Global Jihad*, 137.
32 Ibid., 278–93.
33 Ibid., 372.
34 Ibid., 350–60.
35 Ibid.
36 Ibid., 299.
37 Karsh, *Islamic Imperialism*; Thomas Hegghammer, "The Ideological Hybridization of Jihadi Groups" *Current Trends in Islamist Ideology* 9 (2009) 26–45; *The Hudson Institute* accessed at www.hudson.org/files/public/current_trends_in_islamic_ideology_vol.9.pdf
38 Zabel, "The Military Strategy of Global Jihad."

39 Carafano et al., "Fifty Terror Plots Foiled since 9/11."
40 Nur Aziman Binte Azam, "Al Qaeda's Internet Strategy a Failure? On-line Jihadists Disapprove" *International Center for Political Violence and Terrorism Research* 4 (2012) 1–4 accessed at www.pvtr.org/pdf/ccta/2012/cttafebruary12.pdf
41 *Letters from Abbottabad*, 7, 11–15.
42 Jones, "Al Qaeda's Persistent Sanctuary"; Fernando Reinares, "The Madrid Bombings and Global Jihadism" *Survival* 52 (2010) 83–104.
43 Jarret Brachman and William F. McCants, "Stealing Al-Qaeda's Playbook" *CTC Report* (February 2006) at www.ctc.edu/posts/stealing-al-qaeda-playbook.html
44 Naji, *The Management of Savagery*.
45 Ibid., 40.
46 Ibid., 20.
47 Ibid., 23.
48 Ibid., 5.
49 Ibid., 23.
50 Ibid., 18.
51 Ibid., 51.
52 Ibid., 50–1. Centralization of media operations is an enduring theme of al-Qaeda's strategy to convey a uniform message in a propaganda war against its adversaries and to highlight the transcendental importance of attacking the Western far enemy. Bin Laden prior to his death expresses exasperation with his affiliate's media operations and he sought an agreement with affiliates that would put the central apparatus in charge of approving their communication strategy.
53 Jeremy White, "Al Qaeda Internet and Digihad: The Evolution of Al Qaeda's Media Strategy" *Small War Journal* (November 2012) accessed at www.smallwarjournal.org
54 Ibid.
55 Naji, *The Management of Savagery*, 27.
56 Ibid., 47.
57 Lia, "Does Al Qaeda Articulate a Consistent Strategy."
58 Ibid.
59 Hegghammer, "The Ideological Hybridization of Jihadi Groups."
60 Ibid.
61 Kepel, *The Trail of Political Islam*.
62 Gunaratna, *Inside Al Qaeda*, Preface.
63 Don Rassler, "Al Qaeda's Pakistan Strategy" *CTC Sentinel* 2 (October 2009) 1–4.
64 Mustafa and Brown, "The Taliban Public Space."
65 *Letters from Abbottabad*, 34–7.

66 Bill Roggio, "Al Qaeda's paramilitary 'Shadow Army'" (February 9, 2009) accessed at www.longwarjournal.org/archives/2009/02/al_qaedas_paramiilitia.php
67 Don Rassler and Vahid Brown, "The Haqqani Nexus and the Evolution of Al Qaeda" *Combating Terrorism at West Point* Report (July 14, 2011) accessed at www.ctc.usma.edu
68 Gretchen Peters, "Haqqani Network Financing: Evolution of an Industry" *Combating Terrorism Center at West Point* Report (July 2012) accessed at www.ctc.usma.edu
69 Bergen, *The Longest War*; Reinares, "The Madrid Bombings and Global Jihadism," 83–104.
70 Christopher Swift, "From Periphery to Core: Foreign Fighters and the Evolution of Al Qaeda in the Arabian Peninsula" *FPRI Foreign Fighters Problem: Recent Trends and Case Studies* (2011) accessed at www/fpri.org; Pham, "Foreign Influence and Shifting Horizons."
71 *Letters from Abbottabad*, 34–7.
72 Ibid., 37, 22–8.
73 Shmuel Bar and Yair Minnelli, "The Zawahiri Letter and the Strategy of Al Qaeda" *Current Trends in Islamist Ideology* 3 (2006) 3–51 accessed at www.hudson.org/files/public/current_trends_in_islamist_ideology_vol_3.pdf
74 Gunaratna, *Inside Al Qaeda*, Preface.
75 Ibid., 266.
76 Matt Cianflone, Jason Cull, John Fisher, Dave Holt, Amanda Krause, and Julie Moore, *Anatomy of a Terrorist Attack: An In-depth Investigation into the 2002 Bali, Indonesia, Bombings* (Matthew Ridgway Center of the University of Pittsburg: Pittsburgh, 2006) accessed at www.mercury.ethz.ch/serviceengine/files/ISN/50137/publicationdocument_single_doucment/33258a3.pdf
77 Gunaratna, *Inside Al Qaeda*, 264–6.
78 Ibid., 264–70.
79 Cianflone et al., *Anatomy of a Terrorist Attack*, 38–9.
80 Gunaratna, *Inside Al Qaeda*, 258–62.
81 Cianflone et al., *Anatomy of a Terrorist Attack*, 35–6.
82 Gunaratna, *Inside Al Qaeda*, Preface.
83 Cianflone et al., *Anatomy of a Terrorist Attack*, 33–41.
84 Ibid., 17.
85 Karen Hodgson, "The Al Qaeda Threat in Turkey" *The Long War Journal* (July 8, 2013) accessed at www.longwarjournal.org/archives/2013/07/the_Al_Qaeda_threat_1.php

Chapter 4

1. Text of Osama bin Laden's audio tape given to Al-Jazeera television network April 15, 2004; BBC news (April 15, 2004) transcription accessed at www.news.bbc.couk/2/hi/middle_East/3628069.stm
2. Kimberley Thachuk, Marion Bowman, and Courtney Richardson, "Homegrown Terrorism: The Threat Within" *Center for Technology and National Security. National Defense University* (May 2008) accessed at www.ndu.edu/CTNSP/docUploaded/DTP%20home%2020Grown%20Terrorism.pdf; Robin Simcox, Hannah Stuart, and Houriya Ahmed, *Islamist Terrorism: The British Connections* (Center for Social Cohesion: London, 2010) accessed at www.conservativehome.blogs.com?...?128089320islamist_terrorism_preview.pdf
3. Sageman, *Understanding Terror Networks*; Sageman, *Leaderless Jihad*.
4. Thachuk et al., "Homegrown Terrorism: The Threat Within"; Simcox et al., *Islamist Terrorism*; Javier Jordán, "El terrorismo yihadista en España: situación actual" Study by *Real Instituto Elcano* (September 7, 2005) accessed at www.realinstitutoelcano.org
5. Bruce Reidel, "Al Qaeda Strikes Back" *Foreign Affairs* 86 (2007) 24–40.
6. Hoffman, "The Myth of Grass Roots Terrorism."
7. Jonathan Shanzer, *Al Qaeda's Armies* (Institute for Near Eastern Studies: Washington, DC, 2005); Russell Isaac, "North African Franchise: AQIM: Threat to U.S. Security" *Strategic Insights* 8 (December 2009) accessed at http://mercury.ethz.ch/serviceengine/Files/1SN/111476/...d8d54223.../7.pdf
8. Lorenzo Vidino, *Al Qaeda in Europe* (Prometheus Books: New York, 2005); Radu, *Europe's Ghosts*.
9. Michael Radu, "Radical Imams and Terrorists" *FPRI E-Note* 6 (August 2005) accessed at www.fpri./ww/0606.200508.radu.imamterrrorists.html
10. Javier Jordán, "El terrorismo yihadista en España: evolución despues del 11-M" *Real Instituto Elcano* 7 (February 6, 2009) accessed at http://realinstitutoelcano.org
11. Fernando Reinares, "11-M la conexión: al Qaeda" *El País* (December 17, 2009); Vidino, *Al Qaeda in Europe*; Radu, *Europe's Ghosts*.
12. Gunaratna, *Inside Al Qaeda*.
13. Anthony Celso, "The Tragedy of Al Andaluz: The Madrid Train Terror Attacks" *Mediterranean Quarterly* 16 (Summer 2005) 121–41.
14. Reinares, "11-M la conexión: al Qaeda."
15. Reinares, "The Madrid Bombings and Global Jihadism."
16. Reinares, "11-M la conexión: al Qaeda."
17. Reinares, "¿Acaso 11-3 no se fijo en Bruselas?" *El País* (March 11, 2009).
18. Reinares, "The Madrid Bombings and Global Jihadism."

19 Jordán, "El terrorismo yihadista en España."
20 Reinares, "The Madrid Bombings and Global Jihadism."
21 Jordán, "El terrorismo yihadista en España."
22 Celso, "The Tragedy of Al Andaluz."
23 Fernando Reinares, ¿Expressión de una amenaza compuesta? *El País* (August 3, 2012).
24 Fernando Reinares, "La amenaza yihadista sigue aquí" *El País* (April 25, 2013) 4.
25 Ibid.
26 Radu, *Europe's Ghosts*.
27 Radu, "Radical Imams and Terrorists."
28 Vidino, *Al Qaeda in Europe*.
29 Michael Radu, "Preaching Jihad on Welfare: The Story of Abu Qatada" *FPRI E-Note* (June 2008) accessed at www.fpri.org/enotes/200806.radu.jihadwelfareabuqatada.html
30 Lia, *Architect of Global Jihad*.
31 Radu, *Europe's Ghosts*.
32 Rachel Briggs and Jonathan Birdwell, "Radicalization among Muslims in the UK" *Microcon Working Paper* 7 (May 2009) accessed at www.microconflict.eu/publications/RB_JB.pdf
33 Jodie Reed, "Young Muslims in UK: Education and Integration: A Briefing Paper" The FES/IPPR Seminar (December 2005) accessed at www.library.fes.de/pdf-fies/bueros/london/03682.pdf; Briggs and Birdwell, "Radicalization among Muslims in the UK."
34 Radu, *Europe's Ghosts*.
35 Briggs and Birdwell, "Radicalization among Muslims in the UK."
36 Simcox et al., *Islamist Terrorism*.
37 Ibid.
38 Rachel Briggs, Jennifer Cole, Margaret Gimore, and Valentina Soria, "Anatomy of a Terrorist Attack: What the Coroner's Inquest Revealed about the London Bombings" *Occasional Papers*. Royal United Services Institute for Defense and Security Studies (April 2011) accessed at www.rusi.org/downloads/anatomyofterror/pdf
39 Larry Irons, "Recent Patterns of Terrorism Prevention in the UK" *Homeland Security Affairs* accessed at www.hasj.org/?fullarticle=4.14; Darren Theils, "Policing Evidence: A Review of the Evidence the Police Found" *Police Foundation* (February 2009) accessed at www.police-foundations.oeg.uk/.../policing...evidence/terrorism_review.pdf
40 Sageman, *Leaderless Jihad*.

41 Shaun Gregory, "AQ in Pakistan" *Pakistan Research Unit (PSRU) Brief* 5 (March 1, 2007) accessed at http://spaces.brad.ac.uk8080/download/attachments/748/Brief5finalized.pdf
42 Irons, "Recent Patterns of Terrorism Prevention."
43 Theils, "Policing Evidence."
44 Gregory, "Al Qaeda in Pakistan."
45 "Documents Give New Details on Al Qaeda's London Bombings" (April 30, 2012) accessed at http://articlescnn.com/2012-04-30/world-AlQaeda-documents-london-bombings
46 Radu, *Europe's Ghosts.*
47 Bergen, *The Longest War.*
48 Dame Eliza Manningham-Butler, "The International Threat to the UK" (November 9, 2006) accessed at www.mi5.gov.uk/output/the-international-threat-to-the-uk.html
49 Jay Edwards and Benoit Gomis, "Islamic Terrorism since 9–11: Reassessing the Soft Response" *Chatham House International Security Programme Paper* 10–12 (June 2011) accessed at www.chatamhouse.org/sites/default/files_Edwardsgomis.pdf
50 Raffaello Pantucci, "The Birmingham Terrorist Plotters: Lessons for Counter-Terrorism Today" *RUSI Analysis* (February 23, 2013) accessed at www.rusi.org/analysis/commentary/ref:C51278ADD39211/

Chapter 5

1 From an al-Qaeda internal communique obtained by US Navy Seals in their May 2011 Abbottabad raid; *Letters from Abbottabad*, SOCOM-2012-0000017.
2 Bergen, *The Longest War.*
3 Jean-Charles Brisard, *Zarqawi: The New Face of Al Qaeda* (Polity Press: Cambridge, 2005).
4 Ibid., 15–16.
5 Marc Juergensmeyer, *Terror in the Mind of God: The Global Rise of Religious Violence* (University of California Press: Berkeley, 2000); M. J. Kirdar, "Al Qaeda in Iraq: Case Study 1" *AQAM Futures Project Case Studies Series* (June 2011) accessed at http://csis.org/files/publications/110614_kidar_AlQaedaIraq_Web.pdf
6 Brisard, *Zarqawi: The New Face of Al Qaeda*, 5–6.
7 Nibras Kazimi, "A Virulent Ideology in Mutation: Zarqawi upstages Maqdisi" International Institute Jihadi Websites, *Monitoring Report* (September 2009) accessed at http://sez.isn.ch/ . . . 104.virulentideology.pfd
8 Ibid.

9   Ibid.
10 Gerges, *Rise and Fall of Al Qaeda*.
11 Kirdar, "Al Qaeda in Iraq: Case Study 1."
12 Bergen, *The Longest War*.
13 Brisard, *Zarqawi: The New Face of Al Qaeda*.
14 Ibid., 35–6.
15 Kirdar, "Al Qaeda in Iraq: Case Study 1."
16 Brisard, *Zarqawi: The New Face of Al Qaeda*, 48–54.
17 Kirdar, "Al Qaeda in Iraq: Case Study 1."
18 Brisard, *Zarqawi: The New Face of Al Qaeda*, 54. Amnesties that release jihadists from prison have consistently resulted in many of them returning to the battlefield. This has been the experience in Saudi Arabia, Algeria, as well as Jordan.
19 Kazimi, "A Virulent Ideology in Mutation."
20 Bergen, *The Longest War*.
21 Brisard, *Zarqawi: The New Face of Al Qaeda*, 67.
22 Kirdar, "Al Qaeda in Iraq: Case Study 1."
23 Brisard, *Zarqawi: The New Face of Al Qaeda*.
24 Kirdar, "Al Qaeda in Iraq: Case Study 1."
25 Brisard, *Zarqawi: The New Face of Al Qaeda*, 82.
26 Ibid., 81–2.
27 Ibid., 78–9.
28 Bergen, *The Longest War*, 81–90.
29 Ibid., 119–20.
30 Gerges, *Rise and Fall of Al Qaeda*.
31 Brisard, *Zarqawi: The New Face of Al Qaeda*.
32 Rashid, *Descent into Chaos: The U.S. and the Disaster*.
33 Brisard, *Zarqawi: The New Face of Al Qaeda*, 121–5.
34 Ibid.
35 *Letters from Abbottabad*, Executive Summary.
36 Bar and Minnelli, "The Zawahiri Letter."
37 Brisard, *Zarqawi: The New Face of Al Qaeda*, 121–5.
38 Michael Radu, "The Demise of Abu Musab Zarqawi" *FPRI E-Notes* (June 8, 2006) accessed at www.fpri.org/enotes/20060608.americawar.radu.alzarqawi.html
39 Brisard, *Zarqawi: The New Face of Al Qaeda*, 113–20.
40 Radu, "The Demise of Abu Musab Zarqawi."
41 Kirdar, "Al Qaeda in Iraq: Case Study 1."
42 Ibid.
43 Bergen, *The Longest War*.

44 John McCary, "The Anbar Awakening: An Alliance of Incentives." *The Washington Quarterly* 32 (2009) 43–59. McCary clearly outlines that the arming of Sunni militias and not the surge of US forces was the pivotal factor in denying AQI a sanctuary in the Sunni Triangle. In the course of a few years al-Qaeda was badly defeated in Anbar and was forced to move its major base of operations to Tikrit and Kirkuk.
45 Bergen, *The Longest War*.
46 Brisard, *Zarqawi: The New Face of Al Qaeda*, 137.
47 Kirdar, "Al Qaeda in Iraq: Case Study 1."
48 Ibid.
49 Maura Conway, "From al-Zarqawi to al-Awlaki: The Emergence of the Internet as a New Face of Radical Jihad" Dublin City University accessed at www.isodarco.it/courses/andalo12/doc/zarqawi%20to%20awlakI_V2.pdf; Susan Glasser and Steve Coll, "The Web as Weapon: Zarqawi Intertwines Acts on the Ground in Iraq with a Propaganda Campaign" (August 9, 2005) accessed at www.washingtonpost./wp-dyn/content/article/2005/08108; Fawaz Gerges, "Zarqawi: The Man, the Message and the Video Star" *Institute for Social Policy and Understanding* (May 5, 2011) accessed at http://ispu.org/getarticle/48/1809/publications.aspx
50 Conway, "From al-Zarqawi to al-Awlaki."
51 Ibid.
52 Brisard, *Zarqawi: The New Face of Al Qaeda*, 141.
53 Bergen, *The Longest War*.
54 Brisard, *Zarqawi: The New Face of Al Qaeda*, 145.
55 Ibid., 146. Abu Musab Zarqawi strategy was preconditioned upon the unleashing of sectarian passions to rip Iraq apart making the country untenable to rule for US occupation forces and their Iraqi Allies. The targeting of the Shia was a conscious strategy to ignite sectarian warfare between the Shia and the Sunnis. This strategy was a marked departure for al-Qaeda and was heavily resisted by the central leadership. His February 2004 letter demonstrates a pathological hatred of Shiites, Christians, and Kurds and embarks a sectarian strategy that AQI's successor ISI and its Syrian extension al-Nusra continue to pursue.
56 Kirdar, "Al Qaeda in Iraq: Case Study 1."
57 Bar and Minnelli, "The Zawahiri Letter."
58 Kirdar, "Al Qaeda in Iraq: Case Study 1."
59 Brisard, *Zarqawi: The New Face of Al Qaeda*, 88. The utilization of weapons of mass destruction has always been a central al-Qaeda goal featured prominently in al-Qaeda literature and statements. Abu Bakr Naji in the *Management of Savagery* is explicit in its endorsement.
60 Kazimi, "A Virulent Ideology in Mutation."

61　Ibid.
62　Kirdar, "Al Qaeda in Iraq: Case Study 1."
63　Ibid.
64　Brisard, *Zarqawi: The New Face of Al Qaeda*, 235.
65　"Chronology of Attacks blamed on the Zarqawi Network" accessed at www.newsmonstersandcritics.com/middleeast/feat/article_1171088.phd/chronIraq_Attacks_Blamed_on_ZarqawI_network
66　Brisard, *Zarqawi: The New Face of Al Qaeda*, 235–51.
67　"English Translation of Ayman al-Zawahiri's Letter to Abu Musab al-Zarqawi" *Weekly Standard* (October 12, 2005) accessed at www.weeklystandard.com
68　Ibid. Zawahiri letter to al-Zarqawi is a brilliant piece of political argument as he sways between flattering and condemning Zarqawi's strategy. The inability of al-Qaeda's Central Leadership to control its territorial extensions endures with the Abbottabad correspondence verifying that al-Qaeda's far enemy strategy is not a priority of the organizations regional affiliates.
69　McCary, "The Anbar Awakening."
70　Ibid.
71　Radu, "The Demise of Abu Musab Zarqawi."
72　Brian Fishman, "After Zarqawi: The Dilemmas and Future of Al Qaeda in Iraq" *Washington Quarterly* 29 (2006) 19–36.
73　McCary, "The Anbar Awakening."
74　Fishman, "After Zarqawi."
75　McCary, "The Anbar Awakening."
76　Kirdar, "Al Qaeda in Iraq: Case Study 1."
77　Ibid., 5.
78　Ibid.
79　Ibid.
80　Fernando Reinares, ¿Iraq: pero no era la ocupación military lo que explica el terrorism suicida? *Comentario Elcano* 8 (June 28, 2012) accessed at www.realinsitutoelcano.org/wps/portal/reilcano/conenido?WCM_ . . . html
81　Phares, *The War of Ideas*.
82　Fouad Ajami, *The Syrian Rebellion* (Hoover Institution Press: Stanford, 2012).
83　Michael Broning, "The Sturdy House that Assad Built: Why Damascus Is Not Cairo" *Foreign Affairs* (March 7, 2011) accessed at http://foreignaffairs.com>Features>Snapshots; Tony Badran, "Syria's Assad No Longer in Vogue: What Everyone Got Wrong about Bashar al-Assad" *Foreign Affairs* (March 25, 2011) accessed at www.foreignaffairs.com>Features>snapshots
84　Aaron Zelin, "Deciphering the Jihadist Presence in Syria: An Analysis of Martyrdom Notices" Combating Terrorism Center at West Point *CTC Sentinel* 6 (2013) 7–10.

85 *The Economist* (February 23, 2013) 25–6.
86 Ajami, *The Syrian Rebellion*.
87 Adam Garfinkle, "Syria: Time for Inaction?" *FPRI E-Notes* (March 2013) accessed at www.fpri.org/articles/2013/03/syria-time-inaction.html

Chapter 6

1 Osama bin Laden's May 2010 letter to al-Qaeda leader Sheik Mahmud complaining of the behavior of his affiliated regional branches; *Letters from Abbottabad*, SOCOM-2012-0000019.
2 Rick Ozzie Nelson and Thomas M. Sanderson, "A Threat Transformed: Al Qaeda and Associated Movements in 2011" *Report of the CSIS Homeland Security and Counterterrorism Program and the CSIS Transnational Threats Program* accessed at http://CSIS.org/files/nelson_a_threat_tranformed_web.pdf
3 Swift, "From Periphery to Core."
4 Nelson and Sanderson, "A Threat Transformed."
5 David Shinn, "Al Shabaab's Foreign Threat to Somalia" *Orbis* 55 (2011) 25–37; Pham, "Foreign Influence and Shifting Horizons."
6 Andrew Le Sage, "Somalia's Endless Transition: Breaking the Deadlock" *NDU Strategic Forum* 257 (June 2010) accessed at www.ndu.edu/inns; Shinn, "Al Shabaab's Foreign Threat to Somalia."
7 Rob Wise, "Al Shabaab" *AQAM Futures Project Case Studies Series*: Case Study Number 2 (July 2011) accessed at www.csis.org/; Swift, "From Periphery to Core."
8 Nelson and Sanderson, "A Threat Transformed."
9 Jacqueline Page, "Jihadi Arena Report: Somalia-Development of Radical Islamism and Current Implications" accessed at www.ict.il/Articles/tabid/articlsid/814/currentpage/4/developmetnofradicaljihadism
10 Le Sage, "Somalia's Endless Transition."
11 Wise, "Al Shabaab."
12 Shinn, "Al Shabaab's Foreign Threat to Somalia."
13 Nelson and Sanderson, "A Threat Transformed."
14 Shinn, "Al Shabaab's Foreign Threat to Somalia."
15 Christopher Anzalone, "Al Shabaab's Setbacks in Somalia" *Combating Terrorism Center at West Point* (October 31, 2011) accessed at www.ctc.usma.edu/posts/al-shabaab's-setbacks-in-somalia
16 Shinn, "Al Shabaab's Foreign Threat to Somalia."
17 Anzalone, "Al Shabaab's Setbacks in Somalia."
18 Wise, "Al Shabaab."

19 Christopher Anzalone, "Al Shabaab's Tactical and Media Strategy in the Wake of Battlefield Setbacks" *Combating Terrorism Center CTC Sentinel* 6 (2013) 12–16.
20 Danielle Sheldon, "Al-Qaeda in Yemen-Evolving Threat" (March 5, 2010) accessed at www.ict.org.il/articles/tbid/66/articisid/825/currentpage/4/Developingthreats
21 Swift, "From Periphery to Core."
22 Sheldon, "Al-Qaeda in Yemen-Evolving Threat."
23 Alistair Harris, "Exploiting Grievances: Al Qaeda in the Arabian Peninsula" *Carnegie Endowment for International Peace Middle East Program* 111 (May 2010) accessed at http://carnegieendowment.org/files/exploiting_grievances.pdf
24 Swift, "From Periphery to Core."
25 Nelson and Sanderson, "A Threat Transformed."
26 Swift, "From Periphery to Core."
27 "Anwar al Awlaki: Pro Al-Qaeda Ideologue with Influence in the West" *NEFTA Foundation* (February 5, 2009) accessed at www.neftafoundation.org
28 Bruce Reidel, "Al Qaeda Smells Blood" (September 9, 2011) accessed at www.brookings.edu/opinions/2011/0406_yemen_al_qaeda_redel
29 Sheldon, "Al-Qaeda in Yemen-Evolving Threat."
30 William Thornbury and Jaclyn Levy, "Al Qaeda in the Islamic Maghreb" *CSIS AQAM Futures Case Study* 4 (September 2011) accessed at www.csis.org/publications/al-qaeda-islamic-maghreb
31 Luiz Martinez, *The Algerian Civil War 1990–1998* (Columbia University Press: New York, 2000).
32 Andre Le Sage, "The Evolving Threat of Al Qaeda in the Islamic Maghreb" *INSS Strategic Forum* (July 2011) accessed at www.ndu/press/ib/pdf/statforum/sfno268.pdf
33 Vidino, "The Arrival of Islamic Fundamentalism."
34 Stephen Harmon, "From GSPC to AQIM: The Evolution of an Algerian Islamist Terrorist Groups a Al Qaeda Affiliate and Its Implications for the Sahara-Sahel Region" *Concerned African Scholars Bulletin* 85 (Spring 2010) accessed at www.concernedafricanscholars.org/docs/bullitin85.harmon.pdf
35 Dario Cristiani and Ricardo Fabiani, "Al Qaeda in the Islamic Maghreb: Implications for Algeria's Regional and International Relations" *IAI Working Papers* 11/09 (April 2011) accessed at www.IAI.IT/pdf/docia/iaiwp.1107.pdf
36 "Al Qaeda in the Islamic Maghreb" *Australian National Security* accessed at http://ag.gov.au/WWW/nationalsecurity.nsf/page
37 Le Sage, "The Evolving Threat of Al Qaeda in the Islamic Maghreb."
38 Wolfram Lacher, "Organized Crime and Terrorism in the Sahel" *German Institute for International and Security Affairs* SWP Comments (January 2011) accessed at www.swp-berlin.org/fileadmin/contnets/.../2011-lac-ks.pdf

39 Christopher M. Blanchard, "Libya: Transition and U.S. Policy" *CRS Report for Congress* 7–5700 (December 8, 2011) accessed at www.fas.or/spg/crs/rowl133142.pdf
40 US State Department Advisory Review Board Report on the Benghazi Attacks (December 2012) accessed at www.state.gov/documents/organization/202446.pdf
41 Nelson and Sanderson, "A Threat Transformed."
42 "Al Qaeda in Yemen and Somalia: A Ticking Time Bomb" *Foreign Relations Committee Report to the Senate* (January 21, 2010) accessed at http://gpoacess.gov/congress/indexhtmlwww.foreignservicecommittee/imo/media/doc/yemen.pdf

Chapter 7

1 Letter by AQIM Emir Abdelmalek Droukdel critiquing the religious excesses of his militant's activities in Mali found by Associate Press in Timbuktu after France military intervention driving al-Qaeda from its Malian sanctuary; "Mali: Al Qaida's Sahara Playbook" accessed at http://hosted.ap,org/specials/interactives/.../_pdfs/al-Qaida-manifesto.pdf. Droukdel complaints about the behavior of his militants in Northern Mali and their counterproductive violence and ideological zeal echoes the concern of bin Laden and other in al-Qaeda's central leadership about the brutality of affiliate organizations and how they have lost popular support.
2 Modibo Goita, "West Africa's Growing Terror Threat Confronting AQIM's Sahelian Strategy" *African Security Brief* (February 2011) accessed at http://ndu.edu/press/lib/pdf/Africa-Security-Brief/ASB-11.pdf
3 Michael Tanchum, "Al-Qa'ida's West African Advance: Nigeria's Boko Haram, Mali's Touareg, and the Spread of Salafi Jihadism" *Israeli Journal of Foreign Affairs* 6 (2012) 75–90.
4 Peter Pham, "Boko Haram's Evolving Threat" *African Security Brief* 20 (April 2012) accessed at www.africancenter,org/wp-content/uploads/2012/04/AfricanBriefFinal_20.pdf; Sean Gourley, "Link between Boko Haram and Al Qaeda: Potentially Deadly Synergy" *Global Security Studies* 3 (2012) 1–14; Shannon Connel, "To Be or Not to Be: Is Boko Haram a Foreign Terrorist Organization?" *Global Security Studies* 3 (Summer 2012) 87–93.
5 Tanchum, "Al-Qa'ida's West African Advance."
6 "Is Nigeria's Boko Haram Group Really Tied to Al Qaeda" *Christian Science Monitor* (September 22, 2011).
7 Patrick Meehan and Jackie Speirer, "Boko Haram's Emerging Threat to the U.S. Homeland" *U.S. House of Representatives Homeland Security Subcommittee*

Report (November 30, 2011) accessed at www.homeland.house.gov/.../Boko%20 Emerging%20Threat%20to%20%US%20Homeland.pdf

8 Zachary Devlin-Fotz, "Africa's Fragile States: Empowering Extremists Export of Terrorism" *African Security Brief* 6 (August 2010) accessed at www.nudu.edu/press/lib/pdf/africa-security-brief/asb-6.pdf
9 Fernando Reinares, "FATA in North Mali" *Real Instituto Elcano* Expert Comment 15/2012 (July 31, 2012) accessed at http://realinstitutoelcano.org/wps.portal/rielcano_Eng/content?WC.html
10 Devlin-Fotz, "Africa's Fragile States."
11 John Campbell, "To Combat Boko Haram: Put Down Your Guns" *Foreign Affairs* (August/September 2011).
12 N. D. Danjibo, "Islamic Fundamentalism and Sectarian Violence: The Maitatsine and Boko Haram Crisis in Northern Nigeria" accessed at www.ifra-nigeria.org/.../N-_D_Danjibo_-_Islamic_Fundamentalism_and_htm
13 Gourley, "Link between Boko Haram and Al Qaeda."
14 Pham, "Boko Haram's Evolving Threat."
15 Toni Johnson, "Boko Haram: Backgrounder" *Council on Foreign Relations* (December 27, 2011) accessed at www.cfr.org/africa/boko-haram/p25739
16 Danjibo, "Islamic Fundamentalism and Sectarian Violence."
17 Michael Tanchum, "Al-Qa'ida's New West Africa Map: Ançar Dine, Boko Haram and Jihadism in the Trans-Sahara" *Tel Aviv Notes Special Edition* 6: No. 3 Dayan Center Tel Aviv (2012) accessed at www.dayan.org/sites/default/files/M_Tanchum_AQ_West_Africa_040612.pdf
18 Pham, "Boko Haram's Evolving Threat."
19 Campbell, "To Combat Boko Haram."
20 Emanuel O. Ojo, "Boko Haram: Nigeria's Extra Judicial State" *Journal of Sustainable Development in Africa* 12 (2010) 182–97.
21 Gourley, "Link between Boko Haram and Al Qaeda."
22 Pham, "Boko Haram's Evolving Threat."
23 Meehan and Speirer, "Boko Haram's Emerging Threat."
24 "Nigeria: Timeline of Boko Haram Attacks and Related Violence" *IRIN, UN Council of Humanitarian Affairs* (September 24, 2012) accessed at www.irubbews.org/printreport.aspxreportid=94691.html
25 Gourley, "Link between Boko Haram and Al Qaeda."
26 *The Economist* (April 27–May 3, 2013) 49.
27 Jacob Zenn, "Cooperation or Competition: Boko Haram and Ansaru after the French Intervention in Mali" *Combating Terrorism Center at West Point CTC Sentinel* 6 (2013), 1–9.
28 Ibid.

29 David Kircullen, *Counterinsurgency* (Oxford University Press: New York, 2010).
30 Tanchum, "Al-Qa'ida's New West Africa Map."
31 Tanchum, "Al-Qa'ida's West African Advance."
32 Harvey Glickman, "The Coup in Mali: Background and Foreground" *FPRI E-Note* (April 2012).
33 Reinares, "FATA in North Mali."
34 Tanchum, "Al-Qa'ida's West African Advance."
35 Dario Cristiani, "West Africa's MOJWA Militants—Competition for Al-Qaeda in the Islamic Maghreb?" *Terrorism Monitor Jamestown Foundation 10*, No. 7 (April 6, 2012) accessed at www.jamestown.org
36 Reinares, "FATA in North Mali."
37 Ibid.
38 Gourley, "Link between Boko Haram and Al Qaeda."
39 Tanchum, "Al-Qa'ida's New West Africa Map."
40 Johnson, "Boko Haram: Backgrounder."
41 Wolfram Lacher, "Organized Crime and Terrorism in the Sahel" *German Institute for International and Security Affairs* SWP Comments (January 1, 2011); Lawrence Aida Anmour, "Regional Security Cooperation in the Maghreb: Algeria's Pivotal Ambivalence" *Africa Security Brief* 18 (November 2012) accessed at www.swp-berlin.org/fileadmin/contents/.../2011-lac-ks.pdf
42 Kircullen, *Counterinsurgency*.
43 Martinez, *The Algerian Civil War 1990–1998*.
44 Bing West, *The Strongest Tribe: War, Politics and Endgame in Iraq* (Random House: New York, 2008).
45 "Mali: Al Qaeda's Sahara Playbook."

Chapter 8

1 Osama bin Laden's letter obtained by US Special Forces in their May 2011 Abbottabad raid in which the historic leader comments on the necessity of prioritizing affiliate attacks on the United States; *Letters from Abbottabad*, SOCOM-2012-0000016-HT, 6.
2 Walid Phares, *The Coming Revolution: The Struggle for Freedom in the Middle East* (Simon & Schuster: New York, 2010).
3 Amy Chua, *World on Fire: How Exporting Free Market Democracy Breeds Ethnic Hatred* (Random House: New York, 2003).
4 Vidino, *Al Qaeda in Europe*.

5 Lorenzo Vidino, "The Homegrown Threat to the U.S. Homeland" *ARI Real Instituto Elcano* 171 (December 18, 2009) accessed at www.realinstituto.org/wps/wcm/connect/7b14d08040b690b988eda457bfe70e7
6 Vidino, *Al Qaeda in Europe.*
7 Carafano et al., "Fifty Terror Plots Foiled since 9/11."
8 "Post 9-11 Jihadist Terrorism Cases Involving U.S. Citizens and Residents: An Overview" *Report by New American Foundation-Syracuse University Maxwell School* accessed at www.homegrown.newamericanfoundation.net/overview.html
9 Christopher Swift, "Arc of Convergence: AQAP, Ansar al Sharia and the Struggle for Yemen" *Combating Terrorism Center CTC Sentinel* 5 (2012) 1-7.
10 Naji, *The Management of Savagery.*
11 *Letters from Abbottabad.*
12 Swift, "From Periphery to Core."
13 Iqbal, "Tehrik-e-Taliban: A Global Threat."
14 Watts, "Major Hassan Nidal and the Fort Hood Tragedy."
15 Joseph Lieberman and Susan Collins, "A Ticking Time Bomb: Counterterrorism Lessons from the U.S. Government's Failure to Prevent the Fort Hood Attack" *Special Report of the U.S. Senate Committee on Homeland Security and Government Affairs* (February 3, 2010) accessed at www.hsgac.senate.gov/public/_files/Fort_Hood/FortHoodReport.pdf
16 Watts, "Major Hassan Nidal and the Fort Hood Tragedy."
17 Lieberman and Collins, "A Ticking Time Bomb."
18 Ibid.
19 "Report on the Attempted Terrorist Attack on Board Northwest Flight 523" *Senate Select Committee Intelligence Report* (May 18, 2010) accessed at www.intelligence.senate.gov/100518/1225report.pdf
20 Bill Roggio and Bob Bart, "Charting the U.S. Air Strikes in Yemen: 2002-2013" (April 21, 2013) accessed at www.longwarjournal.org/multimedia/yemen/code/yemenstrikes.php.html
21 Carafano et al., "Fifty Terror Plots Foiled since 9/11."
22 Ibid.

Chapter 9

1 Osama bin Laden's October 21, 2010 letter written to Mahmud al-Hasan designating him as second in command after a Predator drone strike killed his predecessor.
2 Ozzie Nelson, "Al Qaeda and U.S. Homeland Security after Bin Laden" *CERI Strategy Paper* 12 (November 2011) accessed at www.sciencespo.fr/ceri/sites/sciencespo.cer/files/n12_10112011-1.pdf; Bergen, *The Longest War.*

3   *Letters from Abbottabad*, Executive Summary.
4   Bill Roggio and Alex Mayer, "Senior Al Qaeda and Taliban Leaders Killed in U.S. Airstrikes in Pakistan 2004–2013" *Long War Journal*: A Project for the Defense of Democracies accessed at www.longwarjounal.org/pakistan-strikes-hvss.php
5   David Danelo, "Bin Laden's Death and the Moral Level of War" *FPRI E-Note* (May 2011) accessed at http://fpri.org/enotes/201105.fpri.binladen2.html
6   Rohan Gunaratna, "The Arab Spring: Is Al Qaeda on the Wrong Side of History?" *CTTA: Counter Terrorist Trends and Analysis* 3 (September 2011); Phares, *The Coming Revolution*; Gerges, "Zarqawi."
7   Adam Garfinkle, "September 11: Before and After" *FPRI Wire* (October 2001) accessed at www.fpri.org/prewire/0908.2001/10garfinkle.sept11.html
8   Rashid, *Descent into Chaos: How the War*.
9   Bergen, *The Longest War*.
10 Rashid, *Descent into Chaos: How the War*.
11 Peter Bergen, *Manhunt: The 10 Year Search for Bin Laden: From 9–11 to Abbottabad* (Random House: New York, 2012).
12 Bruce Riedel, *Pakistan's Osama bin Laden Report: Was Pakistan Clueless or Complicit in Harboring Bin Laden?* (July 12, 2013) accessed at www.brookings.edu/research/opinions/2013/07/12-pakistan-isi-osama-bin-laden-us-riedel
13 *Letters from Abbottabad*.
14 Ibid.
15 Bergen, *Manhunt*.
16 Ibid.
17 "Al Qaeda No. 2 Killed" accessed at www.gaurdian.com.uk/world/june/05/al-qaeda-abu-yahya-al-libi.pakistan
18 Barak Mendelson, "After Bin Laden" *FPRI E-Note* (May 2011) accessed at http://fpri.org/201105.fpri.binladen.html
19 Cliff Watts, "What If There Is No Al Qaeda: Preparing for Future Terrorism" *FPRI E-Note* (July 2012) accessed at www.fpri.org/articles/2012/07/watts/alqaeda.html
20 Bergen, *Manhunt*.
21 *Letters from Abbottabad*.
22 Ibid., SOCOM-2012-0000006.
23 Ibid.
24 *Letters from Abbottabad*, SOCOM-2012-0000019, 3.
25 "Letters form Abbottabad."
26 Daniel Kimmage, "Al Qaeda Central and the Internet" (March 2010) accessed at www.newamericanfoundation.net/sitesnewamerica.net/files/policydocs/kimmage2_0.pdf
27 Ibid.

28 Roggio and Mayer, "Senior Al Qaeda and Taliban Leaders."
29 Ibid.
30 Peter Bergen and Kathleen Tinderman, "Washington's Phantom War: The Effects of the Drone Program in Pakistan" *Foreign Affairs* 90 (2011) 12–18.
31 Ibid.
32 Barak Obama, *The Audacity of Hope* (Canongate Books: Edinburgh, 2007).
33 "The Military Utility of Drones: CSS Analysis in Security Policy" *CSS ETH Zurich* 78 (July 2010) accessed at http://mercury.ethtz.ch/serviceengine/files/SN/.../en/CSS_Analysis_78.pdf
34 Peter Bergen and Katherine Tiedman, "The Year of the Drone" *New American Foundation: Counterterrorism Strategic Initiative Paper* (February 24, 2010) accessed at www.newamericanfoundation.net
35 Articles.cnn.com/2009-05-18/politics.html
36 Michael Stevens Ilenza, "Targeted Killing: A Defense" *Global Security Studies Spring* 12 (2011) 47–60.
37 Amatai Etzioni, "Unmanned Aircraft Systems: The Moral and Legal Case" *Joint Forces Quarterly* 57 (2010) 66–71.
38 Riedel, *Pakistan's Osama bin Laden Report*.
39 Phillip Seib, "Al Qaeda's Media Machine" *Military Review* (May–June 2008) accessed at www.army.mil/professionalWriting/volumes/volume6/july_2008/7_08_4.html
40 Daniel Kimmage, "Al Qaeda's Media Nexus" *Radio Free Europe/Radio Liberty Special Report* (March 2008) accessed at www.e-prism.org/images/AQ_Medias_Nexus_-_march08.pdf
41 Roggio and Mayer, "Senior Al Qaeda and Taliban Leaders."
42 Ibid.
43 Ibid.
44 Bill Roggio, "Al Qaeda Paramilitary Commander. Haqqani Network Leader Reported Killed in Recent Drone Strike" *Long War Journal* (July 6, 2013) accessed at www.longwarjournal.org/archives/20134/07/al_qaeda_military_co.php
45 Mustafa Qadri, "Public Perceptions of Pakistan's War against Tehrik-e-Taliban" *New Critic* 11 (March 2010) 1–8.
46 Brian Glyn Williams, "The CIA's Covert Predator Drone War in Pakistan 2004–2010: The History of an Assassination Campaign" *Studies in Conflict and Terrorism* 33 (2010) 871–92.
47 Roggio and Mayer, "Senior Al Qaeda and Taliban Leaders."
48 *Letters from Abbottabad*.
49 Ibid.

50 Imtiaz Ali, "Tehrik-i-Taliban's New Ceasefire Offer" *Combating Terrorism Center at West Point CTC Sentinel* 6 (February 2013) 15–18.
51 Steven Cook, "Adrift on the Nile: The Limits of Opposition in Egypt" *Foreign Affairs* 88 (March/April 2009); Michael Browning, "The Sturdy House That Assad Built: Why Damascus Is Not Cairo" *Foreign Affairs* (March 16, 2011).
52 Bruce Fieler, *Generation Freedom: The Middle East Uprisings and the Remaking of the Modern World* (Harper Collins: New York, 2011).
53 Phares, *The Coming Revolution*; Alex Wilner, "Opportunity Costs or Costly Opportunities? The Arab Spring, Osama Bin Laden, and Al-Qaeda African Affiliates" *Perspectives on Terrorism* 5 (2011) 50–62.
54 Phares, *The Coming Revolution*.
55 Juan C. Zarate and David A. Gordon, "The Battle for Reform with Al Qaeda" *Washington Quarterly* 34 (2011) 103–22.
56 Ibid.
57 *Letters from Abbottabad*.
58 Berman, *Terror and Liberalism*.
59 Daniel Byman, "How Secular Uprisings Could Help (Hurt) Jihadists" *Foreign Affairs* (May/June 2011).
60 David Barnett, "Jihadists Denounce Attacks by Egyptian Army in the Sinai" (July 6, 2013) accessed at www.longwarjournal.org/archives/2013/07/jihadists_denounce_a.php
61 Yorum Schweitzer and Gilad Stern, "A Golden Opportunity? Al-Qaeda and the Uprising in the Middle East" *Strategic Assessment* 12 (2011) 29–39.
62 Martinez, *The Algerian Civil War 1990–1998*.
63 *Letters from Abbottabad*.
64 Watts, "What If There Is No Al Qaeda."

Bibliography

Abousouk, Ahmed Ibrahim. "The Ideology of the Mahdi in Muslim History: The Case of the Sudanese Mahdiyya." *Pakistan Journal of History and Culture*, 2009: 43–60.

Ahmad, Aziz. "Mawdudi and Orthodox Fundamentalism in Pakistan." *Middle East Journal 21*, 1967: 369–80.

Ajami, Fouad. *The Syrian Rebellion*. Stanford: Hoover Institution Press, 2012.

Ali, Imtiaz. "Tehrik-e-Taliban: The New Ceasefire Offer." *CTC Sentinel*, 2013: 871–92.

Ambrose, Andreas. "Religious Fundamentalism and Terrorist Acts." *Defense against Terrorism 2*, 2009: 51–91.

Anzalone, Christopher. "Al Shabab's Setbacks in Somalia." *Combating Terrorism Center at West Point*, October 31, 2011.

—. "Al Shabab's Tactical and Media Strategy in the Wake of Battlefield Setbacks." *CTC Sentinel 6*, 2013: 12–16.

Azam, Nur Aziman Binte. "Al Qaeda Internet Strategy a Failure? On-Line Jihadist Disapprove." *Center for Political Violence and Terrorism Research*, 2012.

Badran, Tony. "Syria's Assad, No Longer in Vogue: What Everyone Got Wrong about Bashar al-Assad." *Foreign Affairs*, March 25, 2011.

Bakr, Naji Abu. *The Management of Savagery: The Most Critical Phase Which the Ummah Will Pass*. Cambridge: Harvard University Press, 2006.

Bar, Shmuel and Yair Minneli. "The Zawahiri Letter and the Strategy of Al Qaeda." *Current Trends in Islamic Ideology 3*, 2006: 3–51.

Benjamin, Daniel and Steven Simon. *The Age of Sacred Terror: Radical Islam's War against America*. New York: Random House, 2002.

Bergen, Peter. *Holy War Incorporated: Inside the World of Al Qaeda*. New York: Touchstone Books, 2002.

—. *The Longest War: The Enduring Struggle between the United States and Al Qaeda*. New York: Simon & Schuster, 2011.

—. *Manhunt: The 10 Year Search for Bin Laden from 9-11 to Abbottabad*. New York: Random House, 2012.

Bergen, Peter and Kathleen Tinderman. "Washington's Phantom War: The Effects of the Drone Program in Pakistan." *Foreign Affairs 90*, 2011: 12–18.

—. "The Year of the Drone." *New American Foundation Strategic Paper*, February 24, 2010.

Berman, Paul. *Terror and Liberalism*. New York: W.W. Norton, 2002.

Biddle, Stephen. "Seeing Baghdad: Thinking Saigon." *Foreign Affairs* (March/April), 2006: 2–16.

Blanchard, Christopher. "Libya's Transition and U.S. Policy." *CRS Report 7-5700*, December 2011.
Brachman, Jarret and William McCants. "Stealing Al Qaeda's Playbook." *CTC Report*, West Point, February 2006.
Briggs, Rachel and Jonathan Birdwell. "Radicalization among Muslims in the UK." *Microcon Working Paper 7*, May 2009.
Briggs, Rachel, Jennifer Cole, Margaret Gilmore, and Valentina Soria. *Anatomy of a Terrorist Attack: What the Coroner's Inquest Revealed about the London Bombings.* London: Royal United Services Institute for Defense and Security Studies, 2011.
Brisard, Jean-Charles. *Zarqawi: The New Face of Terror.* Cambridge: Polity Press, 2005.
Broning, Michael. "The Sturdy House That Assad Built: Why Damascus Is Not Cairo." *Foreign Affairs* (March 7), 2011.
Byman, Daniel. "How Secular Uprisings Could Help (Hurt) Jihadists." *Foreign Affairs* (May/June), 2011.
Calvert, John. "The Mythic Foundations of Radical Islam." *Orbis* (Winter), 2004: 29–41.
—. *Sayyid Qutb and the Origins of Radical Islam.* New York: Columbia University Press, 2010.
Campbell, John. "To Combat Boko Haram: Put Down Your Guns." *Foreign Affairs* (August/September), 2011.
Carafano, James Jay, Steven Bucci, and Jessica Zuckerman. "Fifty Terror Plots Foiled since 9/11: The Homegrown Threat and the Long War on Terror." *Heritage Foundation Backgrounder 2682*, 2012: 1–23.
Celso, Anthony. "The Tragedy of Al Andaluz: The Madrid Train Terror Attacks." *Mediterranean Quarterly 16*, 2005: 121–41.
Chambliss, Saxby and Richard Burr. *Senate Select Committee on Intelligence Report on the Attempted Terrorist Attack on Northwest Flight 252.* Washington, DC: US Government Printing Office, 2010.
Chomsky, Noam. *9-11.* New York: Seven Stories Press, 2001.
Chua, Amy. *World on Fire: How Exporting Free Market Democracy Breeds Ethnic Hatred.* New York: Random House, 2003.
Cianflone, Matt, Jason Cull, John Fisher, Dave Holt, Amanda Krause, and Julie Moore. *Anatomy of a Terrorist Attack: An In-Depth Investigation into the 2002 Bali, Indonesia, Bombings.* Pittsburgh: Matthew Ridgeway Center, 2006.
Connel, Shannon. "To Be or Not to Be: Boko Haram a Foreign Terrorist Organization." *Global Security Studies 3*, 2012: 87–93.
Conway, Maura. "From al-Zarqawi to al-Awlaki: The Emergence of the Internet as a New Form of Violent Radical Milieu." Dublin, 2012, accessed at www.isodarco.it/courses/andalo12/doc/Zarqawi%20to%20AwlakI_V2.pdf
Cristiani, Dario and Ricardo Fabiani. "Al Qaeda in the Islamic Maghreb: Implications for Algeria's Regional and International Relations." *IAI Working Paper*, April 2011.

Danelo, David. "Bin Laden's Death and the Moral Level of War." *FPRI E-Note*. Philadelphia, May 2011.

Danjibo, N. D. "Islamic Fundamentalism and Sectarian Violence: The Maitatsine and Boko Haram Crises in Northern Nigeria." *Peace and Conflict Studies Paper Series* (pp. 1–21). Ibadan, Nigeria: Institute of African Studies, University of Ibadan, 2009.

Devlin-Fotz, Zachary. "Africa's Fragile States: Empowering Extremists Export of Terrorism." *African Security Brief 6*, National Defense University, 2010.

Dobson, James. "Who Lost Iraq?" *Foreign Affairs 86*, 2007: 61–75.

Edwards, Jay and Benoit Gomis. "Islamic Terrorism since 2011: Reassessing the Soft Response." *Chatham House International Security Paper*, London, June 2011.

Eikmeier, Dale. "Qutbism: An Ideology of Islamic Fascism." *Parameters* (Spring), 2007: 85–97.

Esposito, John. *The Future of Islam*. New York: Oxford University Press, 2010.

—. *The Islamic Threat: Myth or Reality?* New York: Oxford University Press, 1999.

Etzioni, Amatai. "Unmanned Aircraft Systems: The Moral and Legal Case." *Joint Forces Quarterly 57*, 2010: 66–71.

Fatah, Tarek. *The Tragic Illusion of an Islamic State*. Toronto: John Wiley & Sons, 2006.

Fearon, James. "Iraq's Civil War." *Foreign Affairs 85*, 2006: 2–15.

Fieler, Bruce. *Generation Freedom: The Middle Eastern Uprisings and the Remaking of the Modern World*. New York: Harper Collins, 2011.

Fishman, Brian. "After Zarqawi: The Dilemmas and Future of Al Qaeda in Iraq." *Washington Quarterly 29*, 2006: 19–36.

Franzen, Simon. *Unity in Terrorism: The Relationship between Al Qaeda and the Taliban*. Translated by Institute for Middle Eastern Democracy, October 2012.

Garfinkle, Adam. "Syria: Time for Inaction?" *FPRI E-Note*. Philadelphia, March 2013.

Gartenstein-Ross, Daveed. *Bin Laden's Legacy: Why We Are still Losing the War on Terror*. Hobokon: John Wiley & Sons, 2011.

Gerges, Fawaz. *The Rise and Fall of Al Qaeda*. New York: Oxford University Press, 2010.

—. "Zarqawi: The Man, the Message and the Video Star." *Institute for Social Policy and Understanding*, May 5, 2011.

Glasser, Susan and Steve Coll. "The Web as a Weapon: Zarqawi Intertwines Acts on the Ground with a Propaganda Campaign." *Washington Post*, August 9, 2005.

Glickman, Harvey. "The Coup in Mali." *FPRI E-Note*, Philadelphia, April 2012.

Goita, Modibo. "West Africa's Growing Terrorist Threat: Confronting AQIM's Sahelian Strategy." *African Security Brief*, February 2011.

Gourley, Sean. "Link between Boko Haram and Al Qaeda: Potentially a Deadly Synergy." *Global Security Studies 3*, 2012: 1–14.

Gregory, Shaun. "AQ in Pakistan." *Pakistan Research Unit Brief 5*, March 1, 2007.

Gunaratna, Rohan. "The Arab Spring: Is Al Qaeda on the Wrong Side of History." *CTTA: Counter Terrorist Trends and Analysis 3* (September), 2011.

—. *Inside Al Qaeda: Global Network of Terror*. New York: Berkeley Books, 2002.

Harmon, Stephen. "From GSPC to AQIM: The Evolution of an Algerian Islamist Terrorist Group into an Al Qaeda Affiliate and Its Implications for the Sahara-Sahel Region." *Concerned African Scholars Bulletin 85* (Spring), 2010.

Harris, Alistair. "Exploiting Grievances: Al Qaeda in the Arabian Peninsula." *Carnegie Endowment for International Peace: Middle East Program*, May 2010.

Hegghammer, Thomas. "The Ideological Hybridization of Jihadi Groups." *Current Trends in Islamic Ideology 9*, 2009: 24–45.

Henzel, Christopher. "Origins of Al Qaeda Ideology." *Parameters* (Spring), 2005: 69–80.

Hoffman, Bruce. "The Myth of Grass Roots Terrorism." *Foreign Affairs* (May/June), 2008.

Holt, Grant and David Grey. "The Pakistani Fifth Column: The Pakistani Inter-Services Directorate Sponsorship of Terrorism." *Global Security Studies 2*, 2011: 55–69.

Ilenza, Michael Stevens. "Targeted Killing: A Defense." *Global Security Studies 12*, 2011: 47–60.

Iqbal, Khurum. "Tehrik-e-Taliban: A Global Threat." *Conflict and Peace Studies 3*, 2010: 125–38.

Irons, Larry. *Recent Patterns of Terrorism Prevention in the UK*. London: Homeland Security Affairs, 2009.

Johnson, Toni. "Boko Haram Backgrounder." *Council of Foreign Relations*, December 2011.

Jones, Seth. "Al Qaeda's Persistent Sanctuary." *Real Instituto Elcano ARI 67*, Madrid, April 2011.

Jordán, Javier. "El terrorismo yihadista en España: situacion actual." *Real Instituto Elcano*, Madrid, October 2005.

—. "El terrorismo yihadista en España: evolución despues del 11-M." *Real Instituto Elcano documento de trabajo N7/2009*, Madrid, February 6, 2009.

Juergensmeyer, Marc. *Terror in the Mind of God*. Berkeley: University of California Press, 2000.

Karsh, Ephraim. *Islamic Imperialism: A History*. New Haven: Yale University Press, 2007.

Kazimi, Nibras. "A Virulent Ideology in Mutation: Zarqawi upstages Maqdisi." *International Institute Jihadi Website Monitoring Report*, September 2009.

Kean, Thomas and Lee Hamilton. *The 9-11 Commission Report: The Final Report of the National Commission on Terrorism Attacks on the United States*. Washington, DC: US Government Printing Office, 2004.

Kepel, Gilles. *The Trail of Political Islam*. New York: I.B. Taurus, 1996.

Kircullen, David. *Counter Insurgency*. New York: Oxford University Press, 2010.

Kirdar, M. J. "Al Qaeda in Iraq: Case Study 1." *AQAM Futures Project Case Studies Series*, June 2011.

Knapp, Michael. "Concept and Practice of Jihad." *Parameters* (Spring), 2003: 82–94.

Lacher, William. "Organized Crime and Terrorism in the Sahel." *German Institute for International Security Affairs SWP Comments*, January 2011.

Lahoud, Nelly, Stuart Caudill, Liam Collins, Gabriel Koehler-Derrick, Don Rassler, and Muhammad al-'Ubaydi. *Letters from Abbottabad: Bin Laden Sidelined?* West Point Combating Terrorism Center Harmony Program. West Point, NY: US Army, 2012.

Lewis, Bernard. *The Assassins.* New York: Basic Books, 2002.

—. *What Went Wrong? The Clash between Islam and Modernity.* New York: Harper Perennial, 2003.

Lia, Brynjar. *Architect of Global Jihad: The Life of Al Qaeda Strategist Abu Musab Suri.* New York: Columbia University Press, 2008.

Lieberman, Joseph and Susan Collins. *A Ticking Time Bomb: Counterterrorism Lessons from the U.S. Government's Failure to Prevent the Fort Hood Attack: Implications for the U.S. Armed forces.* Washington, DC: US Government Printing Office, 2011.

Manningham-Buller, Dame Eliza. *The International Terrorist Threat to the UK.* Speech given at Queen Mary College, London, November 9, 2006.

Martinez, Luiz. *The Algerian Civil War 1990-1998.* New York: Columbia University Press, 2000.

McCary, John. "The Anbar Awakening: An Alliance of Incentives." *Washington Quarterly 3*, 2009: 43-59.

McGregor, Andrew. "Jihad and the Rifle Alone: Abdullah Azzam and the Islamist Revolution." *Journal of Conflict Studies 23*, 2003: 92-104.

Meehan, Patrick and Jackie Speirer. "Boko Haram's Emerging Threat to the American Homeland." *U.S. House of Representatives Homeland Security Subcommittee Report*, 2011.

Mendelson, Barak. "After Bin Laden." *FPRI E-Note*, Philadelphia, May 2011.

Moghadan, Assar. "Salafi Jihad as a Religious Ideology." *CTC Sentinel 1*, 2008: 14-16.

Mozaffar, Mehdi. "What Is Islamism: History and Definition of a Concept." *Totalitarian Movements and Political Religions 8*, 2007: 17-33.

Mustafa, Daanish and Katherine E. Brown. "The Taliban Public Space and Terror in Pakistan." *Eurasian Geography and Economics 51*, 2010: 469-512.

Nasr, Vali. *The Shia Revival: How Conflicts within Islam Will Shape the Future.* New York: W.W. Norton, 2007.

Nelson, Rick. "Al Qaeda and U.S. Homeland Security after Bin Laden's Death." *CERI Strategy Paper 12*, November 2011.

Nelson, Rick and Thomas Sanderson. "A Threat Transformed: Al Qaeda and Associated Movements in 2011." *CSIS Counterterrorism Report*, 2011.

New America Foundation/Maxwell School. *Post-9/11 Jihadist* Terrorism *Cases Involving U.S. Citizens and Residents*, n.d.

Novio, Diogo. "Al Qaeda in the Islamic Maghreb: Implications for Algeria's Regional and International Relations." *IPRIS Working Paper*, February 2010.

Obama, Barak. *The Audacity of Hope.* Edinburgh: Canongate Books, 2007.

Ojo, Emanuel. "Boko Haram: Nigeria's Extra Judicial State." *Journal of Sustainable Development in Africa 12*, 2010: 182-97.

Page, Jacqueline. "Jihadi Arena Report: Somalia's Development of Radical Islamism and Current Implications." *International Institute for Counter-Terrorism*, March 3, 2010.

Pantucci, Raffaello. "The Birmingham Terrorist Plotters: Lessons for Counterterrorism Today." *RUSI Analysis*, London, February 23, 2013.

Pham, Peter. "Boko Haram's Evolving Threat." *African Security Brief 20*, April 2012.

—. "Foreign Influence and Shifting Horizons: The Ongoing Evolution of Al Qaeda in the Islamic Maghreb." *Orbis 55*, 2011: 240–54.

Phares, Walid. *The Coming Revolution.* New York: Simon & Schuster, 2010.

—. *The War of Ideas: Jihadism versus Democracy.* New York: Palgrave, 2008.

Qadri, Mustafa. "Public Perceptions of Pakistan's War against Tehrik-e-Taliban." *New Critic 11*, 2010: 1–8.

Qazi, Shazad. "An Extended Profile of the Pakistani Taliban." *Institute for Social Policy and Understanding*, August 2011.

Radu, Michael. "Al Qaeda Confusion: How to Think about Jihad." *FPRI E-Note*, Philadelphia, July 2007.

—. "The Demise of Abu Musab al-Zarqawi." *FPRI E-Notes*, Philadelphia, June 8, 2006.

—. *Europe's Ghosts: Tolerance, Jihadism and the Crisis in the West.* New York: Encounter Books, 2010.

—. "News from Spain: Terror Works." *FPRI E-Note*, Philadelphia, March 16, 2004.

—. "Preaching Jihad on Welfare: The Story of Abu Qutada." *FPRI E-Note*. Philadelphia, June 2008.

Rashid, Ahmed. *Descent into Chaos: The U.S. and the Disaster in Pakistan, Afghanistan and Central Asia.* New York: Penguin Books, 2007.

—. *Taliban.* New York: Penguin Books, 1999.

Ray, Oliver. *The Failure of Political Islam.* New York: I.B. Taurus, 1994.

Reed, Jodie. "Young Muslims in the UK: Education and Integration." *FES/IPPR Seminar*, December 2005.

Reidel, Bruce. "Al Qaeda Smells Blood." *Brookings Institution*, September 9, 2011.

—. "Al Qaeda Strikes Back." *Foreign Affairs 86*, 2007: 24–40.

Reinares, Fernando. "11-M la conexión: al Qaeda." *El Pais*, December 17, 2009.

—. "Acaso 11-3 no se fijo en Bruselas?" *El Pais*, March 11, 2009.

—. *El terrorismo global: un fenómeno polimorfo.* Madrid: *Revista Jurídica Militar*, July 2008.

—. "Expression de una amenaza compuesta?" *El Pais*, August 3, 2012.

—. "FATA in North Mali." *Expert Comment 15*, Madrid, July 31, 2012.

—. "Iraq: pero no era la ocupacion lo que explica el terrorismo suicida." *Real Instituto Elcano Comentario 8*, June 28, 2012.

—. "La amenaza yidadista sigue aqui." *El Pais*, April, 2013: 24.

—. "Las amenazas terroristas en EEUU y el fallido atentado de Times Square." *Real Instituto Elcano ARI 84*, Madrid, May 2010.

—. "The Madrid Bombings and Global Jihadism." *Survival 52*, 2010: 83–104.

Roggio, Bill and Alex Mayer. "Senior Al Qaeda and Taliban Leaders Killed in U.S. Airstrikes in Pakistan, 2004–2013." *Long War Journal*, n.d.

Roggio, Bill and Bob Barry. "Charting the U.S. Air Strikes in Yemen 2002–2013." *Long War Journal*, April 21, 2013.

Sage, Andre Le. "The Evolving Threat of Al Qaeda in the Islamic Maghreb." *INSS Strategic Forum*, July 2011.

—. "Somalia's Endless Transition: Breaking the Deadlock." *NDU Strategic Forum 257*, June 2011.

Sageman, Marc. *Leaderless Jihad*. Philadelphia: University of Pennsylvania, 2007.

—. *Understanding Terror Networks*. Philadelphia: University of Pennsylvania, 2004.

Scheuer, Michael. *Imperial Hubris: Why the West Is Losing the War on Terror*. Dulles: Potomac Books, 2004.

Schwetzer, Yorum and Gilad Stern. "A Golden Opportunity?: Al Qaeda and the Uprisings in the Middle East." *Strategic Assessment 12*, 2011: 29–39.

Shanzer, Jonathan. *Al Qaeda's Armies*. Washington: Institute for Near Eastern Studies, 2005.

Siegel, Pascale. "Al Qaeda's Playbook in Mali." *CTC Sentinel 6*, 2013: 10–12.

Simcox, Robin, Hannah Stuart, and Houriya Ahmed. "Islamist Terrorism: The British Connections." *Center for Social Cohesion*, London, 2010.

Soloman, Robert. *Anti-Semitism: The Longest Hatred*. New York: Schocken Press, 1994.

Sude, Barbara. "Al Qaeda Central: An Assessment of the Threat Posed by the Terrorist Group Headquartered on the Afghanistan-Pakistan Border." *New America Foundation*, February 25, 2010.

Swift, Christopher. "The Arc of Convergence: AQAP, Ansar al-Sharia and the Struggle for Yemen." *CTC Sentinel 3*, 2012: 1–7.

—. "From Periphery to Core: Foreign Fighter and the Evolution of Al Qaeda in the Arabian Peninsula." *Foreign Fighter Problem*, Philadelphia, 2011.

Takeyh, Ray and Nikolas Gvosdev. "Radical Islam: The Death of an Ideology." *Middle East Policy 1*, 2004: 86–95.

Tanchum, Michael. "Al-Qa'ida's West African Advance: Boko Haram, Mali's Touareg, and the Spread of Salafi Jihadism." *Israeli Journal of Foreign Affairs 6*, 2012: 75–90.

Thachuk, Kimberley, Marion Bowman, and Courtney Richardson. "Homegrown Terrorism: The Threat from Within." *National Defense University*, Washington, DC, May 2008.

Thornbury, William and Jaclyn Levy. "Al Qaeda in the Islamic Maghreb." *CSIS AQAM Futures Project Case Study 4*, September 2011.

Vidino, Lorenzo. *Al Qaeda in Europe*. New York: Prometheus Books, 2005.

—. "The Arrival of Islamic Fundamentalism in the Sudan." *Al Nakalah: Fletcher School of Southwest Asian and Islamic Civilization*. Medford: Fletcher School, Fall 2006.

—. "The Homegrown Threat to the U.S. Homeland." *Real Instituto Elcano*, December 18, 2009.

Watts, Clint. "Major Hassan Nidal and the Fort Hood Tragedy: Implications for the U.S. Armed forces." *FPRI E-Note*, Philadelphia, June 2011.

—. "What If There Is No Al Qaeda: Preparing for Future Terrorism." *FPRI E-Note*, Philadelphia, July 2012.

Weekly Standard. "The English Translation of Ayman al-Zawahiri's letter to Abu Musab al-Zarqawi." Washington, DC, October 12, 2005.

West, Bing. *The Strongest Tribe: War, Politics and Endgame in Iraq*. New York: Random House, 2008.

Williams, Brian Glyn. "The CIA Covert Predator Drone War in Pakistan 2004–2010: The History of an Assassination Campaign." *Studies in Conflict and Terrorism 33*, 2010: 871–92.

—. "On the Trail of the Lions of Islam: Foreign Fighters in Afghanistan and Pakistan 1980–2010." *Orbis 55*, 2010: 216–39.

Wise, Rob. "Al Shabaab" AQAM Futures Project Case Studies Series." *CSIS*, July 2011.

Woodward, Bob. *Bush at War*. New York: Simon & Schuster, 2002.

Wright, Lawrence. *The Looming Tower*. Toronto: Borzai Books, 2006.

Zabel, Sarah. *The Military Strategy of Global Jihad*. Carlisle, PA: Strategic Studies Institute, October 2007.

Zackie, M. W. "An Analysis of Abu Musab Sur's Call to Global Islamic Resistance." *Journal of Strategic Security 6*, 2013: 1–18.

Zarate, Juan and David Gordon. "The Battle for Reform within Al Qaeda." *Washington Quarterly*, 2011: 103–22.

Zelin, Aaron. "Deciphering the Jihadist Presence in Syria." *CTC Sentinel 6*, 2013: 7–10.

Zenn, Jacob. "Cooperation and Competition: Boko Haram and Ansaru after the French Intervention in Mali." *CTC Sentinel 6*, 2013: 1–9.

Index

3/11 attack
"buch of guys" theory and, 84-6
network, 88-9
post-, al-Qaeda's network in, 91-3
7/7 attack
al-Qaeda involvement in, 97-8
and network, 95-7
post-, and al-Qaeda plots, 98-102
9/11 attacks origins and, 48-52
9-11 Report, 33, 51, 53

Abdulmutallab, Farouk, 12, 76, 136, 168-70, 171
Abu Sayyaf Groups (ASG), 78, 79
Afghanistan, 3, 9, 10, 13, 25, 29, 32, 37, 41, 42, 46, 47, 64, 67, 69, 70, 75, 78, 80, 87, 88, 93, 94, 97, 102, 106-8, 129, 135, 136, 140, 142, 161, 166-8, 170, 176, 183, 184, 187, 188, 190, 193, 198
Afghan Services Bureau (Maktab al-Khidamat—MAK), 44
Aflaq, Michel, 121
African network, 45-7
Ahmad, Jamal, 89
Ahmad, Mohammad, 20
Ahmed, Abdullah, 99
Ajami, Fouad, 123
The Syrian Rebellion, 122
Akbar, Mohammad Hassan, 167
al-Asiri, Ibrahim, 169
al-Assad, Bashar, 67
al Assad, Hafez, 27, 64, 121-4
al-Awlaki, Anwar, 4, 76, 77, 136-7, 167-9, 172, 187
Inspire (e-magazine), 100, 136, 165
al-Baghdadi, Abu Bakr, 125, 161
al-Baghdadi, Abu Omar, 120
al Banna, Hassan, 21
al Banshiri, Abu Ubaidah, 45
al-Faruk, Omar, 79

Algeria, 26, 29, 31, 65, 107, 130, 134, 135, 138, 139, 141, 143, 150, 151, 155-6
Algerian Islamic National Front (FIS), 138
al-Hasan, Mahmud, 193
al-Hazim, Nawaf, 51
al Imam, Bayat, 107
al Islam, Ansar, 112
Al-Ittihad al-Islamiyya (AIAI), 132
Al Jazeera, 185
al Khalayleh, Ahmed Fadihil, *see* Zarqawi, Abu Musab
al-Kuwaiti, Abu Zaid, 100
al-Libi, Abu Yahya, 186, 187, 193
al Maliki, Nuri, 119
al-Maqdisi, Abu Mohammad, 106, 108, 115
al Maymouni, Mustafa, 89
al-Midhar, Khalid, 51
al-Muhajir, Abu Hamza, 120
Al Muhajiroun (Soldiers of Islam), 94
al-Nusra Front (Syria), 7, 11, 124-8, 161, 179, 197
al-Qaeda, 75-6
affiliates, 129-32
al-Shabaab, 132-5
AQAP, 135-8
AQIM, 138-41
Arab Spring and, 194-7
formation, and far enemy strategy, 31
Abdullah Azzam and defensive jihad doctrine and, 32-5
first Gulf War and, 35-8
Husan al-Turabi and Sudanese patronage (1992-6) and, 38-41
Taliban-al-Qaeda partnership organizational and ideological foundations (1996-2001), 41-4
against United States, 44-54
ideological and religious origins, 16-17
Pakistani Taliban, Uzbek and Haqqani protectors, weakening of, 190-4

plots and attacks against United States
after 9/11
2010 Times Square attack
and, 171–3
al-Qaeda's failed far enemy approach
and, 178–9
AQAP and far enemy strategy
and, 164–6
bin Laden's far enemy strategy
and, 159–61
difficulties in implementing post-9/11
far enemy strategy and, 162–4
failed 2009 Christmas Day passenger
jet attack, 168–70
foiled 2013 al-Qaeda Canadian
passenger train plot and, 177–8
Fort Hood shooting and, 166–8
homegrown terrorist Boston Marathon
attacks (April 2013) and, 173–7
recent plots against NYC public
transport systems, 170–1
transcendental utility of attacking
United States and, 161–2
see also Madrid and London
bombings; *individual entries*
al-Qaeda Canadian passenger train plot
(foiled) (2013), 177–8
al-Qaeda in Iraq (AQI), 5, 8, 11, 26, 77,
114, 115, 118, 120, 125, 126, 135,
136, 139, 161, 191, 199
al-Qaeda in the Arabian Peninsula
(AQAP), 4, 5, 6, 8, 12, 56, 76, 77,
100, 129, 130, 131, 133, 135–8, 142,
160, 161, 163–4, 165, 168–70, 171,
174, 187, 197
al-Qaeda in the Islamic Maghreb
(AQIM), 4, 6, 8, 12, 56, 76, 84,
92–3, 129, 130, 131, 138–41, 142,
144, 145, 148, 151–6, 165, 177, 188,
197, 199
al-Qaeda's post-9/11 strategy and
organizational devolution, 55–8
jihadist doctrines of Abu Musab Suri
and Abu Bakr Naji and, 63–71
and JI partnership, and Bali
attacks, 78–80
Taliban sanctuary destruction
and, 59–63
vexation and exhaustion strategy, 71–8

al-Sahab Institute for Media
Productions, 57, 63, 69–70
al-Shabaab, 5, 6, 8, 12, 26, 56, 77, 129–35,
142, 155, 163, 165, 187, 191, 199
al-Sheeb, Ramzi Bin, 62
al Shehhi, Marwan, 52
al-Shibh, Ramzi Bin, 52, 185
al-Turabi, Hussan, 20
Sudanese patronage (1992–6)
and, 38–41
al-Wahhab, Muhammad ibn Abd, 29
al-Zawahiri, Ayman, 5, 6, 7, 9, 13, 21, 24,
25, 26, 34, 35, 37–40, 61, 65, 70, 77,
84, 91, 92, 98, 102, 109, 115, 118,
125, 126, 134, 161, 165, 179, 184,
186–7, 195, 196
Bitter Harvest, 28
Knights under the Prophet's Banner, 28
Ansar al Sharia, 140–2, 164, 196
Ansar Dine (AD), 6, 143, 144–5, 151–7,
188, 199
Ansaru, 12, 150
Arab Spring impact, and bin Laden's
death, 181–99
Armed Islamic Group (GIA) (Algeria), 12,
26, 64, 83, 84, 86–8, 90, 92, 93, 138,
155, 163, 197
Associated Press, 7
Ataturk, Kemal, 20, 22
Atef, Mohammad, 50, 52–3
Atiyya, Mahmud, 187
Atta, Mohammad, 52, 87
Australia, 80
Awakening Movement, 119
Azizi, Amir, 88, 90, 102
Azzam, Abdullah, 9, 25–6, 31, 49, 74, 106
Defense of Muslim Lands, 33
defensive jihad doctrine of, 32–5

Bahrain, 198
Bakri, Omar, 94
Bali attacks, 78–80
Baqir-al-Hakim, Ayatollah
Muhammad, 113
Bashir, Abu Bakr, 78, 79
Beljad, Youssef, 90
Belmokhtar, Mohktar, 150
Berg, Nicholas, 114
Bergen, Peter, 1, 64

Bergin, Peter, 190
Berman, Paul, 22
Bhutto, Benazir, 56, 74, 192
Binalshibh, Ramzi, 87
bin Laden, Osama, 1, 15, 31, 81, 129, 159
  see also individual entries
Bledsoe, Carlos, 178
Boko Haram (BH), 6, 143, 144–5, 146–50, 154, 155, 157
Bolivia, 66
Bosnia, 135, 140
Bremer, Paul, 112
Brigade 055, 74
Brown, Vahlid, 75
"buch of guys" theory and 3/11, 84–6
Bush administration, 59, 60, 61, 183, 189

Calvert, John, 23
The Camels Hump (e-magazine), 113
Camp David Peace treaty (1979), 27
Canada, 47, 99
Carafano, James Jay
  Heritage Foundation Study, 172
Carafano, Joseph Jay, 66, 163
Casablanca attacks, 89
Chechnya, 135, 140
Chomsky, Noam, 46
Christmas Day passenger jet attack (failed attempt) (2009), 168–70
CIA, 36, 46, 54, 56, 60, 61, 88, 90, 100, 101, 127, 133, 137, 169, 170, 184, 186, 188, 192–3
Clinton Administration, 59, 183
Coalitional Provisional Authority (CPA), 112
Congo, 66

Dadah, Abu, 64, 88, 102
Dar al Harb (House of War), 33
de Mello, Sergio Vieiria, 113
Dishman, Chris, 2
Droukdel, Abdelmalek, 7, 139, 143, 148, 156, 157

Economic Community of West African States (ECOWAS), 4
Egypt, 4, 13, 20, 24, 29, 31, 65, 107, 125, 141, 150, 194–7

Egyptian Islamic Jihad (EIJ), 65
el foco, 9, 10, 65, 66
El Jaauani, Hassan, 177
England, 84
Esseghaier, Chiheb, 178
Ethiopia, 133
Etzioni, Amatai, 190

Fakhet, Sermane Ben Abbdelmajid, 89
Faraj, Muhammad, 24
  The Neglected Duty, 24–5
far enemy strategy, 1, 4–9, 13, 24, 25–9, 93, 109
  of al-Qaeda, 31–54, 80
  AQAP and, 164–6
  of bin Laden, 159–61
  difficulties in implementing post-9/11, 162–4
Foley, Lawrence, 111
Fort Hood shooting, 166–8
France, 83, 84, 87, 138, 139, 153–4, 197
Free Syrian Army (FSA), 124, 126, 127

Gadahn, Adam, 5, 70, 187
Garfinkle, Adam, 127
General Intelligence Department (GID) (Jordan), 107, 115
Ghali, Iyad Ag, 152
Ghana, 169
GICM, 83, 84, 86–90, 92
Global Islamic Media Front, 57, 191
Gramci, Antonio, 22
Guevara, Che, 9, 65, 66
Gunaratna, Rohan, 78, 87

Hambali, *see* Isamuddin, Riduan
Hamburg cell and 9/11 attacks, 52–4
Hamza, Abu, 93–4
Haqqani, Jalaluddin, 62, 74, 75
Haqqani, Muhammad, 192
Haqqani, Saifullah, 192
Haqqani-al-Qaeda, 13
Haqqani network, 74–5, 192
Hassan, Nidal Malek, 4–5, 12, 76, 130, 136, 166–8
Hegghammer, Thomas, 72
Hekmatyar, Gullbuddin, 62
Hoffman, Bruce, 55, 56, 58, 83

homegrown terrorism
  Boston Marathon attacks (April 2013), 173–7
  see also Madrid and London bombings and al-Qaeda's role
Hussein, Hasib Mir, 96–7

Ibrahim, Muktar Said, 99
India, 41
Indonesia, 9, 10, 43, 58, 78–81
Inter-Services Intelligence (Pakistan), 62, 74
Iran, 23, 110–11, 126, 127
Iraq, 2, 3, 4, 8, 10, 11, 13, 27, 39, 57, 58, 67, 69, 80, 82, 84, 85, 91, 97, 98, 103, 105, 109–13, 115, 116, 118, 124, 126, 128, 135, 136, 139, 140, 155, 157, 161, 166, 176, 188, 191, 197
Isamuddin, Riduan, 43, 79–80
Islamic Action Front (IAF), 108
Islamic Court Union (ICU), 132–3
Islamic Movement of Kurdistan (IMK), 110
Islamic Movement of Uzbekistan (IMU), 62
Islamic State of Iraq (ISI), 7, 11, 120, 126, 128
Islamist National Salvation Front (Algeria), 26

jahiliyya (ignorance), 21, 22, 24
Jarrah, Ziad, 52
Jaser, Raed, 178
Jemaah Islamiyah (JI), 2, 10, 43
  and al-Qaeda partnership, and Bali attacks, 78–80
jihadist worldview, 15–16
  al-Qaeda's ideological and religious origins and, 16–17
  Islamist response to foreign domination and, 19–20
  Maududi and Qutb, 20–5
  Qutub's ideological descendants and, 25–9
  war within Muslim world and, 17–19
  see also individual entries
Joint Operations Special Forces Command (JSPC), 188
Jonathan Administration, 149
Jordan, 4, 9, 13, 94, 109, 115, 124

Jordán, Javier, 86, 92
Jund al Islam (Soldiers of Islam), 111–12

Karsh, Ephraim, 18, 19
Karzai, Hamid, 184
Kayam, Omar, 97
Kennedy, Paul, 69
Kenya, 45, 132–4, 183
Khan, Irfan, 100
Khan, Samir, 137
Khan, Sidique, 95–8, 101
Kimmage, Daniel, 187
Kounja, Abenabi, 89
Krekar, Mullah, 110, 111
Kuwait, 36

Lashkar al-Zil (Shadow Army), 74
Lebanon, 11, 13, 124, 126, 127, 128, 197, 198
Lia, Brynjar, 70
Libya, 29, 31, 107, 124, 125, 140–2, 150, 151, 155, 194, 197
Libyan Islamic Fighting Group (LIFG), 27, 140, 163
Lindsey, Jermaine, 96
Londinstan, 83, 168
  United Kingdom's jihadist microculture and, 93–5
The Long War Journal, 170, 188, 190, 192, 193
Los Zetas, 2

Madrid and London bombings, 81–2
  3/11 network and, 88–9
  7/7 network and London attacks and, 95–7
  al-Qaeda involvement in July 7th attacks and, 97–8
  al-Qaeda's Moroccan and Algerian associates and, 86–8
  al-Qaeda's network in post-3/11 Spain and, 91–3
  al-Qaeda's post-9/11 plan and, 89–91
  al-Qaeda's zenith in Europe and, 102–3
  "buch of guys" theory and 3/11, 84–6
  Londinstan and United Kingdom's jihadist microculture and, 93–5
  post-7/7 al-Qaeda plots United Kingdom attacks and, 98–102
  Sageman–Hoffman debate, 83–4

Maghreb, 2, 3, 7, 10, 11, 12, 57, 58, 69, 84, 87, 128, 138–9, 141, 154, 157, 165, 191
Mahdist rebellion, 20
Maitatsine movement, 147
Make a Bomb in the Kitchen of Your Mom, 176
Malaysia, 43, 78–80
Mali, 12, 27, 140, 141, 144, 145, 150, 151, 154–6, 197–9
Manningham-Butler, Dame Eliza, 99
Marwa, Muhammad, 147
Maududi, Abul Ala, 19, 20–1
  Jihad and Society, 21
  The Meaning of the Quran, 21
Mediouni, Nou, 177
Mehsud, Ahmed, 60
Mehsud, Baitullah, 56, 73, 92, 171, 191
Mehsud, Hakimullah, 56, 171, 172, 193
Mehsud, Hekmatyar, 192
Mein Kampf, 37
Millenium Plot and USS Cole bombing, 47–8
Mohammad, Khalid Sheik (KSM), 43, 62, 78–80, 185–6
Mohammad, Nek, 62
moral suasion, 24
Moreh, Muhammad, 101
Moroccan Islamic Combat Group (MICG), 2, 10, 102, 160, 163
Morocco, 4, 9, 13, 89
Moro Islamic Liberation Front (MILF), 78, 79
Morsi, Muhammad, 4
Moussaoui, Zarcarius, 53
Movement for the National Liberation of Azawad (MNLA), 145, 151, 152
Movement for Unity of Jihad in West Africa (MUJWA), 143–5, 151, 152
Muhammad, Khalid Sheik, 114
Muslim Brotherhood (Egypt), 8–9, 13, 21, 25, 64, 67, 121, 182, 196, 198

Naji, Abu Bakr, 3, 11, 24, 32, 37, 55, 58
  jihadist doctrines of, 67–71
  Management of Savagery, 10, 67–70, 114, 165
Nasser, 22, 24, 28
National Salvation Front (FIS), 87

Nayef, Mohammad bin, 169
Nazir, Mullah, 62
near enemy strategy, 4, 8, 9, 11, 25, 26, 27, 29, 34
Netanyau, Benjamin, 127
networks, definition of, 2
Niger, 151, 154
Nigeria, 144, 145, 146, 150, 156
Nizim, Shahrul, 78

Obama Administration, 126, 127, 137, 182, 189–90
Obama's drone war against al-Qaeda and Taliban ties, 188–90
Omar, Mullah, 42, 44, 59, 61, 64
Operation Bojinka, 50, 78, 79, 99
Operation Serval (France), 153
Ottomon Empire, 19–20

Pakistan, 10, 13, 31, 36, 37, 41, 42, 50, 61–2, 73, 75, 78, 83, 84, 90, 91, 93–7, 99, 101, 102, 106, 108, 109, 161, 170–2, 181, 183–5, 188–93, 198
Pan-Arab nationalism, 19
Panetta, Leon, 190
Pan-Islamic Hiz ut Tahrir (Islamic Party of Liberation), 93
Pantucci, Raffaello, 101
Patriotic Union of Kurdistan (PUK), 112
Pearl, Daniel, 114
Phares, Walid
  The Coming Revolution, 162
Philippines, 9, 49–50, 78–80
Protocols of the Elders of Zion, 24, 37

Qutada, Abu, 94
Qutb, Sayyid, 19, 21–5
  ideological descendants of, 25–9
  Milestones Judeophobia, 21, 23, 24

Rabia, Hamza, 90
Rachman, Sheik Abdul, 39, 44, 48, 59
Radu, Michael, 3, 86
Rashid, Ahmed, 41, 60
Rassler, Don, 75
Rauf, Rachid, 98, 102
Reed, Richard, 94, 170
Reinares, Fernando, 57, 86, 91, 151

Ressam, Ahmed, 47
Rigby, Lee, 101
Royal Canadian Mounted Police, 177–8

Sageman, Marc, 11, 52, 56, 57, 58, 76, 81–2, 85, 92, 96
Sahel, 139
Salafist Group for Preaching and Combat (GSPC), 84, 87, 92–4, 139, 163
Samudra, Imam, 80
Saudi Arabia, 40, 42, 43, 44, 124, 125, 183
Shahzad, Faisal, 171–2
Sheik Abdul Rachman Brigade, 141
Shekau, Abubakar bin Muhammad, 148
Singapore, 43, 80
Somalia, 2, 3, 4, 7, 11, 12, 27, 57, 58, 84, 128, 130, 132–4, 141, 157, 165, 182, 191, 197, 198
Soviet Union, 32
Spain, 83, 84, 87–9, 91, 140
Stevens, Christopher, 140, 196
Sudan, 20, 25, 38, 44, 46, 99, 132, 142
Sungkar, Abdullah, 78, 79
Sunni Triangle, 113, 114, 118, 119
Suri, Abu Musab, 3, 9–10, 24, 32, 37, 44, 58, 60, 62, 76, 94
The Call for a Global Islamic Resistance, 9, 63, 64, 65–6, 68
jihadist doctrines of, 63–7
Syria, 7, 11, 13, 18, 39, 65, 67, 109, 110, 111, 113, 115, 125, 127–8, 179, 194, 196, 197
Syrian Jihad, against Assad regime (2011–13), 121–8
Syrian revolt, 4

takfir doctrine, 26, 34, 66, 71, 106, 138
Taliban, 7, 9–10, 12, 28, 31, 41, 56, 58, 64, 70, 75, 83–4, 88–91, 97–9, 102, 110–11, 132–3, 145, 147, 149, 162, 171–2, 183–4, 192
al-Qaeda partnership organizational and ideological foundations (1996–2001), 41–4
destruction of sanctuary of, 59–63
Obama's drone war against al-Qaeda and, 188–90
Tanweer, Shizad, 95–8

Tanzania, 46, 132, 183
tanzim (system not organization) strategy, 65–6
Tawid wal Jihad (Unity and Holy War), 114
Taymiyya, Ibn, 19
Tehrik-e-Taliban (TTP) (Pakistan), 10, 56, 73–5, 83, 160, 163, 165, 171, 172, 182, 186, 187, 191–3
Thailand, 78, 80
Tiedemann, Kathleen, 190
Times Square attack (2010), 171–3
Tora Bora battle, 61
Transitional Federal Government, 133
Trans Sahara Counter Terrorism Partnership, 139
Tsarnaev, Dzhokhar, 173–4, 176–7
Tsarnaev, Tamerlan, 173–7
Tunisia, 4, 9, 13, 125, 194–6, 197
Turkey, 109, 126
Turki, Prince, 35–6
Turkish 9/11, 80

Uganda, 134
ummah, 17, 18, 21, 22, 25, 29, 33, 66
United Islamic Front (1998–2001), 44–5
USS Cole bombing, 79, 183
Millenium Plot and, 47–8
Uzbekistan, 61

vexation and exhaustion strategy, 3, 10, 11, 27, 68–70, 84, 90, 102, 112, 114, 129, 157, 160, 165, 191, 198
of al-Qaeda's post-9/11 strategy of, 71–8
Vidino, Lorenzo, 39, 86, 163
Vinas, Bryant Neals, 170–1

Wahhabism, 29
Wazir tribes, 61–2
West Africa, 143–6
Afghanistan of, 150–4
assessment of jihadist capabilities of, 154–7
Boko Haram and, 146–50
West Point's Combating Terrorism Center, 75, 134, 187
William, Brian Glyn, 193

The World Islamic Front against Jews and
    Crusaders, 45
Wright, Lawrence, 35
    Looming Tower, 34

Yemen, 2, 3, 4, 7, 11, 12, 35, 58, 69, 84,
    128, 130, 134–6, 141, 142, 157,
    165, 169, 182, 183, 191, 194, 196,
    197, 198
Yousef, Ramzi, 48, 49, 50, 59, 78
Yusuf, Muhammad, 147–8

Zarqawi, Abu Musab, 11, 42, 126, 133,
    139, 161, 165
  and 9/11 attacks, and escape to
    Iran, 110–11
  al-Qaeda and Ansar al Islam
    and, 111–12
  al-Qaeda in Iraq post death of, and US
    withdraw, 120–1
  desire, to unleash sectarian civil
    war, 114–15
  fall of, and al-Qaeda's collapse in Anbar
    province, 118–20
  fighting the near enemy, 107–8
  Herat camp of, and early-al-Qaeda
    connections, 109–10
  renewed fight of, against Jordanian
    apostate regime, 115–16
  strategy to defeat Americans in post-
    Saddam Iraq, 112–14
  transition to Arab Afghan, from young
    hoodlum, 105–7
  war against Shia and, 116–18
Zazi, Najibullah, 171
Ziad, Abdel Mehid Abou, 153
Zionist-Crusader alliance, 27, 29, 32, 36,
    37, 44, 48, 53, 69, 162, 164, 182
Zougam, Jamal, 88, 89
Zubaydah, Abu, 47, 62, 109, 185

Made in the USA
Middletown, DE
17 March 2023